D0209266

*Just the Way You Are: How Heredity and Experience
Create the Individual*
(originally published as *I.D.: How Heredity and Experience
Make You Who You Are*)

*The Power of Place: How Our Surroundings Shape
Our Thoughts, Emotions, and Actions*

WORKING ON GOD

WORKING ON GOD

WINIFRED GALLAGHER

RANDOM HOUSE

NEW YORK

All rights reserved under International and Pan-American Copyright
Conventions. Published in the United States by Random House, Inc.,
New York, and simultaneously in Canada by Random House of
Canada Limited, Toronto.

RANDOM HOUSE and colophon are registered trademarks
of Random House, Inc.

Grateful acknowledgment is made to New Directions Publishing
Corporation and Laurence Pollinger Limited for permission
to reprint thirteen lines from "On Being" from
Oblique Prayers, published in Great Britian by Bloodaxe Books
and in the United States by New Directions Publishing
Corporation. Copyright © 1984 by Denise Levertov. Rights in the
British Commonwealth are controlled by Laurence Pollinger
Limited, London. Reprinted by permission of New Directions
Publishing Corporation and Laurence Pollinger Limited.

Library of Congress Cataloging-in-Publication Data

Gallagher, Winifred.
Working on God / Winifred Gallagher.
p.   cm.
ISBN 0-679-44794-6
1. Religion—United States.   I. Title.
BL2525.G33   1999
200'.973'09049—DC21   98-31581

Random House website address: www.atrandom.com

Printed in the United States of America on acid-free paper

24689753

FIRST EDITION

Book design by Carole Lowenstein

For Winifred McCann and
Thomas Gallagher

All the way to heaven is heaven.
—CATHERINE OF SIENA

CONTENTS

INTRODUCTION

This is a book for people who aren't sure about religion. These "neoagnostics" are well-educated skeptics who have inexplicable metaphysical feelings. They regard religion as belief in the unbelievable. Yet they sense something important that eludes their most trusted tools of intellect and learning. Defined by ambivalence and longing, their credos are various: "There may be something," perhaps, or "I'm spiritual, not religious." Neoagnostics are America's most subdued, neglected religious group, yet they are one of its most powerful. They are everywhere, especially at the top.

Religion starts with a question about meaning. *What's true? What matters? Why is there something instead of nothing? Is this all there is? Who am I? What should I do?* Sometimes the question presents itself as rainy-Sunday-afternoon existential blues. A

fear of death. A shadow or hole in a fortunate life. Unlike believers, neoagnostics don't have a ready answer to the question. Unlike atheists, however, they can't help hearing in it
the possibility of something else.

I tried to answer, or at least muffle, the question in all the
obvious ways—love, achievement, stuff, therapy. The question always returned, tantalizing me with hints of an answer
or a glimpse of someone who seemed to know it. I looked
for an answer in nature, then art. I tried science, writing
two books about why our lives are the way they are. But
I got no closer to understanding what they mean. By late
adolescence, I had dismissed religion as anachronistic wish
fulfillment—half Brothers Grimm, half Hallmark, dreadful
at worst and limited at best—that failed to jibe with my
accumulating knowledge and experience. By middle age, I
wearily recognized it as the only road not taken in my pursuit
of the question.

This notion, like any serious expression of interest in religion, can attract odd looks in my urban professional world.
Modern America's brightest and best have long been encour-
aged to disparage the question and to think of churches and
temples as places where one's brains are checked at the door.
Some are atheists or true agnostics, who've concluded that
even if God exists, which can't be proved, God can't be
known. When combined, however, these two groups number fewer than 5 percent of Americans.[1] To their right, but
well to the left of traditional believers, sits the much bigger,
fuzzier group of neoagnostics. If one listens carefully, one can
hear them testify, sort of.

One night, I brought up God at a dinner party. Five years
before, or even three, this would have elicited a brief silence
and averted gazes. But my seven guests plunged into a discussion that lasted the rest of the evening. Like me, they enjoy

the unprecedented benefits of the turn-of-the-millennium American bourgeoisie and yet take for granted situations that until recently were considered crises. Just as I'm the first person in my family to be what my father calls a career gal, I'm also the first to be divorced, a single working mother, a partner in a mixed marriage, and a number of other firsts best left veiled. Living in a time when change itself has become the only constant, my friends and I have stared into chasms opened by family fractures and professional upheavals, depressions and addictions. We wish there were something better than psychotherapy to help us make a big picture out of our lives' mass of details, some of them gory. Superconsumers, we're sickened by relentless materialism. Superachievers, we're repelled by blind ambition and workaholism. "Rugged individuals," we feel a low-grade alienation. From the publisher recovering from cancer who was seeing a "healer" to the college professor who worried about his "pagan" children's moral education to the journalist who was suddenly becoming more interested in his "Jewish half," each person at the table spoke of something lacking in a life more privileged than peaceful, something that seemed to be, to paraphrase the ubiquitous expression, spiritual, if not religious.

After many more such conversations, I realized something that should have been obvious: Like me, the people I talked with had questioned and revised every value they were reared on—intellectual, political, social, aesthetic, sexual, *culinary*—except one. Since their childhood version of it, loaded with familial, developmental, and cultural baggage, had collided head-on with a college education, they had assumed that religion is for intellectual and emotional weaklings. What if the problem wasn't religion, but a childish concept of it? What if religion could be about something else?

There are those who write about what they know, and

those who write *so* they'll know. After some brooding, I decided to investigate religion from a neoagnostic's perspective. One motive for this undertaking was personal: At the end of three years, surely I'd be able to decide once and for all whether religion is right or wrong. My other spur was professional curiosity. While writing about behavioral science, I learned that memory is the cord that binds the individual's different selves into a coherent identity. Over time, I've grown less interested in personality, mine at least, and more interested in what might be called the human condition. Perhaps, I thought, religion might be the thread, running through human experience, that reminds our species of what's most important and real, yet so easily forgotten. Like memory, religion records the past, informs the present, and frames the future. Like memory, it might help us figure out who we are, what we should do, and where we're headed.

William James, a forefather of American psychology and spirituality, said that every religion claims that there's something wrong with the human condition, and that it has the solution. In the wake of the Rancho Santa Fe mass suicide in 1997, America contemplated how the followers of Heaven's Gate, who were not "the faithful" but "crew members," pursued the answer to the human predicament with a pastiche of beliefs and practices drawn from sci-fi movies, gnosticism, and the Internet, leavened with the spirit of paranoia. The grand meaning systems that are the great faiths have been tested by huge numbers of people over long periods of time. Rather than setting myself up as a denomination of one, I decided to center my inquiry on the three traditions I feel most at home with. Historically, my heritage is Christian. Socially, my world—husband, friends, neighborhood—is significantly Jewish. Aesthetically and philosophically, I've long been attracted to Buddhism. Because it increasingly influences these three, and arguably, all Americans, the New Age sensibility figures in as well.

Early in my reporting, I learned that religion had changed since the sixties era, when I dropped out of it. Back then, academe mistook religion's imminent transfiguration for its death throes. As if it were only possible to say what religion is no longer about, attempts to label the new sort are often prefixed by "post-," as in post-Enlightenment, postmodern, postdenominational, postcolonial, postrational, postsecular. No matter the label, religion at the year 2000 concerns questions about how to live at a time of unparalleled change and expresses dissatisfaction with conventional secular solutions— and often those of old-style institutional religion. The most publicized example is least attractive to neoagnostics: recourse to moral and theological certainties, whether by ultraorthodox Jews or evangelical Christians (a small movement until the 1970s, this fervent, creedal, "born-again" faith is now professed by 40 percent of Americans).[2] Another approach, called millennial religion in these pages, regards questions themselves as religious expressions, and in response, offers practices or processes as well as formulations. Both question-oriented millennial religion and the answer-oriented kind differ from the traditional American socially oriented sort that preceded them by their resolute focus on the reality of something else, which is often simply called spirituality.

Millennial religion poses three big questions. The first is the one that, in its various forms, drew me into this inquiry: *What is real?* To our ears, this sounds like a philosophical rather than a religious question, but such a distinction is recent and far from universally accepted. Describing a vast new encyclopedia of philosophy, an admiring reviewer observed that religion and theology occupy so large a place in these ten volumes of conceptual thought that it might have been called an encyclopedia of metaphysics: the knowledge of being and knowing, which assumes that reality is more than what meets the eye.[3] Like Socrates, Huston Smith, America's great scholar of comparative religion, considers probing the nature of *what is* to be life's most essential and moving inquiry. "I don't think that's simply a personal quirk," he says, "but very close to the heart of what religion is. The underlying message of the great faith traditions is that there's another reality radically different from the one that we normally experience daily. You may not believe that. If it is true, however, you may be certain that it's difficult to understand—at least as hard as quantum mechanics." Although it's accepted that it takes at least five years to understand relativity theory and particle physics, Smith says, people assume they can grasp theology's vision of the deepest reality from sound bites or childhood's half-remembered "exposure." After fifty years' immersion in the religious vision of reality, this learned man remains "in *awe* of its profundity."

Along with posing the philosophical question about the nature of what Smith calls "the biggest picture there is," millennial religion is engaged with reality in an everyday, practical sense. Although tolerant of mystery and unanswered questions, its adherents are simply not interested in spiritual doctrines, concerning issues from evolution to homosexuality to women's equality, that contradict their objective knowledge. For the past three hundred years, Western religion has been trapped in an intellectual losing battle with the Newtonian and Enlightenment worldviews. (Eastern religion has wisely refused to be drawn into such conflicts.) In the wake of their own postmodern collapse, wrought by the new physics and events from the Holocaust to the demise of socialism, religion and its former academic rivals are talking again, increasingly in tones of mutual respect. Physicists and theologians borrow each other's imagery. Therapists and clergy speak the language of a new hybrid that might be called psychospirituality. Rather than eviscerating the Bible with the tools of historical and literary criticism, a new breed of scholars has revitalized it.

Millennial religion must be able to coexist with what people know to be objectively true, but it must actively complement their internal, personal reality. Its second question is *What do I feel?* In 1996, MSNBC produced a week of programming called "Is God Alive?" While writing an on-line essay to accompany its special poll on Americans' religious lives, I was particularly struck by one finding. Of the 89 percent of those who considered religion important, only 29 percent saw it primarily as a tradition's beliefs and teachings. As if illustrating the popular term "spirituality," 69 percent regarded religion as their "direct experience of God." Perhaps more than coincidentally, the same number believed in spiritual healing.

This striking comeback of one of religion's most ancient functions epitomizes the new primacy of personal, mind-and-body experience. A third of Americans report they've experienced a "remarkable healing" of a physical or psychological problem.[4] The popularity of healing rituals in churches and temples also bespeaks a related pragmatic question increasingly applied to belief and practice: Does this help me get on with my life? An impressive indication of this shift toward the practical, personal, and democratic is the robust growth of the small-group movement: A quarter of all Americans now meet regularly with others to share spiritual concerns, seeking insight and support from peers rather than institutions and experts.[5]

Critics attribute the new importance of personal religious experience to narcissism. Harvey Cox relates it to a "disenchantment" with institutions, religious as well as secular, that has mushroomed since the 1960s. The Harvard theologian expresses this popular skepticism thus: " 'If it doesn't somehow touch me, I don't know what to make of it, and I'm not interested.' " More than thirty years ago in *The Secular City,* Cox famously predicted religion's decline in the face of modern progress. In *Fire from Heaven,* his most recent work, he recognizes that it's secularism that's headed for extinction.[6] A generation ago, he says, he correctly pointed to "the decline in belief in Holy Church," but missed the parallel phenomenon of "the disabusement of belief among the young concerning those beautiful promises that reason or science or politics were going to deliver us from our misery. All that stuff was oversold and went sour."

Attuned to the real and highly personal, millennial religion also welcomes different traditions' points of view. Its third question is *What are my choices?* In religion as in politics, scholarship, and the arts, sophisticated citizens of a global society no longer look to a single source for all the good ideas, much less Truth. Even within America, an infusion of immigrants from Asia, Africa, and the Middle East over the past thirty years means that neighbors are no longer necessarily Christians or Jews, but Muslims, say, or Buddhists. The number of converts of European ancestry who have embraced these "new" faiths has increased, but remains small.[7] Almost by osmosis, however, religious pluralism has subtly yet significantly modified many spiritual lives, whether by practices, such as Hindu yoga and Zen meditation, or principles, such as reincarnation, which more than a quarter of Americans now accept.[8]

The influential French scholar Danièle Hervieu-Léger describes the new, eclectic approach to religion with a homely metaphor: Rather than being a complete worldview or infallible arbiter of right and wrong, each tradition has become a "toolbox." A person roots through a chest labeled "Christianity" or "Judaism," or even "Catholic" or "Orthodox," ignores the elements that don't seem significant or "right"—

perhaps second-class status for outsiders—and uses the ones that do—sacraments, say, or keeping kosher. Within both Judaism and Christianity, the millennial quest for spirituality has even turned the past and its long-lost practices, such as the kabbalah and healing, into toolboxes of a kind. With them, people build up-to-date, customized religious structures that, like a renovated Victorian house or a brand-new log cabin, retain the *oomph* of tradition. Other individuals borrow tools from an Asian faith, or from the new "theologies" developed by women, say, or gay people.

Individual improvisations on a traditional theme are often disparaged by clergy and scholars as syncretism or mix-and-match religion. To equate the new heterodoxy with lack of seriousness or value is a tremendous, if very common, misapprehension that blinds many, from traditional purists to preacher-politicians to secular commentators, to the millennial revolution going on quietly around them. Those in one ivory tower or another may not like this new "layered" or "blended" spirituality, but huge numbers of people in the trenches do. It addresses their questions and needs in a way that the mostly empty conventional churches and temples clearly don't. If the results can be silly and shallow, they can also be vital, complex, and sturdy—and an important means of renovating dull, lifeless religious forms. As sociologist Wade Clark Roof, who has conducted extensive research on the religious lives of the baby boomers, puts it, "People are in a 'searching' rather than a 'commitment' mode. They have an enormous interest in religion, but in the form of exploring and checking out and mixing things together that may or may not lead to an old-style faith."[9]

After decades of apparent indifference, why are so many thoughtful Americans suddenly interested in religion? Sadly, age explains much of the enthusiasm. Religion, at least the kind of any interest to neoagnostics, is for grown-ups. To Carl Jung and Erik Erikson, the developmental task of midlife—the phase in which a third of us now find ourselves—is figuring out what existence is all about and reconciling oneself to that. A late bloomer, I for one am not much closer to that goal than I was at seven, lying in a pile of autumn leaves and thoughtfully contemplating a vast, burning blue sky. When hormones pushed us to mate and marry, we made a pseudo-religion out of relationships and parenthood, celebrated in the home-as-cathedral and presided over by psychologist-priests. Perhaps some existential gene has turned on now, impelling us en masse toward our next, more philosophical developmental stage.

Culture as well as chronology, I think, figures in this reconsideration of religion. The great experiment in secularism has been running for fifty years, and the results are mixed. There's much talk of a crisis in Judaism as the rate of mixed marriage hovers around 50 percent. Traditionally, this faith has been transmitted by the family as much as by the clergy and in the home as much as in the synagogue. To be Jewish was less about theology than about a culture that had not only its own beliefs but a language, a calendar, customs, food. As Jews have become increasingly assimilated into the American mainstream since the 1950s, Judaism is no longer necessarily "taken in through the pores," as one friend puts it, in a "good Jewish home." As a result, many Jews grew up largely ignorant about what only a generation ago wasn't just a faith but a seamless way of life. Although his secular father's ethnicity inclines him to "feel Jewish," Mike, my half-Christian hockey-playing husband from Minnesota, knows very little about Judaism. To learn, he'd have to attend classes. If we could ever resolve the familiar problem of "what to do about the children," so would they.

Just as there's talk of "post-Jewish" culture, there are rumors that America will soon be a post-Christian society. The same process of homogenization and secularization that affects Jews affects Americans from other traditions, often without their awareness. Nine out of ten citizens now identify in some way with Christianity, but how many of their children and grandchildren will? Although I could no more return to the religion of my childhood than bring my grandparents from their graves, I don't like to imagine their reaction to a great-grandchild pointing to a crucifix and asking, "What happened to that guy?" To the question "Where are you from?" they, if not their suburban offspring, might have answered "Holy Redeemer" or "St. Augustine's." Not just for Irish Catholics like them, but for Swedish Lutherans, African Methodist Episcopalians, Scots Presbyterians, Yankee Congregationalists, and Southern Baptists, religion was not a discrete entity housed in a church. It was part of a way of life that went far beyond beliefs to involve the extended family, a community, and often an ethnic culture. For me, Catholicism means not only grace and guilt, but uncles and aunts, Latin, the Kennedys, handicapped classmates, Gregorian chant, finnan haddie, winning a race at the public playground's "Protestant" Fourth of July celebration—a sweet-and-sour soup that for better and worse my own children will never taste. For centuries, my Christian ancestors and my husband's Jewish ones had an understanding of the way things are and how they fit together that we now wistfully call holistic, and religion was knitted into its smooth fabric. That life is different for us can be regarded as progress or decline, or even some of both, but there must be consequences.

On hearing the dreaded "R" word, numerous people, from my gynecologist to my accountant, have shaken their heads and observed that religion is to blame for terrible things, from wars to persecutions. Along with large-scale intolerance and inequity, it has created private hells of ignorance, superstition, and guilt. I agree, yet side with the Berrigan brother-priests, who said, "The church is a whore, but she's our mother." If religion—the record of our struggle to understand why we exist and what we should therefore do—has tragic flaws, so do the modern secular "faiths" of Marx and Freud that not long ago seemed destined to replace it.

When I began this book, I had no religious life. After a few months' research and thought, as I undertake my first reporting trip, I'm caught up with my first question. *What is most real?* Intellectually, pursuing it—God or no God—brings moments of philosophical grandeur, beauty, and pleasure. Emotionally, I feel *better.* Does this lifting of spirits have to do with a change in perspective? I wonder. With the mere idea of something larger than me and my vicissitudes? Already, I wonder why religious professionals spend so much of their energy on preaching to—or squabbling with—the converted, rather than trying to figure out and engage with what's going on in neoagnostic minds. I'm beginning to grasp that religion needn't focus on beliefs, but can at least begin with trust in your own experience of what is, but is mysterious—a different kind of challenge for a neoagnostic. I sense religion's capacity to bring order to internal or external chaos. Sometimes, for a few moments, I'm even buoyed by what St. Paul calls "the peace that passes all understanding." Most important, I'm thinking of religion as a process of working on God.

PART ONE

THEMES

CHAPTER ONE

SPIRITUALITY: JUST DO IT

A T FOUR-FIFTEEN on a cold, starry morning in California wine country, I slip out of my sleeping bag and into leggings, two layers of fleece, and sandals. Forgoing toothbrush for flashlight, I head up one of the steep, dew-soaked wooded paths that lead to the heart of the Sonoma Mountain Zen Center. Once an old redwood barn, the warm, oil-lamplit *zendo* has the soothing feel and smell of a sauna. A bell rings, and some thirty black-robed people, ranging in age from nineteen to the mid-seventies, commence the rapid execution of 108 full prostrations to Buddha. This is a workout, and by the halfway point, a few simply bow. Outside, the wind howls. At a neighboring farm, fighting cocks crow.

When the grueling ceremony is completed, we file out

in barefoot, silent pairs for a short break before getting down to the morning's real business: *zazen,* or seated meditation, and related rituals that will last until eight-thirty. Down in the farmhouse that's the social center for this community, or *sangha,* I clutch a mug of herbal tea and consider my mute companions' sleepy faces. The thick gray dawn presses against the windows. As my quadriceps turn to wood and my stomach rumbles futilely, I recall the reservations politely voiced by Jakusho Kwong-roshi, the abbot, about a raw beginner's joining them for three days of a rigorous silent Zen retreat called *sesshin,* meaning "to touch the mind."

In the fading starlight, a great gong sounds. We troop back to the *zendo* for two forty-minute rounds of *zazen,* the practice that's at the heart of this form of Buddhism. When I arrived yesterday, I had a brief tutorial with Kwong-roshi, one of America's handful of Zen masters, whose special authority has been transmitted from teacher to teacher through centuries. With his Chinese features, shaved head, robes, and aura of calm cheer, he could be a Hollywood lama. First he showed me how to sit cross-legged toward the edge of the hard round black cushion, resting my folded knees on a thick cotton underpad. After trying several postures, he decided that the Burma pose, which resembles yoga's half-lotus, suited me best. The thumbs of my nested hands pointed upward too much, he noted, which conveyed tension; I quickly corrected at least the digital component of the problem. Next, Kwong-roshi took a yardstick and measured the right place—about twenty-four inches from the floor—for my half-lidded gaze to fall when meditating. "We don't close our eyes," he said. "That may create other problems." Although this posture was comfortable enough, I knew that it wouldn't remain so.

Next, Kwong-roshi demonstrated the long, slow Zen breathing, which gives more energy to the exhale, "like you do when having a baby or using the rest room." He explained that a fetus breathes only once or twice a minute, and a Zen adept a mere five times or even fewer; with the slower, emptier unborn mind that results, conditioning drops away, "and we are able to see our basic goodness." One night, he said, he was driving with his four sons, now grown, when they came upon a terrible automobile accident. He rushed from his car, only to find one man already dead and another gravely injured, "lying in a pool of blood, staring up. I could hear his breathing, and it was *unshu*—Zen breathing. The man said to me, 'The stars are so bright tonight.' His eyes, too, were brilliant. Then an ambulance came and took him away."

My body taken care of, Kwong-roshi turned to my mind. I must simply concentrate on counting my breaths, he said, going back to "one" each time I'm distracted. "We usually let our thoughts just go," he said, "and our breath follows them, all over the place. Here, we make our thoughts follow the sound of our breath, so they naturally slow down and drop away. Breath sweeps mind." Before dismissing me, Kwong-roshi said that after doing Zen practice for a while, "you begin to live differently." Comparing *sesshin* to an express train, he advised, "Just get on and go." I nodded but didn't really understand either of these two comments as well as I would even a day later.

Now, finding my assigned place in the *zendo*, I perch carefully atop my cushion for forty minutes of *zazen*. Trying to remember all the roshi's instructions, I inhale and, especially, exhale—the optimum starting point for all activities. The redwood building, too, seems to breathe, creaking and groaning in response to the wind. After rushing around on planes and California's freeways for the past few days, I am relieved at first just to be still in the soft dawn darkness. Sitting tall, I earnestly try to do nothing.

A gong rings, and we rise stiffly for ten minutes of *kinhin,* or silent walking meditation. As if choreographing *Waiting for Godot,* we baby-step in single file around the *zendo,* going no place slowly. Gradually, the circulation returns to my right leg. Outside, songbirds announce daylight.

The gong sounds again, summoning us back to our cushions for the next round of *zazen.* All novelty evaporates, exposing deep holes in my concentration. As a writer, I'm accustomed to recording what's going on, even if it's only in my own head. Giving up thoughts, which are not only my business but my pleasure and existential defense, seems not only hard, but wrong. Some of this difficulty is cultural. The style of meditation I'm familiar with, as a Westerner, involves thinking *about* something, whether a bit of Scripture or world peace. Could this Asian thinking about nothing but counting my breaths be "better" than focusing on some worthy concept or image? Kwong-roshi said that his own master had taught that before one uses a calculator, one must clear it. Although empty mind eludes me, just gunning for it slows down and reduces the number of my thoughts.

Suddenly, the electrical outlet slightly to the left of my official gazing locus starts to get on my nerves. What is the point of sitting here in this uncomfortable position at a hellish hour of the morning, staring at a wall plug? I devise a koan, or Zen paradox: Why does Zen seem so smart and simple when you read about it and so dumb and hard when you do it? When the bell rings for morning "work practice," the prospect of chores seems Dionysian.

Time flies until ten-thirty, and the particularly grueling triple *zazen.* With *kinhin,* chanting, and a ritual meal, we'll be in this room, mostly locked into one position, for nearly four hours. I feel twinges of panic as I lower myself gingerly onto the now dreaded pillow. Familiar with this reaction from starting a long run, I give myself the same moronic, effective pep talk: If they can do it, I can do it. Because counting breaths doesn't feel right to me, I decide to repeat silently a simple phrase instead: "Here. Now." This is probably cheating, I think, despite trying not to.

By the light of the enigmatic, sound-of-one-hand-clapping Zen literature, I'm not sure that what I sense during *zazen* is "right." I can best describe it as an experiential version of a perception that helped to create modern painting. The elements of life's background—from breathing to consciousness, the sound of the wind to the *zendo*'s barny redwood smell—come to the surface, revealing themselves to be as vital as the more "important" things that usually occupy the foreground, and our attention. There's an awareness of *natura naturans*—nature naturing. Then, too, I can't help but notice that my thoughts and sensations come and go, but something else doesn't. Although my *zazen* state has no religious content in the usual sense, I'm reminded of theologian Paul Tillich's definition of God as the "ground of being."

During the afternoon work period, I invoke journalistic license to break the *sesshin* silence and talk with Helen, an energetic seventy-three-year-old. The retired director of a school for disturbed and disabled children, she does volunteer work with "people who need . . . things," she says. "When I die, I want to be like an old slipper." Living spaces here are shared, but her years and notorious snoring have entitled Helen to an old trailer in the parking lot. In this cozy home, I ask her why she practices Zen.

After some thought, Helen says, "I do it because I like it. I don't like to shop or go on cruises. My husband talked me into going on one of those, once. Zen is what I enjoy." She has studied here for ten years, "which is nothing in Zen, but an eternity for an American," she says. "Everything we do seems to last about ten years!" She esteems Kwong-roshi because she's "wary of charismatic teachers who push big causes and Asian teachers who don't understand Americans. Roshi's personal, one-man-in-the universe-right-now-here approach has a lot to offer Western Buddhism. In *dokusan* [a formal, private student-teacher interview], I don't go to him for answers, but I leave beaming with a sense of peace and comfort."

Although she was long a church member, Helen prefers Buddhism's worldview, which she first encountered as a child in Japan, where her family lived for a time. In the Judeo-Christian West, she says, "there's a hierarchy of God, then man, then nature. In Asia, there's not. We don't like to acknowledge what being a human *is*—just part of nature, an animal. We could all be killers in an instant!" She laughs merrily. "Every time you take a step, you kill." Within Buddhism, Helen prefers the Soto Zen tradition to the Rinzai school, which puts more stress on intellectual practices such as koans. "Here, it's what you do, not what you think, that counts," she says. "Marin County Buddhism is too intellectual for me! Here, people aren't always quoting at you. They're busy working and doing."

Asked what Zen practice has done for her, Helen stops to think again. "Rounded my rough edges," she says finally. "Sanded me. I'm not quite as righteous or irritable. I see now that harmony doesn't have to depend on two people thinking alike. With my husband, for example. After I had been practicing for a while, I said to myself, Helen, he's not perfect, but neither are you. We get along better now. I live now in more harmony with . . . whatever." She pauses again, then says, "Zen changes your view of the world from inside. First it turns it on its head, so that you think you're going insane." I laugh in a way I wouldn't have yesterday. "Then," says Helen, "it's just different. You realize that all you can concentrate on is what's in front of you, by being alert every second. There's still fire and flood, but all's right with the world anyway, and you're at peace."

On the second day of *sesshin*, no rays of light or seraphic voices have poured from my brown plastic wall outlet. *Zazen* remains extremely difficult. Aching legs and backs have driven a few people from the floor to chairs set against the wall. For me, the toughest part remains emptying my mind. The shifting light outside subtly alters the *zendo*'s atmosphere, just as thoughts and sensations alter my head's. Like the shadows, my internal states—boredom, contentment, frustration—come and go, while I just sit there, trying to pay them no mind. After the second sitting of the midday marathon, it's hard to believe there's a third. Wake up! scream the fighting cocks. Distinctions blur between them and me, there and here, consciousness and reality. Wake up! Wake up! (Later, Kwong-roshi says that the name Buddha derives from *buddh,* which means "awakened.")

A few months before *sesshin,* I went to the Museum of Modern Art to see the Picasso portraiture exhibition. Shrine-like, the small, final room held a triptych of three very late self-portraits. One painting, done about a year before the artist died at the age of ninety-two, portrayed that confrontation with mortality that not even the most protean creator is spared. A modern version of an ascetic saint contemplating a skull, it showed the artist with brain raddled and nerves exposed, tongue protruding and sparse hair standing on end. The features of the fragmented face are wildly sprung, as if from the coils of an old mattress. The right eye is upended, flat, as sightless as a dead fish's. Within this desolation, the only vital sign is the left eye: alert, unaccountably blue, and earnestly focused upward. The question is unavoidable: *At what?* One of art's greatest thieves, perhaps Picasso had appropriated a motif from religious carvings, Asian and Celtic alike, in which contemplation is signified by a face that has one eye open and one closed. A neuroscientist who studies consciousness once told me that our ideal state is this "quiet alertness," which is the goal of a lot of drug use, prescription and otherwise. Amidst his own disintegration, the blue eye in Picasso's death's head remains quietly alert.

The Zen art of paying attention is epitomized by *oryoki* ("just enough"), a special dining ritual from which the famous tea ceremony derives. During *sesshin,* meals are eaten ceremonially in the *zendo* after the final round of *zazen,* in silence and seated for meditation. Beside each person's cushion is a pretty nest of three bowls and wooden spoon and chopsticks, wrapped up in pale linen. Three times a day, we untie this bundle and sequentially arrange the cloths and implements just so. Heralded by dramatic drumming, designated servers bring food in large pots from the kitchen, bow before each person, ladle, bow again, and move on until everyone has been helped. Then, as one body, one mind, we tuck into the mysterious but very good vegetarian fare, a kind of spiritual comfort food. Sadly, custom calls for it to be eaten at a furious pace. Then, like members of some strange clean-plate club, we discreetly scrape our bowls and lick our utensils, rinse them with tea, drink our "dishwater," wipe our bowls dry, and tie up the whole business for the next meal. As I soon learn, the second one stops focusing, a bowl gets put in the wrong place, a chopstick falls with a clatter, a cloth is folded in half instead of thirds.

One night, just as I congratulate myself on finally getting the hang of this alien business, I pour tea all over my place mat. A server silently hands me a napkin that's folded into her belt for just such emergencies. As a server myself one morning, I forget to help the person sitting behind the big gong, until the emphatically rolling eyes of several otherwise immobile Buddhas signal my mistake as surely as fire alarms. I find *oryoki* maddening, but it poses a question: How much of my life do I waste on thinking of one thing while doing another, badly?

As my hours in the *zendo* accumulate, too much pointless thinking and feeling begin to seem like the cranial equivalent of overeating. During breaks, I sit on the stoop of the rustic wooden hut that I share with a mysterious silent, black-robed roommate (she turns out to be a very nice lawyer, soon to be married). I mostly just watch the California spring unfold: Red spiderweb / Moss-covered dime / Pale quarter-moon / Outside my door.

Sesshin simplifies my definition of religious experience to "the heightening of reality." (Kwong-roshi would say "the revealing of reality" instead.) The volume of what is is suddenly amplified, so that the usual faint tinkling becomes a symphony. Literature is full of illustrations of this intensification, from Huck's fusion with the Mississippi he drifts on to haughty Prince Andrei's deathbed realization that in the end, he is "a particle of love." Like Huck, Americans are inclined to have religious experiences in nature. In "Of Being," the poet Denise Levertov wrote:

> *I know this happiness*
> *is provisional:*
>> *the looming presences—*
>> *great suffering, great fear—*
>> *withdraw only*
>> *into peripheral vision:*
> *but ineluctable this shimmering*
> *of wind in the blue leaves:*

this flood of stillness
widening the lake of sky:
this need to dance,
this need to kneel:
this mystery:

My sense of the numinous is generally keenest upstate, in the fields and forest that surround my old schoolhouse. In winter, there's no plumbing and only a stove for warmth, but I'm willing to chop wood and carry water for a few days of crackling silence. One freezing morning, crouched in a snowbank by the creek brushing my teeth, I understood why monastic life has traditionally been rural and short on comforts. In a warm bathroom I would have missed this sere elegance of black crows and fir trees piled white. After a winter of such ablutions, what would spring mean?

One day last summer I was walking down a dirt road when suddenly, in an overgrown meadow, a bear rose up on its hind legs. So unexpected was this sight a mere two and a half hours from Times Square that at first I saw only a huge dog, standing with its front paws on a hidden rock. But the creature was as erect as a man, and as tall, too. The bear saw or perhaps smelled me, dropped to all fours, and disappeared into the tall grass, away from my neighbor's beehives and toward the forest. For years I've read about bears, but seeing one a few hundred yards from my house was something else again. Jolted out of automatic pilot, my perception sharpened and focused on the unexpected truth. There are real bears in the woods! Things aren't necessarily what they seem. There's more to reality than meets the eye. A so-called transformative experience, this ursine epiphany not only filled me with a need to dance, to kneel, but changed my perception of the world and my place in it.

Once in a while, too, it seems that something else is suddenly present. My five senses can't discern it, yet it seems quite different from a thought or other product of my brain. It calls for awe. I think, What great holiness! I think, too, that I'm getting only a fraction, a glimpse, a flicker, of this thing, because, as if it were electricity, I couldn't withstand more. Then, as mysteriously as it came, it goes.

Because of my science background, I'm intrigued by fleshy components of religious experience. While researching a story about the neurophysiology of orgasm, I learned that because it's a reflex, the nerve impulses that generate orgasm don't reach the cognitive areas of the brain; thus, the event can be neither exactly remembered nor simply produced by will. This universal yet evanescent, novel, giftlike quality is also characteristic of profound spiritual experiences. Perhaps they, too, are rooted in the instinctual, emotional midbrain— which in turn may help explain why intellectuals are so often uneasy about spiritual matters.

For most people, an experience of heightened reality is exceptional. For some of the great souls of Buddhism, Judaism, and Christianity, it's just the way it is. A research psychiatrist once told me that a baby wouldn't notice the effects of LSD, called "God in a pill" for its reliability in producing short-lived mystical states; the drug blocks a particular serotonin receptor, which seems to inhibit the adult's habitual perceptual filters, which an infant has yet to acquire. Perhaps what's true of a baby is true of a saint.

At *sesshin,* I inquire about *kensho,* or "see nature," which is Zen's term for the sudden, transformative perception of reality, including one's true essence. My questions elicit primness: "We all have special experiences, but we don't talk much about them. We don't focus on them, but on authentic practice." Talk is sparing in *zendo*s but often cheap in other sanctuaries. Many people who go to a church or temple seek-ing *kensho* get moralizing sermons instead. The fresh, deep consciousness they desire, which is true religious experience, may not even be mentioned, creating the impression that it's either a chimera or too "holy" to speak of or be enjoyed by the likes of them.

Known as a poet-philosopher, Ralph Waldo Emerson (1803–82), the father of American spirituality, began his ca-reer as an ordained minister. While pastor of a Boston church, he had doubts about the nature of the sacraments, resigned his position, and took off for Europe, where he visited Words-worth and Coleridge. After returning home, he developed his transcendental philosophy, which posits the divine as humanity's guiding principle and thus complements Ameri-can ethics of idealism, egalitarianism, and common sense. "I like the silent church before the service begins," he wrote, "better than any preaching." Many of his fellow citizens have given Zen a warm reception in the thirty or so years since it arrived from Asia largely because this silent, individualistic re-ligion is felt rather than believed. Indeed, there's some argu-ment about whether Buddhism and Zen are, in the usual sense, religions at all. Buddha himself was an atheist. Some prefer to describe the tradition he left behind as nontheistic, implicitly leaving room for something else. Most certainly, however, Zen is less a set of beliefs than a practice for the here and now.

Like all great geniuses of religion, Buddha was a master psychologist who focused on the human thirst for meaning and on relief from life's inevitable pain. After intense analysis of society and self, he concluded that all our misery results from the illusion of a separate "me" and the failure to appre-hend reality's transitory nature. According to his "four noble truths," life is full of suffering, most of which can be traced to desire, which in turn can be overcome, yielding peace. To pursue these truths, one must walk the "eightfold path," living with right views, resolve, speech, action, livelihood, effort, mindfulness, and concentration. Anticipating cognitive and behavioral therapy by some twenty-five hundred years, Buddha observed, "All we are is the result of what we have thought" and "all things can be mastered with mindfulness." His own grueling spiritual struggle had proved to him that enlightenment cannot be produced by intellect alone, but through something close to what we call a "gut feeling" that must be rooted in experience. To achieve this state, Buddha advocated the direct physical and mental practice of meditation that became Zen's core.

Many Americans think of Zen when they hear "Buddhism," but in fact Zen is an offshoot of the larger Buddhist tradition that began in India in the sixth century B.C.E. Zen's roots also extend to Japan and China, where the third-century sage Lao-tse taught simplicity, nonattachment, and attunement with the *tao,* or spontaneous, creative power of the universe—concepts that complemented Buddha's "way." Advocating a *caveat emptor* approach to religion, Buddha urged interested parties not to buy on faith, but to road-test the merit of his teachings themselves: "Come and see." Zen regards even its own sacred literature as illusory, compared to direct experience. When I asked Kwong-roshi how he described his religion to the uninitiated, he said, "I don't usually talk about Zen unless someone asks me a question. Then I may say something. Sometimes you don't speak about religion, but the other person gets a sense of who you are. That's a Buddhist attitude—thinking in terms of what someone else can experience with you."

Despite its Asian trappings, in important respects Zen is as American as apple pie. Like the nation's secular religion of sports, it teaches that peak performance looks simple but requires, as Buddha said, pushing forward like an "ox that marches through the deep mire." If I had to describe *zazen* in one word, it would be "exercise." On my hard cushion, I appreciate for the first time a systematic how-to approach to spiritual development that one *does*. Rather than ignoring the body or regarding it as a source of trouble, as in many forms of Western spirituality, Zen uses it. Like sports, this religion has clear rules, coaches, and equipment—a whole technology that helps people to become "addicted" to the activity and benefit from its unexpected side effects. Like working out, this spiritual practice unites body and mind, brings order to life, whispers that this too shall pass, and makes one feel good when it's over.

Zen suits America in other ways, too. It shares her anarchic, playful sensibility, articulated by artists from Walt Whitman to Kurt Vonnegut: "I tell you, we are here on Earth to fart around, and don't let anybody tell you any different." Like Jeffersonian democracy, it values independence and interdependence. Like Emersonian spirituality, it sees "big mind" embodied in each person, and life's beauty and joy contained in everyday moments.

As the millennium approaches, the experiential, individualistic thread remarked so long ago by Emerson runs brightly through America's religious fabric. Among nations, only India is demonstrably more spiritual. Ninety-five percent of Americans say they believe in God. (In what might be a head count of neoagnostics, sociologist Wade Clark Roof estimates that upwards of a third of baby boomers "affirm in one way or another a divine power or presence, even if they admit to uncertainty in their belief," and even though they also entertain "individualistic meaning systems," and remain "highly secularized in their conceptions of the forces governing life.")[1] Forty percent of Americans attend services weekly—an astounding rate when contrasted with the United Kingdom's 2 percent, say, or Italy's 5 percent. Interestingly, 90 percent of Americans engage in private religious experience. Of the 70 percent who pray daily, almost half feel that in some way or other God has spoken to them personally. Most Americans also believe in miracles, including more than 70 percent of those who have postgraduate degrees.[2] This do-it-yourself, "privatized" faith is rooted not only in Emerson's "God within" and John Muir's idea of nature as cathedral but also in the political principles of religious freedom and the separation of church and state. Even traditional believers are apt to feel that individuals should decide for themselves what to think, and that being a good Christian, say, or a good Jew doesn't depend on institutional standards, such as attending services.[3]

Of all forms of religious experience, Americans have traditionally been strong on the "community spirit" that's so often missing from postmodern life. On Sonoma Mountain, it's based not on superficial social similarities or weekly attendance at brief services but on the sharing of "big mind" and long-term practice. One of the paradoxes of *sesshin* is that silence creates solidarity, even intimacy. Soon, imposing chit-chat on others seems almost violent. In the quiet atmosphere, too, one appreciates the few things that do get said. Washing dishes one morning, I'm annoyed by one of my workmates, who rubs at invisible spots on pots I've already cleaned and generally acts the fussbudget. Then I notice the funereal calla lilies framed by the kitchen window, which, because I've been reading the Gospels, make me think of Easter and resurrection. A little chatting is a perk of kitchen duty, so I free-associate aloud, mentioning a thought-provoking biblical detail: Before raising Lazarus from the dead, Jesus joined the mourners and wept for his dear friend. Towel suspended, my fellow dishwasher nods happily and says, yes, yes, that *is* interesting. Standing stiffly over a steaming sink on a chilly morning after three hours of meditation, two unwashed, uncombed, barefooted people with not terribly compatible temperaments nonetheless beam at each other in peculiar understanding. Accustomed to "knowing" what someone else is like, or is thinking or feeling, I'm taken aback on the following morning by a brief exchange with a stern-looking, black-robed senior monk. Sure that he considers me a bumbling dilettante, I'm mortified to be caught before *zazen,* furtively trying to limber up with a runner's stretch against the *zendo's* outer wall. "It's not moving," he whispers. Much silent Zen hilarity!

On the final night during *zazen,* I'm summoned for *dokusan* with Kwong-roshi. On the first night, I had walked into the small chamber beside the *zendo,* plopped down, and said hi. Now, tutored in the protocol, I enter, walk to the left, bow to the shrine, bow to Kwong-roshi, do a full prostration, make another bow, and then sit as if for meditation. On the wall is a picture of his own teacher, Shunryu Suzuki, the late author of the splendid *Zen Mind, Beginner's Mind,* now in its twelfth printing.[4] A Japanese roshi, he came to America on a visit in 1958 and stayed to found the first Zen training monastery in the West. Even in a photograph, Suzuki-roshi exerts magnetism. Earlier, during a talk to the community, Kwong-roshi recalled that before his teacher died of cancer, their customary calligraphy sessions had become an ordeal for Suzuki-roshi, who was "so sick the brush fell from his hand. But we kept making the character for 'same.' He would point to it and tell me, 'We are the same.' I didn't grasp the meaning then, but as the years go by, I'm beginning to discover that it's true. Finally, because he was so frail, I stopped showing up for calligraphy. But that was a mistake. The Zen way is to keep going."

A minute of *dokusan* makes plain that the medium is the message, and Kwong-roshi is it. The feeling that there's nothing that I couldn't say to him (a sense I'll repeatedly have in the presence of the spiritually advanced) paradoxically makes the discussion of earth-shattering issues unnecessary. On another, surely lower, level, however, I'm a reporter, and I want to get to the bottom of this Zen business. I ask our species' most practical spiritual question: What happens when we die? Wonderfully, Kwong-roshi says, "That's being taken care of." Zen adepts don't fear death, he adds, because they've "practiced for it. Sitting kills the self. You see what that's like, so you're not afraid of it." When I say that I've noticed that the *zendo* isn't an environment for egomaniacs, he smiles.

The historian Arnold Toynbee predicted that one of the great developments of the twentieth century would be the coming of Buddhism to the West. Kwong-roshi agrees: "The transmission of mindfulness—not just the thinking mind, but the unconditioned one that you might call God and we call big mind or Buddha nature—is a whole new concept here." Rather than seeing mindfulness as a kind of talent, like artistic flair or musicality, he believes that everyone willing to make the requisite effort can attain it. "You wash your face every day, and then it gets dirty again," he says. "The conditioned mind keeps getting tainted, and you have to wash it—that's all. Meditation and physical practice just restore mindfulness." Buddhists don't believe in a god outside themselves—"you and I are Buddha," Kwong-roshi says. Yet he "doesn't have a problem" with theistic religions or their practitioners who increasingly borrow from Zen, "as long as we know we're talking about something that goes back beyond Jesus, Buddha, God—they're all just names."

Before taking leave of Kwong-roshi (I had been correctly instructed that I'd "just know when it's time"), I tell him about my mantra. Somewhat to my surprise, he says it's okay to use words rather than counting breaths, because "it's important that the practice works for you." I shouldn't get discouraged about empty mind: "Just release your thoughts by not entertaining them, and shift your attention to your breath or mantra." Reminding me that in two days it will be Buddha's birthday, "which means it's your birthday, too," he sends me off to sleep.

Late on the next afternoon after the final *zazen,* we form a farewell circle and offer comments on *sesshin.* The seemingly severe spiritual warriors smile and laugh; some cry. Kwong-roshi tells us, "Now you know what is available in yourself." Someone offers me the Zen compliment: "I admire your practice." I know that this means, "Even though clueless, you showed up for all the sittings and sat till the bell rang." But I'm pleased anyway.

After the electric atmosphere of *sesshin,* normal life is bittersweet. On Saturday night, like circus clowns, five retreatants jam into a compact car and head to Sonoma for dinner. The opportunity to bathe hasn't presented itself in three days, but courtesy of *oryoki,* my jeans are pleasantly loose and my good Italian jacket, pulled from a duffel bag, once again covers a multitude of sins. We eat fine food with forks, drink a lot of local chardonnay, and, unhindered by social posturing, talk about real things. We laugh a great deal, and at one point, the waitress gently chides us, in Californese, "for having such a good time."

On Sunday morning, just before the big celebration for Buddha to which the public is invited, I take a walk in the mountain meadows. My brain is like a room that's just been cleared out, scrubbed, and left with its windows open. Not much is there, but the space is clean, cool, and sunlit. All the things that worried me when I arrived—a sick parent, deadlines, a gripe with a friend—could worry me still. I'm just less inclined to engage with them. When the bustling for the celebration begins in earnest, I take a quick peek at the birthday boy's gorgeously beflowered shrine, and slip away. As I leave, Helen smiles and says, "Have a good . . . whatever!"

One evening after returning from California, I visit B'nai Jeshurun, a Conservative synagogue about a ten-minute walk from my house, for the celebration of Simchas Torah. On this holy day, the "people of the book" give joyous thanksgiving for their sacred Scripture. Although it's Saturday night in New York, there's standing room only, even in the balcony, where I end up among mostly young and middle-aged men and women dressed in casual weekend clothes. Downstairs on the *bimah,* the congregation's two rabbis, Rolando Matalon and Marcelo Bronstein, chant in sonorous Hebrew before the half dozen Torahs draped in red velvet. Then they invite the oldest congregants to carry the scrolls up and down the cheering aisles. Next, the more robust are invited to take the Torah to the street, followed by twelve hundred congregants. Musicians on a raised bandstand play klezmer tunes against the backdrop of the starry sky and the building's Romanesque façade.

It's a Methodist church. In 1991, the collapse of the original synagogue's ceiling became a blessing in disguise when B'nai Jeshurun's charismatic rabbi, Marshall Meyer, accepted the offer of the congregation of St. Paul and St. Andrew to share its roof. As I look at the crowd, it's hard to believe that just a few years ago, B'nai Jeshurun, like St. Paul and St. Andrew and many other older urban congregations, was moribund. Led by Meyer, and after his death in 1993 by his former

Argentinian students Rabbi Matalon and Rabbi Bronstein, B'nai Jeshurun has developed into a booming postmodern congregation.

Of the many ways in which B'nai Jeshurun could illustrate a textbook on millennial religion, the most obvious is its embrace of America's increasing religious pluralism. Without blurring or watering down their own traditions, Jews and Christians share the same sacred space and social ministry in their neighborhood. The synagogue's rich community life includes singles' Shabbat dinners and an employment bureau. A homeless shelter, soup kitchen, and tutoring project attest to its engagement with modern realities, as do adult education courses such as "I Can't Read Hebrew, I Never Went to Yeshiva, and I Want to Study Talmud." Although this is a Conservative, or more traditional, synagogue, Rabbi Yael Ridberg has recently joined the staff, and women not only wear yarmulkes and prayer shawls and read the Torah—practices previously reserved for men—but also serve on the board of directors. But most millennial of all is B'nai Jeshurun's emotional, experiential liturgy.

In America, where most Jews belong to the Reform and Conservative movements, most synagogues are sedate places that, with their pews, stained glass, and mostly English prayer, are not unlike mainline churches. Tonight, B'nai Jeshurun is closer to a Hasidic shul. With the strongest members holding the heavy Torahs aloft, we dance, clapping and singing, in circles and snaking lines, celebrating God's gift of words and wisdom. Over the festive din, Rabbi Matalon shouts instructions, which are not always immediately followed. Even the tough New York cops manning the roadblocks that divert traffic around the scene smile to see the city night throbbing with holy joy.

When I ask him later about why B'nai Jeshurun is so special, Rabbi Matalon, who is universally known as Roly, could be describing the classic millennial congregation. "We're an inclusive community where people can know each other, increasingly through small groups. We don't check at the door to see if you're rich or poor, gay or straight, have a religious background or not. Second, because religion can't stay within the sanctuary, we're dedicated to action and justice. God doesn't need our prayers, but our partnership in changing the world. Most importantly, we're spiritual. We look beyond the material life of paychecks and security to some echo of the truth that lasts and is meaningful when everything we take for granted crumbles around us. We believe in liturgy done with passion. Whether painful or joyful, life must be lived intensely, especially when standing before God."

Later, I attend one of B'nai Jeshurun's long Saturday-morning Shabbat services. Covering the Christian mosaics in the front of the sanctuary is a huge banner that reads, "How good it is when brothers and sisters dwell together in harmony." On Sundays, a big wooden cross is brought to the altar where a portable ark containing Torah scrolls now rests. To help congregants find Judaism's spiritual core, the synagogue offers several levels of Hebrew instruction each week. (Although some American Jews can follow the Hebrew liturgy as if it were in English, many more have learned only how to recite the language, much as Catholics once did with Latin.) In a way that English can't, the ancient language helps open "the gates of prayer," Roly explained to me, because it's "tailor-made for the ideas and values of this people." To illustrate, he offered the word *kadosh*. Its English translation is "holy," which calls up in the Christian grand images of angels and haloes. But *kadosh*, which derives from the everyday term for "to set aside," simply means that something has been made special, such as food or time, as in Shabbat. "Holy" and *"kadosh,"* said Roly, "open very different doors in the mind. In Hebrew, sanctity is anything that God wants me to set aside for a special purpose. God is the most *kadosh* of all. In English, we'd lose all these associations. For us, Hebrew isn't just words, but value concepts."

As at the *zendo,* the service's experiential quality is striking. Music plays a big part in the B'nai Jeshurun experience. As the congregation filters in on this Saturday morning, Ari Priven, the cantor and music director, plays soft keyboard melodies that have a meditative, settling-down quality. After welcoming the congregation, Roly draws our attention to Israel, where the spirit of the Oslo accords has been rapidly fraying. Perhaps, he says, peace is the "lost property" that today's Scriptures insist must be restored to its rightful owners. Then, the prayers of praise that begin the service are accompanied by a rippling improvisational mix of mystical songs and Israeli folk melodies played on guitar, keyboard, and organ. The combination of music and fervent Hebrew soon impels me to daven—rock back and forth in prayer.

Up at the *bimah,* within a few minutes' time, several engaged couples dance under an improvised *chuppah* (canopy), mourners stand to commemorate their loved ones, and the sick come forward to pray for healing near the ark. With dispatch, the whole human condition is lifted up and sanctified, gracefully creating what psychotherapists call a corrective emotional experience. Without any preaching, each of us is gently put back in our proper place in the great scheme of things. Like the people who dance, mourn, and ask for healing, we too have been and will be happy, sad, and ill. Like them, we're in good hands. Faces relax, smiles are shared. At one point, the members of the congregation, mostly seated as couples, friends, or families, put their arms around one another's shoulders and sway to the music. When a tall stranger next to me, who has his whole family in tow, slings his arm across my back, I blink away tears.

Already, my reporting has confirmed an insight gleaned long ago from two very different interviews. The first was with an astute psychiatric researcher at the National Institute of Mental Health. While discussing neurotransmitters, he suddenly looked at me and sighed. "The great problem in life," he said, "is how to balance your need for privacy and independence with your need for others and for love. The wrong ratio in either direction can drive you crazy." A complementary and more personal observation came from a cheerful Italian Franciscan. "You have that *Irish* energy," he told me. "It's wonderful when it's going outward, but when it goes inward . . ." He shook his head.

If I had to give one reason why religion is worthwhile, it would be that it's guaranteed, as the friar would put it, to direct one's attention outward, or as the psychiatrist would say, to balance the me:them ratio. A major distinction between a religious experience and other internal events of beauty or import, whether aesthetic, intellectual, or emotional, is that religion points a person, like Scrooge on Christmas morning, away from narcissism and toward compassion. All the great faiths promote loving-kindness and charity. Research shows that America's religious institutions are the major source of community volunteers, and that their members are far likelier than others to donate to charities.[5] When all is said and done, they're arguably society's greatest influence for good behavior.

Toward the end of the three-hour service, the day's bar mitzvah boy reads his Hebrew text and is then gently questioned by his teacher, Marcelo. Asked what the Torah is for, the boy says "it's about creating a just society." How does one know that one has done enough to bring that about? the rabbi wants to know. "It's hard to tell," the boy says—a fine answer, in my opinion. "We in the United States have more than enough, yet we don't do enough," says Marcelo. "It's immoral. In Judaism, it's not enough just to feel compassion without acting on it. For us, it's always love and action together." Finally Marcelo prays that God will give the young man "the courage to believe that he can make a difference and change the world. If the caring unite, they can make a new world."

Before we leave, we hear a few words from a special guest. Rabbi Jonathan Omer-Man, the director of Metivta, a center of Jewish spirituality in Los Angeles, is a highly respected teacher who studied with some of the greatest masters of kabbalah, or Jewish mysticism. His long white hair and embroidered cap set off a droll, sophisticated face that soon makes one forget about the crutches made necessary by polio long ago. In a flutey British-inflected voice, the rabbi addresses the day's Torah portion; in Judaism, rather than speaking off-the-cuff, it's customary to comment on a set text.

Today's reading from the First Book of the Kings concerns the in-your-face activist prophet Elijah and his run-in with Jezebel. Rabbi Omer-Man refreshes our memory of the details: The "urbane" wife of King Ahab decided to "put some spice in her life" by adding a coterie of pagan priests to her court. When Elijah, "one of the most uncomfortable people one could have around," killed fifty of them, Jezebel "put out a contract on him." Fleeing alone into the Sinai desert, Elijah went through an ancient version of Outward Bound. The first stage of his experience was self-pity: He had made a mess of things, and "wished he had never been born." Next came self-evaluation: What had he done with his life? As soon as Elijah softened up, nature kicked in. A great wind blew, says the text, but God was not in it. Next came fire and earthquake, but still no God; despite their power, these events didn't bring understanding. Finally, there came a quietness, says the rabbi, "implying that whatever would happen to Elijah would happen in silence."

To us, says Rabbi Omer-Man, the wind, fire, and quake seem to signify God. To the Jewish mystics, however, they stood for speech, imagination, and emotion. For them, God was in the silence, he says, "because that's the thing that allows you to reevaluate your life and make the necessary changes. Elijah had to be quiet before he could figure out that he needed to stop being so aggressive." As it was for the prophet, so it is for us. "Only in silence can we find forgiveness," says the rabbi. "We can't change our past deeds, but in quiet we can reflect on them, and then change our future course."

When I leave the Shabbat service, conducted mostly in a language I don't understand, I've smiled and wept, thought and felt. In my busy house of five children, Saturday afternoon is usually a hectic time of getting various athletes to various playing fields and doing all the errands that couldn't be crammed into the week. Today, however, I stroll home in the sunshine, humming Hebrew melodies. In broad daylight, I go to bed with my husband and stay put for a two-hour nap. For the rest of the day, I sing and smile. If the *zendo* provided one sense of experiential religion, B'nai Jeshurun has offered another.

On the following day, I meet with Rabbi Omer-Man to discuss millennial religion. Thinking of Shabbat, I wonder aloud why I'm so moved by ritual, even unfamiliar ones. "Spiritual community," he says immediately. "It gives a sense of meaning and direction, and of life that's bigger than one's own. It's healing without therapy." One of his most interesting classes, in fact, consists of psychotherapists "who realize that they've reached a place where they have no more answers," he says. "I think Western individualism has gone mad in its quest for individual fulfillment. That has had incredible benefits, but it has gone off track, until people now really think the individual exists separately from society and family."

Of those who "rebel against the cult of the self," says Rabbi Omer-Man, some look to the past, drawn to the tribal feeling and respect for tradition emphasized in fundamentalism. This style of religion leaves many unmoved, however, particularly neoagnostics. Describing Judaism as "the dream of the Jewish people," he says, "What happens is that rabbis—or priests, in Christianity—come along and say, 'This is the order in which you dream.' You say, 'But an angel was there on the hill and waked me.' And they say, 'No, he was in the valley.' Religion must have structure, accumulated wisdom, and even authority, but it can't be based on power. Imposing compulsory beliefs is like trying to make one part of the brain control the other."

With roots in Europe and Israel, Rabbi Omer-Man has a clear-eyed perspective on the difficulties thoughtful Americans face when trying to find a spiritual home. Although very religious from its early days, he says, the country is also pragmatic, results-oriented, and materialistic—tendencies antithetical to spirituality. To complicate matters, particularly for neoagnostics, a strong anti-intellectual streak runs through the country's religious history. Fortunately, he says, "when you go into the synagogue, it doesn't matter whether you believe in God that morning." We pause for a laugh. "You're worshiping the divine, whether you believe in it or not."

If some spiritually inclined Jews react against fundamentalism and its putative ownership of the faith's mysticism, others have been turned off by twentieth-century hyperrational Reform Judaism. When I ask Rabbi Omer-Man about the new trendiness of kabbalah—a spirituality du jour in the entertainment and fashion worlds—he rolls his eyes. This emotional form of Jewish mysticism began in eleventh-century France and flourished in medieval Europe, until it was gradually buried, outside of Hasidism, by Judaism's stress on rationalism and the law. The basic premise of kabbalah is that the words, letters, and numbers of the Scriptures hold mysteries that can be decoded with the help of esoteric texts. Once they gain knowledge of the ten "emanations," or forms of divine presence in the world, the initiated can sanctify every aspect of life and "repair the world." As throughout history, says Rabbi Omer-Man, "people want the cream without the milk." Some are drawn to kabbalah by its mysticism, while others hope for a kind of Jewish astrology, he says, "a head game of doing the different intellectual combinations of the emanations and levels of reality. The problem isn't that people are studying kabbalah, but that they're studying mostly bad kabbalah. It's meant to be a Jewish mystical tradition that leads you on the long, *long* path to enlightenment. Not the once-a-week seminar, but the long path."

When trying to distinguish between good and bad religion, Rabbi Omer-Man uses a simple gauge: "If it makes you work," he says, "there's a chance it might be a good one. If not, it's just another commodity for consumers. People want gimmicks. In the seventies, the Reverend Moon had some powerful tricks that gave people an instant spiritual experience. He'd get them exhausted, then march them up a mountain for sunrise, and they'd say, 'Without dope, I saw God!' That's a gimmick, not a practice. Spirituality is not a simple technique."

After *sesshin,* this muddy-boots approach to mysticism doesn't surprise me. "My number-one lesson in Jewish meditation is boredom," says Rabbi Omer-Man. "I don't know if this will attract millions, but it's like marriage. You have to woo people with some sort of experience; then things get less exciting. Some congregations have a problem in that they're afraid of boring people, so they entertain them instead. That's one good thing about the fundamentalists—they don't entertain."

When I ask just how one does Jewish meditation, Rabbi

Omer-Man says obliquely, "There are four or five ways. Sometimes using an image or a concept. More frequently a sound. There's watching the mind . . ." Remembering my hard cushion at *sesshin,* I complain about how grueling it is just to sit down and shut up. "Those were the first words my first teacher said to me," he says, beaming. "I had been asking him all these questions—and we weren't in California, but in Jerusalem, where people are much ruder!" When I despair of keeping an empty mind, he sympathetically says that no one can: "The mind is like a vacuum. All you can do is control what comes in." Simply limiting the sheer number of thoughts seems to help, I allow. "Exactly," he says, harking back to Elijah. "Silence is a *practice.* It isn't just going out into the desert or turning off the phone. It's maintaining a practice, learned over years, of creating little islands of silence within life."

When I ask Rabbi Omer-Man how much of a person's spiritual life is up to God, his trace of irritation reminds me that I should know better. Jews consider it unseemly for the likes of us to speculate about the divine nature or what God should or shouldn't be up to. "I'm just one person doing my job," he says, "and I don't know. Clearly, that's very important." Fools rush in, so I say that it seems unfair to me that, as with artistic or intellectual ability, some people seem to have a great capacity for spirituality and others little. "I don't think we can apply the word 'fair' to grace, which by definition is random," says the rabbi. "For years I've noticed that some of the most undeserving young people can have the most incredible spiritual experiences, often with chemical intervention, while older ones who work and work get little glimmers every three years. That's okay."

As I leave, Rabbi Omer-Man offers some advice. "Find a teacher or group," he says. "Be discriminating. Find a teacher who had a teacher. It's like buying a used car. Who drove it before you?" His last words on spiritual matters, however, are "Lighten up."

Of things that are hard for me to lighten up about, Christianity and its founder are near the top of the list. Nevertheless, since the 1970s, from the new evangelical megachurches to the Internet, they are prospering. At the millennium, one of three people on the planet and nine out of ten Americans identify themselves as Christians. The world's fastest-growing religious movement is a supremely experiential form of evangelical—"born-again," fervent, Gospel-based—Christianity known as Pentecostalism. (Its name derives from Pentecost, or the day when the Spirit's fire descended on the first frightened Christians, inspiring them to spread the Good News.) Although few readers of this book would be inclined to embrace it, in important respects, Pentecostalism is a bellwether of millennial religion.

Rather than creedal dogma, Pentecostalism emphasizes experience, particularly the here-and-now-on-Earth activity of the Holy Spirit, manifested during its liturgy in high emotionality and special "gifts and signs" such as speaking in tongues. Particularly popular in the Latin American, Asian, and American megacities, Pentecostalism claims one in four Christians, or 450 million people. In *Fire from Heaven,* his study of the movement, Harvey Cox argues that in failing to supply people with answers and meaning as anticipated, secular culture paradoxically triggered a global religious renaissance. To him, Pentecostalism is the most dramatic expression of "God's revenge on 'God is dead.' " In its "primal spirituality," he also sees a "mystical-experiential protest against an existing religious language that has turned stagnant or been corrupted."

When I first moved to New York City, my goal of securing the biggest apartment for the least money led me to a lively, run-down neighborhood that might have been airlifted from San Juan. The first night in my new home explained its attractive rent. By seven in the evening the walls were vibrating to the electric guitars, keyboard, and booming "alleluias" from a barely noticeable storefront church next door. Many years later, I remember two things about my Pentecostal neighbors. They literally lived the Gospel mandates of charity and inclusiveness. Their church doubled as a crisis center, which harbored addicts trying to kick their habits, wives of violent spouses, and others down on their luck. Just as I had never seen essential, give-all-you-have-to-the-poor Christian charity of this sort before, I had never seen such spiritual fervor.

My new neighbors' services usually began with loud music and praising the Lord, accompanied by clapping and swaying and testifying. Next came ardent prayer "in the Spirit," a sermon, more singing, and some simple refreshments. On special occasions, the whole operation moved outside, where the guitars throbbed and the reverend hollered the Good News through a microphone. I would peek from my window as certain congregants "got the Spirit," doing a kind of nervous dance and even falling to the pavement as if having a seizure. Americans of northern European descent may be squeamish about such overt manifestations of spiritual experience, regarding them as hysteria, neurosis, or fakery, but in many cultures, they are religion's sine qua non, and are understood as expressions of what is beyond words.

Pentecostalism's exact origins are disputed, but Cox traces it to Los Angeles in 1906. Turning from empty rituals and artificial barriers of race and class, William Seymour, a black preacher, and his congregation of the black and white working poor gathered to seek direct experience of the divine. These first Pentecostals were criticized for de-emphasizing the usual church hierarchy and doctrine; some of their modern successors are fundamentalists in their beliefs, but many aren't. "Pentecostals don't have a creed, or even a single denomination," says Cox. "Rather than being written down in a single volume, their theology is diffused among songs, prayers, sermons, and testimonies that challenge the secular worldview. You take your orders from the Spirit—your own experience of Pentecost."

Reservations about Pentecostalism resemble those voiced about experiential millennial religion in general, and not surprisingly, often come from institutional religion. Does a culture prone to search for God in a pill, prescription or otherwise, expect the same instant gratification from "designer" religion? Is the new "spirituality" motivated by a quest for authenticity or by narcissism? By feeling good or doing good? Rather than being shallow or trendy, however, Pentecostalism is just the latest illustration of how Christianity periodically leans more heavily on one of its "four pillars": Scripture, reason, tradition, and experience. The early church's focus on experience gave way to an emphasis on ecclesiastical tradition, which was fought by Luther and Calvin, who focused on Scripture. The Reformation was in turn challenged by the Enlightenment's stress on reason, which set off highly emotional forms of revivalism such as John Wesley's Methodism. In the twentieth century, American Protestantism, like Judaism, became increasingly "desacralized," or rationalistic and concerned with social issues. Voting with their feet, many people left mainstream religion for neoagnosticism or the fervent spirituality still often cherished in more orthodox traditions as well as in Pentecostalism.

Nearly seventeen hundred years ago, Gregory of Nyssa, an ascetic father of the early church, wrote, "For truly barren is profane education, which is always in labor but never gives birth." Many centuries later, even students at the nation's most elite—and traditionally secular—universities are less rationalistically and scientifically minded than their parents and grandparents. They're not fundamentalists or even conventionally observant, but they are interested in the spirituality of the great traditions. As an example of this "very big change," Cox says that Harvard's Jewish students "generally are far more serious about their religion today, although it doesn't necessarily pay off in weekly synagogue attendance. The young are vulnerable and have a touching need for something for which they're searching, and they go back to see what their ancestors did. The students can be very fond of their parents, but their construction of the world, goals, and values aren't exactly what the young want. They're drawn to the original vision—the core experience—of the different traditions, including the one they might have been brought up in."

Like Harvard students, most neoagnostics will never go to a Pentecostal church, yet they often have important things in common with those who do. Great numbers of Americans now question both secular materialism and religious dogma, prefer the intuitive to the canned, and opt for problem solving over rules and regulations. If he were to rewrite *The Secular City*, Cox says, he would explain that the sixties did in fact see a real erosion of religion as measured by attendance at church, say, or checklists of creedal beliefs. However, time has proved such standards to be "a very narrow way of looking at religion. What's happening is neither a secularization of, nor a return to, traditional religion, but a *change* in religion, of which the Pentecostals are one expression."

Despite the booming Pentecostal movement and Jesus' ubiquity on magazine covers and in bookstore windows, mentioning his name remains a highly effective way to cast a pall over a conversation among neoagnostics. Some of this aversion derives from the fact that he has been nearly kidnapped by the religious right, so that Jesus is identified with ranting televangelists, and "Christian" is often used as a synonym for "fundamentalist" or "reactionary." Then, too, a certain intellectual and cultural snobbery mandates that virtually any religion, from shamanism to Zoroastrianism, is better than the homegrown kind available down the street. Despite my ambivalence about Christianity, there's something appealing about its political incorrectness.

Christianity's main problem, however, at least in my world, is that Jesus symbolizes belief in the unbelievable. The unattractive figure many of us encountered in childhood went around saying things like "Blessed are the mournful," demanding that people accept him as God, and separating them into sheep and goats or wheat and chaff. I always knew which group I'd be in, and secretly thought that in real life only a creep would talk that way. On the other hand, Jesus' dour outlook was understandable, considering that he had been born so that he could be tortured and killed to appease his own father's rage at the rest of us, sinful from conception. Protection from this gloomy deity and his ferocious parent depended on belief in his divinity, which in turn depended on believing that Jesus had walked on water and performed other miracles. Within weeks of arriving in the brave new world of college and just in time for the sexual revolution, I left Christianity and its censorious founder behind.

At a loss about how to reapproach Christianity but determined to go someplace and do something, I join six thousand other people and several hundred remarkably composed dogs in New York City's huge Episcopal Cathedral of St. John the Divine for a celebration of St. Francis of Assisi, Santa's ecologically correct cousin. In an astoundingly beautiful liturgy that could rival any Lincoln Center performance, more than a dozen choirs, two dance companies, African drummers, the voices of humpback whales and timber wolves, and most of the passengers from Noah's ark join the Paul Winter Consort in celebrating Winter's festive Missa Gaia, or Earth Mass. When a black musician rises from clouds of incense to blow into a great white conch shell, the flower-strewn altar swarms with masked bird-dancers preening in brilliant spandex and feathers. Preceding the bearers of the ceremonial bread and wine, the drummers march down the two-block-long nave behind leaping dancers in golden sarongs. *"Ubi caritas et amor, Deus ibi est"* (Where abideth charity and love, God is ever there), sings the choir, mixing Gregorian, Yoruba, and Khemitic chants. Finally, in a breathless quiet, an elephant, looking as intricate and elegant as a jewel in the vast space, leads a procession of animals—camel, monkey, owl, llama, boa constrictor, hawk, even a hive of bees—down the aisle, radiating a magical civility and the wonder of creation that intoxicated St. Francis.

Under this glorious sensory bombardment, it's simply impossible to remain disengaged. The crowd reflects the cathedral's position, literally straddling impoverished Harlem and privileged Columbia University and figuratively, a staid WASP institution and the new urbanized, pluralistic America. If some here profess a devout Christianity, surely many have, like me, drifted away from it after childhood. Others, like my "half-Jewish" husband and our children, have never had a religion to reject. No matter what our backgrounds, we sway, weep, clap, hug, smile, exclaim, cheer. Thousands of strangers clasp hands and raise our voices in harmony. Better than the most eloquent preaching, we create an eschatological tableau that evokes Christianity's Great Commandment, drawn from the Torah: to love the Creator and the created as oneself.

Sitting in the church for three hours, I have plenty of time to take in the iconography of millennial religion. Along with the usual statues and holy pictures, the small shrines flanking the great nave hold AIDS and Holocaust memorials, fossils, a giant crystal, a bronze bison, a sculpture of the Wolf of Gubbio once tamed by St. Francis, and the living flora and fauna of the Hudson River aquarium. The Poets' Corner includes the names of Walt Whitman, Ernest Hemingway, and other writers not known for their conventional piety. The church bulletin lists not only traditional liturgical and community services, but also a healing ministry, an environmental studies center, and a pastoral psychotherapy program. The Sh'ma Israel, which is perhaps Judaism's quintessential prayer, is sung at the Scripture readings, and the ranks of religious dignitaries include not only black and female priests and ministers, but Zen monks and Native American spiritual leaders. From the great sunflower-decked pulpit, Swami Vivekananda, a Hindu sage, offers a prayer: "*Om.* God, there's nothing but you. Help us see all the unity in diversity."

The cathedral's millennial tone is largely the doing of the Very Reverend James Parks Morton, its dean. (He has since left that position to run an interfaith center in New York.) Over the past twenty-five years, the dean, a large, glamourous, open-natured Harvard man by way of Texas, re-created the cathedral variously as the church of peace, urban activism, the arts, the environment, and religious tolerance. Throughout his swashbuckling ministry, many doubters of high and low degree, from East Side grandes dames to street people, were lured into church by the dean's way of showing God's "kingdom" rather than talking about it. Exuberantly going about his business—championing low-income housing, vamping at a society wedding, exhibiting an image of a crucified woman, weeping unashamedly at prayer—the dean became a poster boy for a certain brand of Christianity—indeed, millennial religion. Where many saw broad-mindedness, warmth, and innovative spirit, however, others found imprudence and a religious promiscuity, if not heresy. Even his supporters allow that the dean occasionally drove them crazy. Nonetheless, as one priest later tells me, "On their deathbed, everyone wants Jim. I sure would."

Later, trying to explain how the St. Francis liturgy somehow re-created the Garden of Eden before the Fall, I come up with two elements: an unfamiliar sense of self and others, and a hint of something else. Most intriguingly, the magic had nothing to do with believing the unbelievable, but came from trusting one's own experience of mystery. Perhaps the final blessing, given by Dean Morton, says it best: What we experienced was "the peace and joy that passeth all understanding."

Impressed, but still not ready for traditional Sunday services, I return several times to the cathedral for vespers. The church's early-evening office, or prayer rite, is traditionally conducted in candlelight. The flames are meant to represent God's power over chaos, and perhaps our proper place in a universe in which we are but flickers. Vespers is particularly soothing when one enters the church in daylight and leaves in darkness. Throughout the ritual, the setting sun progressively dims the great nave and brightens the candles, wordlessly replacing us into nature's diurnal rhythms, which the city's glitter and round-the-clock light often overwhelm. By gently recognizing realities, from the sunset to our day's-end fatigue to the many others in need of prayers, vespers restores my sense of place in the world and stirs a longing for something larger that contains us all. In the old stone church, listening to the ethereal medieval and Renaissance music, I recall C. S. Lewis's observation that we can't give up on the idea of heaven because our own experience suggests it.

One evening, the short homily is given by Canon John Luce, who artfully distinguishes between religion and spirituality. The problem with institutional religion, he says, is that it "often keeps Jesus locked up in the church and out of the world, which doesn't jibe with his teaching at all." But the church has a good side: community. To Canon Luce, "spirituality" means "I don't need the church because I can go to God directly," yet Martin Luther King, Desmond Tutu, and Dorothy Day, the founder of the Catholic Worker Movement, came from organized religion, not spirituality. He tells about walking down Chrystie Street in New York's tough Lower East Side one day with Dorothy Day, "who had *nothing*—a chair, some cookies." They encountered a hideous, stinking, sore-covered beggar. Day embraced him tenderly and chatted with him for a few minutes. When they proceeded on their way, Luce asked, "Who is that?" She said, "Why, John, it's Jesus." Imagining myself in Day's shoes, my heart sinks. Throwing up his arms, the priest says, "It's because we're Christians that we can embrace all others regardless of differences. We do it because that's what Jesus does."

The cathedral, says Canon Luce, is "inclusive, not exclusive. We Anglicans are Incarnation Christians, who celebrate God in the flesh. Jesus talked about a brand-new tribe or society— the people of God. The cathedral's premise is 'Let's behave like the Kingdom is already here! Don't just preach it, but do it! Let's show each other how it can be!' " Surely, I think, the Kingdom must be something like what was summoned up on St. Francis day. Heart on fire, the holy old man who has spent his life ministering to the poor tells us, "Religion demands a leap of faith. Its only question is 'On what are you willing to bet your life?' Then, you must live your answer. Just try it!" He laughs. "Do it! Love everyone! Fight injustice! See what happens!" In this invitation, as in the little story that preceded it, I recognize the heart of the Christian message, feel its push-pull, and stay away from church for a while. I would much rather study or meditate than fight injustice or love everyone.

After a few weeks, I brave one of the cathedral's low-key weekday Eucharist services. Part of the huge church's genius loci is that, like a vast forest, it contains many microenvironments that give a sense of shelter and intimacy. Held at noon in the small St. Martin's Chapel, one of several in the semicircular apse just behind the great altar, the Eucharist attracts an eclectic little group of about fifteen or twenty Columbia folk, clergy, office workers, and the occasional shopping-bag lady. The rough gray stone walls glow softly with light filtered through the old stained glass. The only sound is the abundant birdsong from the close. There's little in the way of decoration, other than a small cross and a serene Joan of Arc, eyes modestly cast down; she reminds me of Kwan Yin, a female Chinese bodhisattva.

The Eucharist is celebrated by Canon Jeffrey Golliher, a compact, bearded Southerner with a quiet but intense manner. Listening to the Bible readings, I cautiously allow to myself that being here feels okay. In his brief sermon, in which he seems to be just talking about how life is, the priest addresses this very thing: Why *should* we feel okay? Even good? First, he repeats a line from Psalm 139: "For it was you who formed my inward parts; you knit me together in my mother's womb. I praise you, for I am fearfully and wonderfully made." Some people like to talk about salvation, he says, but he prefers to think in terms of awakening or remembering—and of course, sleeping or forgetting. Salvation, he says, is when we remember that God knew us before we were formed in the womb, and always will know us. Being lost is when we forget. Salvation is waking up to a world pervaded by the sacred, and being lost is being asleep to that fact. Salvation means putting our faith in this different reality, he says, "so that we aren't yanked all over the place by random events we can't control or by our own emotions. It's a disciplined, wide-awake calm that comes from remembering what's really true, and from prayer. Jesus said that prayer is an exploration. 'Open your hearts.' 'Don't judge, so that you won't be judged.' Those are magnificent ways to say 'Be open to the world'— to new possibilities, including who you think you are, and transcending a lot of what you were taught.'"

The roomy way in which Canon Golliher talks about such things is about the only kind of Christianity I can handle. One day, we have coffee in the Hungarian Pastry Shop, a hallowed sanctuary of West Side artists and academics that's just across the street from the cathedral. Jeff explains that he was an anthropologist and a professor in the college-degree program at Attica prison before his midlife ordination and now directs the cathedral's healing and environmental ministries, along with serving as an Anglican observer at the United Nations. It already seems to me that he's also a laid-back, low-key missionary to neoagnostics.

Most of the time, Jeff says, he doesn't talk much about ecology or healing, which he sees as the same thing, or even about religion, but about "meaning in life. I try to have really honest conversations that create sacred space, in the sense of making a place where you can tell the truth to yourself. That's it. That's a religious experience in itself. A lot of us don't have it often, as we didn't in our childhood churches and temples. Once that sacred space is available, people will have questions about how to live respectfully. Simplicity becomes available, at least as a thought, a possibility?" The more important the subject, the more Southern he sounds, ending his sentences, even declarative ones, on an upswing, as if they were questions. In this engaging way he can quite emphatically tell you something while seeming to be just wondering. "Then," he says, "people might want to make some changes in how they live?"

From Jeff's perspective as both professor and priest, working on God is a good thing. "I don't have an intellectual model of God," he says. "For the time being, and maybe forever, I don't want people to have preconceptions about what God's supposed to be. I want them to get rid of a lot of images so they can see God as a mystery that's real in everyday life." If pressed to define the divine, he says, "I'd say that there's this thing called spirit—I'd leave it at that—which, when encountered, makes you feel like you've woken up after being asleep?" As a Christian clergyman who has also learned from Central American shamans, he says, "the distinction between theology and culture is not a particularly real one to me. Whatever we call it, I'm interested in meaning and how we organize our worlds. Religion should give a sense of 'This is what the universe is like' that's more real than the standard version. To me, there's a sense of well-being, compassion, and a strange kind of neutrality about how the universe works, not in the sense of 'uncaring,' but in there being a peace beyond thinking about or testing—*shalom* 'that passeth all understanding.' God's a name for all that mystery?"

Gained in a *zendo,* synagogue, and cathedral, my recent experiences have given me a new sense of religion as relying on intuition more than belief. Yet for neoagnostics, trusting our own experience in such a matter is a challenge; it means going with our deep, personal perceptions of what is, which our education urges us to doubt. Since the Enlightenment, religion has lain at one end of a philosophical spectrum and science's version of reality at the other. To interest neoagnostics, however, just as religion must be "real" in the experiential sense, it must also harmonize with what we intellectually know to be true. Next, I decide to investigate the improbable rumors that after more than three hundred years of warfare, there are signs of a truce, if not peace, between science and religion.

CHAPTER TWO

RELIGION GETS REAL

There are a sort of men who are well trained in
the liberal sciences, but this does not content
them. They do not hold back until they behold in
its greatest extent and perfection the full blaze of
Truth, whose splendor, even now, shimmers
beneath the surface of such sciences.

—AUGUSTINE OF HIPPO

HIGH IN THE SHANGRI-LA of Berkeley's hills, I pass a late Sunday afternoon in the sunlit parlor of Huston Smith, author of *The World's Religions* and of one of my favorite remarks: "A man trying to understand God is like a dog contemplating man. He knows something about the other, but not everything."[1] For fifty years, he has studied and taught the world's eight great spiritual traditions in secular bastions such as the university here and the Massachusetts Institute of Technology. After a few minutes with this tall gentleman silvery with wisdom, age, and grace, Merlin unaccountably comes to mind.

High on religious experience, I go on about its millennial triumph over institutional belief. After the courtesy of a moment's consideration, Smith says, "I'm not sure I agree. Stale doctrines that have lost all vitality get you nowhere. But experience comes and goes. The word is as amorphous as any our language possesses and has a shadow side, which is the touchy-feely thing. For some, if not all, people, religion begins with being bowled over by a new vision of the nature of things. Hope must be anchored there, if it's to inspire conviction. Such views of reality can change but are more stable than personal experience."

To Smith, humanity's most important question is, "*What is the nature of reality? The big picture? The final way things are?* Kafka says, 'In your struggle with the world, bet on the world,' and he's right! The big picture is 'the world' in its ultimate sense." Is this hyperreality God? I wonder. "Or any other name one might wish," says Smith. "In Islam, it's Allah. In Hinduism, Brahman. In Taoism, the Tao. They all refer to the final nature of reality."

Taking heart from the thought of my old Labrador retriever pondering me, I venture a guess as to the essence of this thing, as the medieval philosopher St. Anselm said, "than which nothing greater can be conceived." It must be, I say, some kind of consciousness? "It is aware, and more like mind than a birdbath, for sure," says Smith. "But it's infinite mind, which is as much beyond ours as yours is beyond your dog's. Brahman's characteristics are infinite being, awareness, and bliss. We can have only the most rudimentary notion of what that infinity is."

In the age of psychology, Smith's discussion of religion is philosophical, even in the old definition of the term as inclusive of science. Both religion and science, after all, concern ontology: the study of the nature of being, or the fundamental, unchanging essence that underlies all else. Considering the magnitude of this big picture, whether drawn by physics or religion, it's not surprising that most people focus on a much smaller one: the self. Although he allows that therapy can help certain types of problems, Smith says, "it's a poor substitute for religion, which takes one out of oneself in commitment to something greater and trivializes the ego by comparison with the larger self one can identify with and become."

If a religion's heart is its compelling vision of the nature of reality, Smith says, it isn't surprising that so many sanctuaries are empty. Although he wants religion to be more like science in regaining the ontological focus it once had, he would expect the two ontologies to be very different. In science, ultimate reality is the deepest structure of nature, Smith says, but "science deals only with nature, which is only part of reality. For all its power, it's a radically limited instrument, because its crux is the controlled experiment. Because we can only control things inferior to us, those are the only things science can tell us about. It speaks to technology, not wisdom." In an effort to fit into secular, science-minded society, modern mainstream American religion has often compromised, if not surrendered, its unique spiritual and philosophical perspective.

Neoagnostics in particular perceive an either/or relationship between the scientific and the religious worldviews. The postmodern challenge, however, is not choosing between them, but recognizing the proper sphere of each: nature and a reality that is something else, which is deeply related to life's meaning. With nearly evangelical fervor, Smith asserts that instead of articulating "a robust alternative to the conventional worldview, mainline liberal churches have tailored their theologies to the standard outlook of today's intelligentsia." Pointing out that these churches' memberships have declined by 25 percent in as many years, he traces a disastrous domino effect in which professors in mainline seminaries look up to their closest counterparts in the prestigious universities and take on their styles of thought, which are secular to the core. "True, one still hears the *word* 'God' in seminaries," says Smith, "but what is the cash value of that word in a worldview that is architected by Einstein, Darwin, Marx, Freud, and Nietzsche, and to which God can be added or not according to taste? Traditionally, human beings saw themselves as divinely created and only slightly inferior to angels. Darwin positions us somewhere above other animals." Unsatisfied by this secularized religion so popular in intellectual seminaries, many congregants vote with their feet, turning to conservative traditions, Asian religions such as Sufism and Buddhism, or New Age spirituality, all of which vigorously champion what Carlos Castaneda called "a separate reality."

Like the philosopher Alfred North Whitehead, Smith thinks that the future depends on the relationship between history's two most powerful forces. "First, religion had the power," he says, "and used it badly to try to strangle some of the sciences in the cradle. Now science has the power, but not the adequate worldview. A major task of the next millennium is for them to settle into a respectful relationship that recognizes the competences and limits of each."

The relationship between science and religion looms large in neoagnostic minds. In short, because science proved to be right about nature—evolution as opposed to the Garden of Eden, the heliocentric versus the geocentric universe—religion would seem to be for dummies. This idea is rooted in the era of the Enlightenment and the birth of what is now called classical or modern physics—the old-fashioned kind I was taught. For more than three hundred years after Isaac Newton, perhaps history's greatest scientist, physics focused on the atom as reality's most basic unit. Because it was first thought that atoms don't alter through time, change was assumed to be the result of their movements. Simply the sum of its parts, the universe was a mechanism that, given appropriate technology, could be completely, empirically explained. The truth about it came not from personal experience but from "the numbers," or hard data. This clockwork worldview was complemented by the rational philosophy of the Enlightenment, whose rosy vision of progress presided over by governments, not gods, is epitomized by the U.S. Constitution.

For all their glorious achievements, Enlightenment philosophy and classical physics created profound disruptions in the West's inner life. Suddenly, creation and creatures had become machines. Sacred mysteries became things that science simply hadn't yet explained. The new "God of the philosophers" was an engineer who had once thrown the switch of a cosmic assembly line and then retired. The new high priests of quantification began to address humanity's great questions, including the most basic: Why does anything exist? "Incredible coincidence," said science.

As the public grew increasingly impressed by science's achievements within its proper domain, such as technology, religion was inexorably banished to an intellectual netherworld where science could more or less be ignored. After Kant tried to "save" religion by arguing that it concerns a different order—morality—it increasingly gravitated toward what amounted to social work. By the 1960s, God was widely reported as missing and presumed dead.

Theology wasn't paying much attention, but since Einstein's theory of relativity, the clockwork of Newtonian physics had been ticking erratically. Cosmology—the study of the universe, or largest thing—proposed the big bang theory: Instead of just *being there,* the universe began, started by an uncaused cause. Perhaps even God? Leading cosmologists such as Stephen Hawking and Freeman Dyson asserted that the probability of the coincidences required for the existence of life in the universe is near zero, and Hawking even dined with the pope.

From the opposite end of the spectrum—the science of the motion of subatomic particles, or the smallest things—quantum mechanics proposed a new vision of reality that inclines physicists to sound like theologians. (Some even cross professional lines: Cambridge particle physicist John Polkinghorne became an Anglican priest and author of books such as *Quarks, Chaos, and Christianity.*) According to its principle of "nonlocality," reality consists not of individual, isolated entities, such as particles of matter, but of sets of fundamental relationships. (For example, a single molecule doesn't have temperature, which is a collective phenomenon that arises from the interaction of many molecules.) Instead of looking like a clock, quantum reality looks like "chaos," where seemingly hard boundaries are revealed as active and blurry. Even former apples and oranges such as energy and matter aren't discrete. One no longer speaks of waves and particles, but rather "wave-like" and "particle-like" properties, or even "wavicles." Nor is physics the only science that has embraced this more complex paradigm of reality. In biology, the cell is no longer studied in isolation, because its functioning is so much affected by its neighbors' electrochemical activity. Where behavior is concerned, the most sophisticated investigations of why we are the way we are reveal a psychobiological "second nature" that genes and environment create between them. In short, rather than elaborating on Newton's blueprint of reality as a giant gadget built of widgets, the deeper scientists probe, the more nuance and interrelationship and the less mechanistic determinism their picture of reality reveals. This doesn't assume God or creation, but it can accommodate, even sometimes imply, such things.

By challenging the way we usually think and expanding our capacity for wonder, science itself sometimes seems to suggest new approaches to what has been described as the supernatural. According to quantum theory, for example, the smaller a thing, the more powerful it becomes, which can bring the idea of God to mind—mine at least. Certainly concepts and terms from physics crop up frequently in conversations about religion these days—and vice versa. I like the paradoxical quantum language, which evokes an ancient, esoteric Christian prayer tradition known as apophatic spirituality, or the *via negativa*. By its dark lights, because the human mind is incapable of comprehending what God is, we can only accurately determine what God *isn't;* the sole certainty is that any name for or theory about God will be inadequate. In the Zen saying "The mountains are always moving," and Psalm 114, which says that when the Israelites were delivered from Egypt, "the mountains skipped like rams, and the little hills like young sheep," there are intimations of wavicles.

One day I talk about the new dialogue between religion and physics with Robert John Russell, a physicist and theologian who is the director of the Center for Theology and the Natural Sciences at Berkeley's interfaith Graduate Theological Union. "We talk about God as a disclosure of ultimacy in immediacy—our ordinary present experience," he says. "What could that mean? Perhaps it's like wavicles and other quantum paradoxes that assert something while also denying it. Both physics and religion are riddled with essential paradox and point to the numinous that goes beyond language. Each relies on analogies to illuminate a phenomenon that they also must, in the end, leave shrouded in its inherent mystery."

As someone who's committed to both religion and science, Russell is one of an increasing number of respected intellectuals who are dedicated to bringing about their right relationship. "Science without religion is lame," said Einstein. "Religion without science is blind." If physics becomes the key to reality, important phenomena that lie outside its domain, such as consciousness, are overlooked, says Russell, "and you end up with a mechanistic system." In his view, theology's much broader view of human nature demands that it "push back on science and say, 'Look, you give us a window on the world. But if that becomes the only clue to reality, it's like fishing with a two-inch fishnet and saying there can't be one-inch fish.' "

What I know of physics amounts pretty much to wonderment at the vastness at one end of its inquiry into the nature of things and the minuteness at the other. I must take the word of cognoscenti that its new vision of reality gives religion's ancient one some elbow room. Yet as I continue my reporting I grow less concerned about agreement, or lack of it, between religion and science. Academics on both sides of the fence are understandably concerned with battling ontologies; some now hold on to two contradictory concepts in the hope that the effort will give birth to a new way of thinking. As they go about their lives, however, most people find a way to entertain both science and mystery, as they do other very different viewpoints.

According to the "pluralism" of the late Oxford philosopher and social theorist Isaiah Berlin, there are certain important values, each as "true" as the other, that are simply incompatible, and that's that. In an essay called "The Romantic Revolution," he points out that most people subscribe to principles from both of modernity's great wellsprings: the Enlightenment and Romanticism. Although these philosophies conflict mightily, we nonetheless weave their rational and emotional worldviews into the fabric of our lives. There's no need for such principles to fight it out or conflate; they need only to be civil, allowing people to enjoy the benefits of both.[2] Making a similar case, the eloquent physicist Freeman Dyson points out that other traditions regard science and religion ("a way to live") as two different domains that needn't conflict. Christianity alone wars with science, he argues, because both are rooted in Greek thought and its quest for absolute truth. Science plumbs nature for it, while theology pursues the science of God. Each claims its vision of reality is the only correct one. Yet, says Dyson, "Just as science can live without certainty, religion can live without dogma, and the two can live together without conflict."[3]

So they did in the mind of Blaise Pascal. A deeply devout Christian, the French scientist and philosopher discovered the theory of probability and the properties of the cycloid, and advanced the fields of differential calculus and hydraulics. After his death, this note was found sewn into his coat's lining: "FIRE. God of Abraham, God of Isaac, God of Jacob, not of the philosophers and scholars. Certainty. Certainty. Feeling. Joy. Peace. 23 Nov. 1654."

Signs that antipathy to religion is no longer virtually an intellectual credential are cropping up everywhere. The relationship between science and faith inspires an increasing number of intellectual books and conferences. In 1997, the prestigious journal *Nature* reported that 40 percent of scientists believe not just in some vague cosmic force, but in a God who's in communication with humanity and answers prayers. Hard scientists, such as physicists, chemists, and mathematicians, seem even more inclined to hold such beliefs. A long profile of Bill Gates, the high priest of computerdom, included a number of references to religion that would have been hard to imagine in such a story even a few years ago. Asked if there might be something special, even divine, about the human soul, Gates doesn't sneer but says simply, "I don't have any evidence on that." Calling the mind a "creation," he says that although it can be explained in software-like terms, "it shouldn't be compared to software. Religion has come around to the view that even things that can be explained scientifically can have an underlying purpose that goes beyond the science. Even though I am not religious, the amazement and wonder I have about the human mind is closer to religious awe than dispassionate analysis."[4]

Even among neoagnostics, there are few experts on physics. Regarding the knowledge at the other end of the scientific spectrum, nearly all consider themselves adepts. At the millennium, like physics, psychology is one of the prisms through which we see reality.

One afternoon at the Sonoma Mountain Zen Center, I walk up the road to the home of Shinko Kwong, a monk who is the wife of Kwong-roshi. During *sesshin,* I had been impressed by how this small, sturdy woman, in Zen parlance, "sat like a mountain." When I ask about her evolution from daughter of secular Chinese immigrants to graduate student in psychology to mother of four sons to monk, she begins with a classic adolescent existential crisis à la J. D. Salinger's Franny. Recalling how her perky childhood persona as a pom-pom girl and good student began to fray in college, Shinko says, "I'd look at all these people rushing around and wonder, What for? What does it all mean? What's the *point?*" When the girl most likely to succeed stopped getting A's and started having crying jags, Shinko and her family feared an emotional breakdown. One day, an anthropology professor gave her the Upanishads, the classic Hindu exposition of reality as based on Brahman—the universe's eternal, conscious ground—and atman—the individual's inner core.

After reading the Upanishads, Shinko says, "I knew my unhappiness was about a religious question. As soon as I understood that, I was okay. But what if things had gone another way? What if that one person hadn't given me a book? That act is why I'm here today." Like many deeply religious people, Shinko doesn't believe in coincidences. "Every time you meet someone," she says, "it's a unique opportunity. You can go 'oh,' or 'Ohhh!' That teacher affected the course of my whole life."

Only after their marriage did Kwong-roshi, then a commercial artist, begin to study Zen Buddhism with the charismatic Shunryu Suzuki. As an independent woman in prefeminist times, Shinko recalls, she said to herself, "If my husband is doing Zen, *I'll* do something else." (When Kwong-roshi arrives home during our interview and seems about to contribute some remarks, Shinko lifts a hand, and he disappears.) Yet with four small children and no extramural outlet of her own, she also envied her mate. One day, worried about the quality of her life and her sons', she visited Suzuki-roshi by herself. "We had tea," she says. "He didn't say much. Afterwards, though, I was extremely calm. I still had all the complaints about my life, but I was feeling okay. I said to myself, 'If my mind was calm then, it could be calm anywhere I go.'"

Impressed by her experience with a state that psychotherapy aspires to produce, Shinko began attending Suzuki's talks. " 'You don't need to come here to find peace,' he'd tell us," she says. " 'You can find it everywhere.' " At home, her life changed from drudgery to a "journey," she says. "I was still only sitting once a week, but surrendering to wherever I was. As soon as I stopped 'just taking care of the kids' and started doing a practice, I felt a challenge, an opportunity to gain enlightenment. Instead of being like getting the spaghetti on the table in five minutes, life became like *oryoki*."

Listening to Shinko describe her journey—a term almost as popular at the millennium as spirituality—I think of how most clinicians would regard a young woman like the one she once was: an unhappy, well-educated, middle-class mother with no career. A psychopharmacologist might give her an anti-anxiety agent, or even an antidepressant. Detecting signs of so-called self-defeating behavior, a therapist would probably push her toward fulfillment outside the home. Religion offered a different solution—a new way to approach reality—but interestingly, one no less "psychological."

For most of history, there were no hard lines between the intellectual, emotional, and spiritual. When the Jews were exiled to Babylonia in the sixth century B.C.E., they used religion to cope with the devastation. Deprived of their homeland and the temple at the heart of their hitherto sacrificial tradition, they emphasized the Torah and their distinctiveness as "people of the book." To foster some identity and order in a world turned upside down, they devised religious "purity" laws, including kosher dietary principles, that also gave a sense of control over daily life. The church, too, played therapist. She not only forgave sins, but also forbade scrupulosity, drunkenness, gluttony, despair, and suicide in an effort to discourage what we would call obsessive-compulsive disorder, addiction, and depression.

A hundred years after the emergence of modern behavioral science, attributing mental illnesses to sinfulness, weakness, or demonic possession and "treating" them with ritual seems brutish. Even the world of only a few decades ago, in which there were no antidepressants and psychotherapy was regarded by many as navel-gazing for liberal intellectual wimps, sounds primitive. At the millennium, therapy is a multi-billion-dollar industry. Particularly in the neoagnostic milieu, it is almost as much a given as college. Even those who've never had a single session are bathed daily in ubiquitous therapeutic messages from the media and the neighbors' conversation about stress and compulsiveness, passive aggression and fear of commitment. Civic events, from a speech by President Bill Clinton to the funeral of Diana, Princess of Wales, illustrate how thoroughly "the people's science" pervades modern life. Psychology's principles concerning self and relationships help structure our personal lives and provide the lingua franca for discussing them.

At the millennium, however, there's a growing realization that psychology, long touted as a secular religion, cannot replace the original. Both are interested in transformation, but of different kinds. One attempts to develop the self, the other to transform it into something else; one judges, the other doesn't; one focuses on the individual, the other also on community; one embraces history and tradition, the other questions them. At the same time, many people find that neither religion nor psychology is quite enough. Efforts to combine the former's insights on meaning, mystery, and the commonweal, and the latter's on fulfillment, have created a new hybrid sensibility that might be called psychospirituality.

A religion's success now often depends not just on what it says but on how it says it. Buddhism's popularity among well-educated, sophisticated Americans a mere thirty years after being imported from Asia is a good example. Zen in particular both talks psychospirituality's talk and walks its walk. Like cognitive and behavioral therapies, it focuses on patterns of thinking and acting *now*. Indeed, part of "right effort" is ridding the mind of negative states so that positive traits, such as compassion and concentration, can take root. Its upbeat, take-charge approach is a big part of Zen's appeal to Americans: There's something we can do—cultivate mindfulness—that can prevent our lives from becoming a mere reaction to the things that happen to us.

When talking about good and bad, right and wrong,

Shinko sounds more like a psychologist than a monk. When I ask her about how to address one's faults—erstwhile sins—she says, "First, you just become aware of them and go 'Oooohhh!' Then the vessel becomes bigger and can include those parts. Once you can do that, you can shift and change them. They become something you can use."

I mention one of my own most irksome flaws, a tendency to feel inappropriately responsible for others. Shinko's response is one I'll think of repeatedly in months to come, as I experiment with Zen's psychoactive effects. First, she graciously says she's "the same way. But practice enables me to see through that. To see that there's helping, then a point where it's not me helping. Practice also lets me see that I can leave people alone, and not give too much feeling to something that may not even be so. Staying with the breath shows me that I have a self that's not dependent on whether a son does this or that. It's stabilizing *to allow to be what is.*"

Her background in psychology enables Shinko to see some profound overlapping between it and Zen, but she stresses the two shouldn't be confused. Although practice increases self-knowledge, intuition, and focus, those are merely secondary benefits. Like all great religions, too, hers differs from psychology in its strong outward dimension. "Zen isn't motivated by the desire for self-fulfillment," she says, "but by a deep experience that's beyond the psychological." Asked to elaborate, Shinko talks about identity, but with a twist. "Zen practice gives the most direct experience of a 'me' that's universal and authentic—more than just some 'personality me,'" she says. "I can directly experience myself as part of reality and as a complete whole at the same time. I can see that there's no gap between me and cooking, or others. I feel satisfied, and that I don't have to prove anything. From that place, I can actualize my life. Practice makes me feel most naked and most true, like being seen by God. It makes me feel clean, more human, more direct. I practice because it keeps me honest."

As I leave, I tell Shinko that I've been working on incorporating Zen into my new, rather experimental inner life. "We're here to allow people to experience something authentic," she says. "They can call it whatever they like. *Zazen* and the rituals are only skillful means."

If Zen is at the forefront of psychospirituality, other religions are catching up fast. In many sanctuaries, prayer has become "meditation," and old-fashioned terms such as "doubt," "repentance," and "observance" are recast as "seeking," "personal growth," and "mindfulness." At one of the weekday-noon Eucharists at the Cathedral of St. John the Divine, I listen to Canon Jeff Golliher talk about a passage from the Gospel according to St. John, in which Jesus tells his friends not to worry when he's no longer among them in the flesh, because he'll be in them, and they in him. "Our worst times are when we feel alone and that we can't do anything," says Jeff. "That's the world talking." At such dark moments, he says, we need to remember that although we can't always control events, we can have peace by tapping the presence that Jesus was talking about. Even if it doesn't feel like it's there. No matter what, we don't have to lose touch totally with that—"the joy inside." In his variation on Jesus' anxiety-assuaging theme, Jeff says, "We don't have to fix reality. Only God can do that." The congregants give an almost audible sigh. "Jesus—and life—just ask that we keep showing up and being as honest as we can be." Rapt at the thought, the faces around me suggest that people can't hear this message enough.

Tapping his anthropological skills, Jeff once conducted a study of religious experience—specifically, that of the Eucharist. He found it has two phases, which might be called opening the door and remembering. The first often depends on a good sermon, meaning one that speaks personally. Once the door is opened, a memory appears. One woman, for example, recalled a honeymoon sunset on the beach with her new husband. Remembered in the eucharistic setting, the memory was spiritualized, says Jeff, "or put in a God context," so that it renewed her love, reminded her that life is good, and even served as a metaphor for the soul's relationship to the divine. As Jeff sees it, "The Eucharist is the doorway for different people to experience God in different ways." Although the institutional church often cherishes other ideas, as far as the people in the pews are concerned, he says, "they just want the encounter with the mystery."

Like sermons in the age of psychospirituality, pastoral counseling, too, has changed; no longer does it consist of the time-honored platitudinous pep talk and a prayer in the rector's study. One day, I have coffee at the Hungarian Pastry Shop with Canon Susan Harriss, who's the vicar of St. Saviour's parish, as the cathedral's permanent congregation is called. A wife and mother of three, she's a provocative preacher, author, and chaplain of the Cathedral School.[5] Talking about how many issues that used to be black and white have become gray, she recalls a recent discussion of abortion. Susan was impressed by a mother of several children who said that while she could perhaps have an abortion, she "wouldn't expect to be the same after." In the polarized way in which such difficult issues are discussed publicly, this kind of gray-area nuance, which most people feel, gets lost.

As we sip, I start talking about a difficult situation that I shouldn't technically feel guilty about but do—a kind of retroactive codependency scenario. First, Susan says that "figuring out who is to blame isn't always helpful." Then, rather than talking do's and don'ts, she helps me think compassionately yet clearly. I'm surprised by how different from either a friend's or a therapist's her priestly attention feels. Instead of looking to the past, she wonders if there's anything I should do in the present. After some discussion, it seems the answer is "nothing." When she faces this kind of complicated situation in her own life, Susan says, "I don't pray for an outcome, but for some peace or centeredness." Finally, she says, the sacrament of confession sometimes helps one deal with the past, because the ancient ritual "can be a way of letting go."

There was much talk of confession in the church of my youth, but I never heard anything about "letting go." To learn more about this sea change in clerical vocabulary, I enroll in a theology course at the General Theological Seminary in Manhattan. Walled off on all sides by its mostly Victorian buildings, the Episcopalian seminary's block-square quadrangle was first presided over by Rector Clement Clarke Moore. Perhaps he, like me, once saw General's jewel-box landscape silver-plated by an ice storm; some such magic must have inspired *The Night before Christmas.* For two hours each Thursday afternoon, I enter this secret garden to hear Professor Elisabeth Koening lecture on the Christian spiritual masters whose lives and works are the center of a new discipline called ascetical theology. (As Elisabeth says tartly, "Christians can and should be as articulate about their spirituality as Buddhists.") Most of my fellow students are preparing for ordination, but a few are laypeople, including therapists who are training for a second, quintessentially millennial, career in "spiritual direction." As one of them explains, her patients often seem to need something in addition to what treatment alone can give them.

At heart, says Elisabeth, ascetical theology concerns "the process of falling in love with God and then, creation." Historically, the stereotype has been that "thinkers" write theology, while spirituality is consigned to "feelers." This dualism, and the complementary notion that experience plays second fiddle to intellect, is crumbling. As people grow more interested in spirituality, meaning experience, and less so in religion, meaning dogma and rules, Christians are drawn more to the faith's mystics—John of the Cross and Teresa of Avila—than to its theologians and disciplinarians—Thomas Aquinas and Benedict. Endowed with resources that only an ancient tradition can command, Christianity can survey its vast toolbox and select the saints that suit the times. The increasing interest in and respect for Hasidism and its emotive spirituality—long eschewed by rationalist mainstream Jews—bespeaks a similar shift in Judaism.

After a few weeks, psychospirituality seems less like a revolution than a renaissance. Like us, says Elisabeth, the masters we study, from the early church's *abbas* and *ammas,* or monastic fathers and mothers, to the contemporary Anglican theologian Rowan Williams, have regarded the individual as engaged in a continual process of becoming, or "seeking." Their objective, however, has been an identity that differs from the one sought in a therapist's office. More starkly aware of human weakness and fallibility than we like to be, the early fathers of the church taught that true self-knowledge requires acknowledging dependence on the Creator, thus kinship with all other creatures. "It is not I," said Anthony of the Desert, an early sage, miracle worker, and pioneer of monasticism, "but the grace of God which is in me."

One of the more pragmatic benefits of the popular interest in mysticism is the emergence of some of the church's long-neglected female spiritual masters. Although women were forbidden to teach or preach, not even popes could prevent them from experiencing and recording God's personal revelations to them, whose tone often contrasted with that of the church. After two millennia of typifying the "male" qualities of authority, judgment, and linear thinking, Christianity needs the juice of the "woman's" sensibility that celebrates nurture, nature, and a kinder, gentler worldview.

Julian of Norwich, a well-known writer in her day and Chaucer's contemporary, underwent a near-death experience that included visions of Christ's passion, which she describes in her book *Showings*. Julian's drawn-out, Technicolor vision of Jesus' agony first strikes me as a hysteric's sadomasochistic hallucination: "I saw his dear face, dry, bloodless, and pallid with death. . . . it turned a blue color, gradually changing to a browny blue, as the flesh continued to die." Yet when Elisabeth puts Julian in the context of her dark, often nightmarish fourteenth-century world, in which the Hundred Years' War with France raged while three waves of the plague devastated Norwich, I can see her vision as a means of coping with seemingly senseless suffering by identifying it with Christ's.

Plumbing the horror that surrounded them for some meaning, Julian's contemporaries often attributed it to God's wrath at their sinfulness. As reactions to the AIDS epidemic and natural disasters make plain, many people still respond in this way. In November 1996, a cyclone tearing through Balusutippa, India, killed an estimated two thousand people and destroyed a half million homes and a million and a half acres of unharvested crops. "It is our fate," one Indian farmer explained to a reporter. "God must be angry with us. We all know it, the pot of sinfulness has been full for a long time. There is adultery, and so much else. So perhaps the pot has finally overflowed, and we are being punished for our sins."[6] Yet as Elisabeth points out, Julian uses the crucifixion not to induce guilt and fear of punishment, as the institutional church often does, but to prove the depth of divine solicitude. In one passage, contrary to doctrine and much to Satan's dismay, Jesus even redeems sinners from hell itself. Julian's overriding message is that, as God tells her, "You will see for yourself that every sort of thing will be all right."

It's easy to see why Julian's advice was much sought. She was a psychologist centuries before the term existed. Describing how she deals with her own fluctuating moods, she begins one passage, "So happy spiritually that I felt completely at peace and relaxed: nothing on earth could have disturbed me." With the unsentimental acuity of a Zen master, she continues, "But this lasted only a short while and I began to react with a sense of loneliness and depression, and the futility of life; *I was so tired of myself that I could scarcely bother to live* [italics mine]. No comfort and relaxation now, just faith, hope, and charity, and not much of these in feeling, but only in bare fact." Writing elsewhere of the ups and downs of spiritual life, she remarks, "It is not God's will therefore that we should grieve and sorrow over our present sufferings, but rather that we should leave them at once and keep ourselves in his everlasting joy."

If Julian was a master of mood management, few have been as expert in effecting personal change—a millennial obsession—as Ignatius of Loyola, the Spanish aristocrat and founder of the elite Society of Jesus. After being wounded in battle, the young army officer was sent to recover in a remote fortress, where he had only the lives of Jesus and the saints to read. The vain, ambitious young man soon noticed that their spiritual ideals inspired him more than his customary worldly goals—this was the first of his important "discernments." After a year of solitude and prayer, he wrote his *Spiritual Exercises,* which four hundred years later remains a popular step-by-step guide for Christians on religious retreats.

Prefiguring modern psychological techniques such as visualization and cognitive therapy, Ignatius portrayed each soul as playing a role in a cosmic war that good and evil have waged throughout history. He also devised a vivid form of meditation in which a person imagines actually hearing, seeing, and otherwise sensing and participating in biblical events. Like Julian, he was sensitive to the power of moods, which he recast as "desolations" and "consolations" that respectively spur the soul to confront God and sustain it on its journey. Hundreds of years after Ignatius, in a nay-saying, fatalistic, overly cerebral world, the phenomenal success of movements as diverse as Alcoholics Anonymous and Pentecostalism suggests that the Jesuit was right: Fervent religion can help people to change by tapping deep emotions. For those for whom pricey amenities such as psychotherapy are barely imaginable, the fruits of Ignatian psychospirituality can be as pragmatic—sobriety, industry, marital fidelity—as they are religious.

Those interested in subtler transformations may find a patron saint in Augustine of Hippo, one of history's great philosophers and Christianity's most influential thinkers. The figure I previously knew was a gloomy, unsympathetic academic whose dour mind helped develop some of the church's least appealing concepts, including its Platonic suspicion of the flesh, the doctrine of predestination, and the idea of a spiritual "elect." Elisabeth presents another side of Augustine, whose long, difficult struggle of working on God makes him seem a proto-neoagnostic.

Born a pagan in 354 C.E., Augustine, the last of the great Romans, was a classical rhetorician who was baptized as a Christian in adulthood, after years of agonizing. He was not only the first autobiographer, but also the first psychologist of the self. In his ancient world, the person was regarded from an externalized perspective, almost as a generic human entity. Philosophers spoke of what "a man" should or should not be or do. Augustine, says Elisabeth, reached toward a more modern, complex, internalized self. In the *Confessions,* an intricate self-analysis perhaps comparable only to Freud's, he described a person who was a personality: far more particular, unstable, and dependent on context and relationship than the classical archetype. Written more than fifteen hundred years ago, the *Confessions* makes eerily modern reading. Smart and well-educated, Augustine demands an intellectually rigorous religion rooted in ontology. For him, as for most characters in modern fiction, however, reality lies within. As Augustine tells God, "You were there in front of me, but I had wandered away from myself. And if I could not find my own self, how much less could I find You?"

His major character flaw has made Augustine a favorite subject for posthumous psychoanalysis. In a revelatory passage from the *Confessions,* he describes mere adolescent high jinks—tossing some pears at pigs—not as a silly prank, but as a moral catastrophe. Just as the cliché would have it, his narcissism is usually laid at his mother's feet. Monica, a Christian, both idealized and demonized her pride and joy. The resulting sensibility of feeling both special and bad, self-absorbed and unworthy, that underlies the *Confessions* is the hallmark of narcissism.

Augustine's greatest accomplishment as a historical figure was the intellectual bridge he threw up between the ancient and modern worlds, including their religions. As a human being, says Elisabeth, his triumph was the healing of his gaping narcissistic wound. In psychospiritualese, Augustine was an insecure superachiever whose religious journey was also a search for an integrated self. With enormous prescience, he intuits a cutting-edge psychological principle: A personality is made up of many different selves knit into a whole by memory. Brilliantly combining scientific and theological insight, he reckons that only God, the sole witness of total reality, can "remember" all the different Augustines all the time, thus making him whole. Moreover, by definition, God not only sees exactly who Augustine is but also accepts and loves him—a Parent who finds him good enough. At last, Augustine finds himself upon finding God: "Too late I came to love thee, O thou Beauty both so ancient and so fresh, yea too late I came to love thee. And behold, thou wert within me, and I out of myself, where I made search for thee."

So ancient and so fresh, Augustine's understanding of God as both transcendent and immanent pervades millennial religion. His anxious, intelligent, ambivalent search resembles those of highly individualized neoagnostics who, weighed down by the peculiarly modern mixed blessing of self-fulfillment, feel both entitled and flawed, self-centered and lonely—and never quite satisfied. "Thou hast made us for Thyself, O Lord," says Augustine, "and our hearts can find no rest until they rest in Thee."

In learning and thinking about Christianity's spiritual masters, retooled for the millennium, I find another way to re-approach my own conflict-laden religious heritage. In their lives and work, I find much to admire and much that overlaps with those of other faiths' great souls. Working on saints is much easier than working on Jesus.

One night, I attend a very different kind of class, called "Memory and Hope: The Politics of African-American Spirituality." Offered by Auburn Theological Seminary, which sponsors educational programs for laypeople as well as clergy, it's held at Auburn's quarters at the famous Union Theological Seminary in New York City. The teacher is James Washington, professor of religion at both Union and Columbia University and author of *Conversations with God,* a collection of African-American religious writings. Along with his academic credentials, Dr. Washington is the inspirational black Baptist preacher squared. From the moment this larger-than-life man offers a sonorous opening prayer that marks the gathering in of the evening and the desirability of putting away the day's cares, an almost palpable fellowship descends on those seated around the long conference table. This has become a safe place to talk, even about painful things hard to bring up elsewhere.

Right away, Dr. Washington blends insights from psychology with religion and politics. By masking their hurt and refusing to acknowledge their history, he says, African-Americans, like victims of child abuse, ultimately prevent themselves from letting go of their pain: "We're haunted by our pasts, and must recover and confront them before we can forgive others and go on to know and be ourselves. We're in a crisis caused by having more information than knowledge, particularly of our buried selves."

Identifying psychotherapy as a "legatee" of the priest's ancient medicinal work, Dr. Washington observes that religious ritual is a way of managing, if not curing, evil, which he defines as "the experience of obstruction of whatever type." Along with pointing out "the fetishizing of the ordinary," the clergy's task, he says, is "freeing people through explanation. How liberating to understand how you got into the hell you're in! And that's what religion can do."

Borrowing a term from child psychology to describe the hell in which the most disadvantaged African-Americans reside, Dr. Washington speaks of "soul murder": the intentional breaking of a person's will, accomplished by depriving him of affection or respect and inciting him to despair. When soul murder is visited on those described as a "permanent underclass," life loses any apparent meaning or worth. The result can be "suicide, infanticide, parricide," says Dr. Washington, "even deicide." Once a person has been spiritually eviscerated, he says, "without Providence, there's no hope."

To illustrate hope and redemption, Dr. Washington reads

an account, taken from a nineteenth-century issue of the *Atlantic Monthly*, about a pretty young African-American woman who caused a commotion at a big prayer meeting. Rushing forward in the utmost distress, she announced, "Something has taken me over that causes me to hate myself! Pray for me!" Although she was totally focused on herself, particularly her pain and badness, says Dr. Washington, "the girl's narcissism was a trigger for getting help. She came to a church—*a hospital!*" Before the words are out of his mouth, smiles and amens flash around the table. Unlike the troubled girl, those assembled here know what's about to happen. Suddenly, I'm surrounded by that joyous, infectious sense of being upheld, no matter what, by a tremendous power for good, a spirit that's said to have been characteristic of Martin Luther King. "The primary business of religion is to take away the pain!" thunders Dr. Washington. "If a church doesn't do that, shut the door! We get so weary as it pours in faster than we can shovel it. But once in a while, grace suddenly descends . . . *like a spaceship.* And we live for the next such moment."

Amidst the nods and chuckles, Dr. Washington asks an elder for a concluding prayer. The man has a tough act to follow. (Later, I meet a rabbi who, at an interfaith service, had the misfortune of having to read a long Hebrew prayer right after one of Dr. Washington's spontaneous outpourings.) Without missing a beat, however, the elder draws the Lord's attention to the late hour, our hopes of a safe trip home, our confidence that despite our human frailty, he will accept and assist us "just as we are," and our thanks for his faithful servant James. In a chorus of amens, we go our separate ways, with one person at least wondering at a vast spiritual reservoir so often untapped by a culture in such need of it. (A few months later, at the age of forty-nine, Dr. Washington died suddenly;

he was mourned throughout the city and for ten days at Union Seminary.)

At a large secular conference, I sat in on a workshop in which successful professionals discussed the search for meaning. After a number of people had recounted their quests, I realized their stories had two least common denominators: a struggle with a painful problem, and the support of a small group of some kind—one of the most widespread, under-remarked manifestations of religion getting real.

CHAPTER THREE

THINKING
FOR
OURSELVES

A T NEARLY NINE O'CLOCK on a Tuesday night, about forty men and women assemble in one of B'nai Jeshurun's meeting rooms for a weekly meeting on psychotherapy and Judaism. First, Rabbi Marcelo Bronstein, who practiced as a therapist before his ordination, helps us shed the day's concerns by leading us in a meditative, hum-along Jewish melody. Next, this brawny, sanguine fellow, whose English and Hebrew retain the lilt of his native Argentina, leads us in a visualization exercise. We are resting by a river, he says, when suddenly, we realize that a terrible deed from our past is about to surface again: "Feel the fear and terror of it."

Thus primed, we break into small groups. In the classic Jewish style, we won't just "share our thoughts" about religion and therapy willy-nilly but will consider them in relation to a passage from the Torah. Each of us will be a *hevruta*—study partner—whose role is to help the group find, question, and clarify the text's meanings. "The way in which we approach tonight's text is the way in which we approach life's," says Marcelo. "Do we adapt the text to life or life to the text? These have always been the two great schools of Judaism, which are now expressed as movements—Orthodox, Conservative, Reform."

Marcelo distributes our xeroxed Torah portion, which is a juicy one. When the story opens, Jacob is filled with dread over his impending confrontation with Esau, his estranged brother; twenty years earlier, Jacob had tricked him out of his patrimony. That night, Jacob has a strange dream and a wrestling match with a particularly mysterious angel, after which he limps and is blessed.

An Irish girl from Philadelphia in a town where psychoanalysis is described as the fourth branch of Judaism, I take a deep breath and greet my *hevruta* partners. Like rabbinical students, these three therapists—two women and a man—immediately begin to pull apart the text with that peculiarly Jewish combination of intensity and humor, high seriousness and earthy practicality, moving easily between religion and psychology, Jacob's problems and their patients'. After fifteen minutes, when Marcelo asks for interpretations, lots of hands shoot up. Among the offerings:

Like Jacob's way of getting his father's blessing—a good thing—by impersonating his older brother—not so good—many situations in life are ambivalent. Only after divesting himself of his worldly goods can Jacob wrestle, just as a patient must jettison his psychic baggage in order to face his real conflicts. Who, exactly, is this angel? The God within? Jacob's "other side"? When you wrestle, you get better. You're always marked by your struggles, so that even though Jacob is better off after he wrestles, he also limps. In order to change, you have to give up something. Maybe you have to be injured to be healed?

After some discussion of Jacob's clay feet, Marcelo asks, "Why is someone like him, or Abraham, who gave his wife to Pharaoh, a patriarch? Because they're us—liars and cheaters, guilty and saintly. They are models of life's depth." In the Bible, he says, Jacob is first described as "crooked." Later, he's "straightforward." Is his limp, the rabbi wonders, a kind of interim diagnosis? A transitional stage between his crookedness and straightness? One purpose of a diagnosis, says Marcelo, is to help a person see himself clearly—as crooked, depressed, manipulative, or whatever—so that he knows what has to change.

Raising psychotherapy's—and perhaps adult life's—major issue, Marcelo asks, "What can change, and what's fixed? There's a saying that not even God can alter the past, but sometimes it's hard for people, including your patients, to let those events go and move on." People come into therapy because they want understanding and change, he says, "but—this is terrible to say—I wonder how much of the therapeutic mind goes into immersing the patient in something that should have ended a long time ago, rather than creating change. The spiritual reality tries to fly free, but psychology is a rational phenomenon. My question is, 'In the service of what?' "

After polling our opinions on the Bible's attitude about our potential for change, Marcelo professes amazement at the overwhelmingly affirmative response. His own reading, it seems, is not so optimistic. With the prophets' no-balm-in-Gilead fervor, he turns to his own experiences as a therapist, saying, "This is the pain of my life that I'm sharing!" When one of his clients improved, he confesses, he was usually "mystified" about exactly why. Consider, he says, a couple so acrimonious that he expected them "to come to their next marriage counseling session in separate cars. Instead, they arrived holding hands. What is the magic that happens when people get better? I haven't a clue."

Reminding me of Isaiah Berlin's concept of pluralism, Marcelo says that as a psychologist, he's "conflicted by the realization that there's a psychological reality and a spiritual reality, and they're not the same. When I was a therapist, people would come to me with some of the same problems that they do now, but they would need at least a year to open up and get to the core of the pain. They come here to a rabbi, and in one appointment—boom! Everything comes out with such trust in the wisdom of the tradition."

This different reaction to religion bespeaks what Marcelo calls "a component of hope. Hope in something soothing and outside the self. Some light that's going to take the person on a spiritual journey. The journey part is very important, especially because it's not solitary, but made with others. Just being together in community—religion's most basic element—can be very restorative." Every Shabbat, he's amazed at the number of tough New Yorkers who step forward during the service to ask for healing. "That's telling everybody that you're broken," says Marcelo. "Many cry as they share their vulnerability, surrounded by people who are standing up for them. Forget about the theological question about whether God answers prayers! There's a healing power in just being there. Not performing, just being. The simplest things! This realization should help psychologists not to feel so omnipotent. The vast ocean of a human mind and soul can't be fully understood, much less by any one school of thought. Psychotherapeutic theories are all rationalizations, because the real element of change is mysterious."

Turning back to the Bible, Marcelo finally offers his answer to the big question he posed earlier—What can change and what can't?—by quoting Rabbi Akiba. The legendary first-century Torah scholar synthesized the Bible's message thus: "Everything is fixed, but permission is given." According to Marcelo's interpretation, this means that by the lights of Torah, "free choice in the Western sense is an illusion and the quest for it, a neurosis." Spreading his hands a foot apart, he says that to him, "what Akiba meant was that the fact that I live between this wall and this wall"—built of givens such as gender, intelligence, temperament, family, nationality—"is set. But, I have permission to *live* fully within those limits— to explore, develop, evolve, within them. Part of the sickness of our time is that we don't accept the idea that we have limits. We choose things for ourselves that are beyond our spiritual, human, or intellectual boundaries, which causes pain. I'm not saying that a poor peasant must accept the burden of poverty for life. For him, living fully might mean changing those economic boundaries, which aren't his real ones, but are imposed on him unjustly. Wisdom means knowing who we are in every sense of the word and trying to live fully within those limits." Holding his hands apart again, he says, "This is my life—from here to here. I can only fully develop within those boundaries. When I accept that, I have a radical change of perspective."

"If it is possible to go one mile to the east, that means it is possible to go one mile to the west," said Shunryu Suzuki. "This is freedom." Whether from rabbi or roshi, this message doesn't fall easily on American ears, particularly therapists'. My partners, who are after all dedicated to the business of change, resist it, but with an equanimity that's part of Jewish study. Who could settle in one evening a question that the rabbis have pondered for millennia?

By the end of our discussion, I realize that although nothing has been settled, joining others in looking at the issue of personal change through the frame of a wise old tradition has given me a new perspective. Before heading off into the cold night, we hum another little song, then chat for a few minutes. I'm impressed when one of my partners says with great feeling, "What interests me is what we, as Jews, can bring to our work that's special."

One Wednesday evening, I join a group at the cathedral for a weekly discussion of the different but complementary teachings of St. Benedict and St. Francis. The former invented an enduring monastic "rule," or way to structure daily religious life; the latter infused spirituality with openness and spontaneity. Tonight's goal is not to pursue religious scholarship but to consider how some ancient Christian values expressed by these two figures might be relevant to our lives today. Coming straight from work, thirty-five adults—black and white, men and women, mostly middle-aged and middle-class, with a few Gen-Xers sprinkled in—gather in a large parlor at Cathedral House, one of those endearing ecclesiastical settings that combine creaky robber-baron splendor with folding chairs and plastic cups. Before delving into our rather esoteric subject, we partake of a five-dollar dinner of pasta and salad.

Tonight's session is led by Canon Susan Harriss, whose bright blue clerical shirt and chinos emphasize her collegiate air. Back in the sixth century, she says, Benedict of Nursia got sick of secular society and left Rome for what would become the great monastery of Monte Casino, near Naples. His Benedictine rule is followed by many Christians today, not all of whom are monks and nuns. In fact, says Susan, it was written "by a layman for laymen as a getting-through-the-day manual. A way to be in the world, but not."

The most familiar part of the Benedictine rule is its daily

schedule of prayer. Its "offices," or services, such as vespers, are spaced throughout each twenty-four hours to satisfy the scriptural injunction to praise God seven times daily. If those gathered here have one thing in common, it's a sense of not having enough time. The idea of reciting the daily offices elicits much eye-rolling and head-shaking. Susan's remarks on Benedict's ideals elicit even more grimacing and shifting in chairs. The rule's prologue is filled with references to obedience, which we all hate. Susan laughs and says that Benedict was also very big on humility, or "ascending by descent." When we break into small groups of four or five for discussion, it's comforting to see others' dismay at the thought of these stern, old-fashioned Christian virtues.

The evening ends soothingly with compline, one of Benedict's offices. As is so often the case upon leaving a religious gathering, I immediately behave badly. I had hoped to stroll home alone in the moonlight but am joined by a chatty woman who enthuses about spirituality. My barely suppressed irritation points up my deficiencies in Benedictine community spirit—a realization that in itself strikes me as a validation of the small-group movement.

On the following Wednesday, Canon Jeff Golliher's remarks about the hipper, more millennial St. Francis gently touch on another important function of the small-group phenomenon: defining morality in an age of ambiguous ethics. Before we begin, he announces that the evening must end promptly so he can get to the airport and to his mother-in-law's deathbed. Like so many modern American families, Jeff's mixes spiritual traditions—Southern Baptist, Jewish, Anglican, Hindu—in a way impossible to imagine only a relatively short time ago. Although Jewish, the dying woman has asked him to recite at her funeral St. Francis's famous prayer that begins, "Lord, make me an instrument of your peace."

One thing that spiritual masters as different as Akiba, Benedict, and Francis have in common is a talent for articulating grand, simple concepts that can transform a life. Just as Susan gently exposed our own attitudes toward Benedict's austere virtues of order, obedience, and humility, Jeff helps us rethink Franciscan values, especially poverty. This doesn't mean penury, he says, "as much as not giving *things* the utmost importance." For Jeff, this holy poverty is "the antidote to greed, which Francis considered the worst sin." We prefer to picture a Disneyesque St. Francis talking to animals than to think about the materialism that's wrecking their world and ours, but to the cathedral staff in general and Jeff in particular, the environment is a profoundly moral issue. Adding a personal dimension to this social one, he says that greed is "not only material, but emotional, sensual, and perceptual." Like a depth charge, the idea that it's sinful to hog not just things but *experience*—attention, even affection—quietly sinks into my brain.

Next, we form the inevitable clusters and read "The Cave," a brief story written by a Franciscan, and then discuss it. To me, it's about the fear of exploring one's own inner darkness. Most people, however, see the cave as a kind of hermitage where we should spend more time than we do—a constant theme in the gatherings and conversations I take part in these days. When a woman remarks that it was much easier to be spiritual back in a monastic agrarian society than it is today in a law office, heads nod vigorously.

Not long ago, mine would have, too. But the more reporting I do, the more I suspect that the real spiritual problem usually isn't scheduling; it's the painful climb out of old, comfortable ruts of habit that true change requires. Then, too, I grow less wistful about a spirituality that would exclude 99 percent of us, and the numinous moments that occur while we are taking the kids to school, working, or making love. Most of all, overglorification of monasticism strikes me as destructive in that it almost allows those who can't do everything to do nothing. Aloud, I say that I'm attracted to the Jewish idea of a sanctity compatible with life in the world of marriage, family, community, even business. At least one person takes offense at my perceived Christian-bashing: "I think some of us do pretty well!"

As seems to be the way of such gatherings, however, the evening ends hopefully. As if she too had discussed Jacob's dream at B'nai Jeshurun, an older black woman sitting next to me quietly rereads a line from "The Cave": "Only soul and body can become spirit, and their union takes place deep inside where our humanity waits for the wrestling that becomes embrace." I'm not even sure what that means, but I feel peaceful when she says firmly, "When that happens, you can breathe."

As in the B'nai Jeshurun group, no one at these cathedral meetings proselytizes, or even teaches in the conventional sense. Rather, these democratic evenings simply present an opportunity to test our own experience against a spiritual tradition, to regard our lives from a different angle. In their way, they are educational, even provocative, but when I try to describe their effect in a word, I'm surprised that it's "consoling."

Far from being unusual, meetings like those held at B'nai Jeshurun and the cathedral are just two of hundreds of thousands of such events that take place in America's churches, temples, and homes each night. After conducting a national survey in 1992, Robert Wuthnow, a sociologist who is the director of the Center for Study of American Religion at Princeton University, discovered what he calls a "quiet revolution" of small groups.[1] Tradition has it that Americans crave autonomy, but research shows that recent generations increasingly value social relationships. According to Wuthnow, an astounding *40 percent* of Americans regularly meet in small groups to provide each other with information, insight, and support.

Clichéd accounts of "encounter groups" and lachrymose victims in perpetual crisis belie the significance of this massive, grassroots movement. Some 750,000 of these regular gatherings concern a shared secular interest, such as books, politics, or hiking. Of the 500,000 self-help groups, the most ubiquitous is the mother of all: Alcoholics Anonymous. Others support breast-cancer survivors and single parents, crime victims and bereaved families, AIDS and Alzheimer's caretakers.

The stereotype of the chronic whiner notwithstanding, Wuthnow found that most people don't join groups out of a sense of neediness and desperation. Nearly three quarters of his subjects were motivated by the desire to "grow as a person." Almost half sought a "more disciplined spiritual life." Only one in five persons joined because of personal problems, and just one in ten because of loneliness. Nor are members merely seeking novelty or indulging a whim; more than half have gathered at least twice monthly for an hour or more over periods of at least three years. Among the benefits group members most often cite are learning to give and take, navigate ups and downs more gracefully, and be more open, honest, and forgiving. Two of three people in all groups, not just religious ones, say the collective experience has brought them closer to God.

Some pastors joke that there's more religion going on in the church basement than in the church, and statistics suggest they may be right. Almost two thirds of participants in the huge small-group movement, or 24 percent of all Americans, meet under the aegis of a religious organization and share some spiritual concern. Along with 900,000 Bible-study groups and 800,000 adult religious classes, there are "house churches," ex-Catholics who celebrate the Eucharist themselves, and the *hevruta* movement for home study of the Torah. There's even a twelve-step program called Religious Abuse Anonymous, designed for people "addicted" to simplistic, destructive doctrine. Like those focused on Benedict and Francis or Judaism and psychotherapy, most groups attempt to make religion relevant to "real life." In creating safe spaces for intimacy, they also combat the isolation and social fragmentation that epidemiologists implicate in so much illness and malaise.

Just as he distinguishes between worship and the "more self-interested pursuits" that increasingly go on in the same building, Wuthnow also distinguishes between "the person who's in AA, for example, and talks from a very deep level about dependence on a higher power, and someone who reads the latest self-help, angel, or soul book and it's all sort of the same." Such differences notwithstanding, he says, "there's a lot of searching going on, and much of it is outside traditional institutions or in the spaces between and among them. The boundaries between religion and nonreligion are very blurry now. People who ten years ago wouldn't have thought they had any interest in such things now find themselves talking about 'spirituality.'"

To Harvard's Harvey Cox, the proliferation of small groups is linked to the millennial struggle to identify right and wrong in a morally ambiguous world. Citing "a change in what we respond to as authoritative," he says, "here, religious institutions have a lot to learn, and be careful about, from the various self-help and twelve-step programs—and also the early church." Before it turned monarchical and bureaucratic under Constantine, Cox thinks, Christianity worked more like modern support groups than like congregations in which passive audiences are lectured to by experts. In small groups, he says, "problems can be hashed out and sorted through with reference to tradition, sometimes including prayer, as well as others' similar experiences. People know they can't completely trust their own, because they might be mistaken, and they want opportunities to test things out." Although they continue to strike their traditions' major experiential chords, in celebrating the Eucharist, say, or Shabbat, Cox feels that many congregations "are evolving from an audience to a participatory style."

Although their creedal, evangelical theology isn't attractive to most neoagnostics, the phenomenal popularity of the megachurches has millennial underpinnings. Some sponsor up to a hundred weekly support meetings. Like their professional counselors, high-tech audiovisuals, and determinedly secular architecture, the groups proclaim the churches' understanding that, as Cox puts it, "the old formulaic Gothic building with huge red doors and rigid rituals just doesn't correspond to people's reality." However, he thinks that given some retooling, traditional houses of worship can also deliver what postmodern people want. Recalling one Easter at the cathedral when, amidst trumpets and lilies, "they dressed me up and sent me down that two-block-long aisle," Cox says that such settings allow a person to "feel part of something that seems to be in motion and big. You can choose to be anonymous, too, at least for a little while, which many people want. Because [the cathedral] also offers small study, prayer, and action groups, it can feel user-friendly, too. Many people want to be part of the big show, but also of something more intimate."

Although they too wish to be part of a large spiritual movement that addresses their personal concerns, some Americans aren't willing or ready to walk into a church or temple. An increasing number simply log on to their computers. The major on-line services offer hundreds of bulletin boards, for Muslims and Scientologists, Orthodox Jews and Mormons. On the Web, Jains and pagans, Jesus freaks and Tibetan Buddhists, find kindred spirits. For institutions, electronic religion is an important new way to evangelize. For individuals, the attractions run from exchanging views with theologically strange bedfellows to having a cool format for potentially embarrassing personal discussions.

While some find religion on the Internet, many more still turn to older electronic pulpits. Each day, twelve million Americans tune in to Dr. Laura Schlessinger, the author of the best-selling *How Could You Do That? The Abdication of Character, Courage and Conscience.* Although she has a doctorate in physiology and a license in marriage and family counseling, Dr. Laura's more important credential is her Conservative Judaism. As one profile put it, she "is not interested in your pain, your suffering, your heartbreak. She does not care about your low self-esteem and your lousy childhood. She is shrink as aerobics teacher: Stop feeling sorry for yourself. Stop blaming other people. Stop thinking about yourself so much. Forget victimhood, empathy or therapy as anodyne. In other words, suck it up, bucko."[2] As Dr. Laura observes, "Whether something is right or wrong is not an issue in therapy. Modern therapy promotes self-centeredness. Everything is rational or relative. I'm not. My morality is based on the Old Testament and the Talmud. Whenever I can, I try to push people toward religion."

Taking a softer approach, Jeff Weber, a production executive at Odyssey, a national cable television network, ministers to a subgroup of the third of Americans who watch religious television each week. Unlike the stereotypical fundamentalist fans of the "dollar and holler" televangelists, many of his viewers have "more questions than answers," says Jeff. "They're searching for a sense of purpose beyond taking care of business." Of these "thinking people," he says, "many grew up in a religious tradition, and then, in the sixties, said, 'I don't have a lot of use for this.' Now, they're saying, 'Maybe I didn't have to throw out the baby with the bathwater.' " Still others have profound thoughts and emotions that they don't recognize as religious and can't put a name to. In making programming decisions for these skeptical seekers, Jeff differentiates between "religion, which is associated with tradition and beliefs solidified into dogma that gets practiced in a building, and spirituality, which is far broader. It has to do with the search for meaning and feeling at home in the world, and doesn't necessarily have to connect with God. To me, spirituality is being aware, awake, living a life that's present."

If Odyssey's viewers are united by any one interest, it's psychospirituality—in the station's parlance, "exploring life's journey." Bringing up a recent series called "Discovering Everyday Spirituality," Jeff describes it as an antidote to "this myth that if we only had time to close the door and meditate more often, read and talk more, we could be more spiritual. In my own life, I've become more appreciative of everyday things. To me now, spirituality is about paying attention. I'm trying to get to a place where I'm just more attentive to the quiet, ordinary things, so that they achieve a kind of sacredness."

The middle-aged, middle-class yearning for wholeness that Jeff expresses, magnified by millions, is addressed not only by Odyssey but by an explosion of books and guides, tapes and seminars, aimed at the new high-minded, hardworking, quality-time psychospiritual consumer. In the world of the thinking person's religious search, even finding a common language for talking about God can be tricky. Partly because of psychology, the traditional divine portrait has changed. For many, the stern creator and judge has come to resemble a modern dad. Permissive, generally benign, easygoing where behavior, even filial duty, is concerned, this cozy, firm-but-kind deity is tolerant of challenges to his role and authority, no stickler about homework, and used to being consulted mostly in times of trouble. For others, psychology has strengthened the idea of the God—or Buddha nature—within, whether located in the individual or a group. Still others wrestle with the question of whether religion is a creation of our emotional need or a genuine leap toward something else. "I'm still trying to figure that out," says Jeff. "I'm not sitting here saying 'Yes, there's a God and he's my personal savior.' But I do the work I do because I'm obsessed with that question. What I threw out was the prepackaged religious stuff. After we'd learned from science, psychotherapy, and all those things, dogmatic formulas just didn't make sense anymore or jibe with what we knew."

Like a good therapist or millennial clergyperson, Jeff doesn't try to "hit people over the head with answers, but to help them on their journey with resources and tools to make their lives more meaningful." Quoting the host of one of the network's popular shows, called "Common Sense Religion," he says viewers are concerned about "the three H's—hope, help, and home." Indeed, when he talks about his own suburban church, Jeff could be one of them. "What I love is the wonderful mixed bag of fellow seekers who have a lot of scars and limps and come together to affirm that in each other and ask questions," he says. "We're committed to living a life that has some justice and grace, but in the sixties, religion got preoccupied with the justice part. Back then, many of us thought we'd 'find ourselves' in a community, but somehow our inner lives got neglected." Nonetheless, the issue of trying to balance the personal and social leaves Jeff feeling "tremendously torn. Do I have time for community issues when I should be spending more time with my own family? I live with this guilt that my time commitments aren't matching my ultimate concerns. If I *say* that the most important thing in my life is my kids, why am I not spending more hours with them? Why am I obsessed with my work, in the office from seven in the morning till eight at night? I think that a lot of us urban professionals, and others, too, are characterized by tremendous tension. Now, there's more of a need for religion to minister to people's internal hurts."

Of the social movements that are rooted in and identified with the small-group phenomenon, feminism is one of the most important. Its first "consciousness-raising" meetings thirty years ago generated much of the energy that inspired women to change the world. In speaking of how women have changed religion, Huston Smith first says that "in thinking that they have gotten the muddy end of the stick in history and that everything should be done to correct that, I am a feminist. My NOW card is in my wallet." Then, he turns to what he sees as two important developments. Of women's new presence in positions of leadership, he says that "it remains to be seen if they can bring new vitality to the churches and other congregations. That's still up in the air." Reiterating that he's "all for rectifying injustice," he makes a second point: "Feminism has taken its toll on mainline religion by absolutizing the issue of justice for women. Using that criterion and reading it backwards, [feminism] has seen the traditions as patriarchal. Since patriarchy is bad, the religions are bad, too. So why stay with them? By making a political position the bottom line, it relativizes religion's other dimensions, which saps people's belief, affection, and respect."

In going about my reporting, I've been repeatedly surprised

by how moving I find it to hear a woman's voice from the pulpit. It's hard for me to imagine that this experience in itself isn't revitalizing institutions that had previously silenced half the human race—and the majority of their regular congregants. But I have reason to ponder Smith's other observation during a radiant October week in 1997, when hundreds of women gather in New York to attend "Speaking in the Open: The Public Vocation of Women's Theologies," a three-day conference convened by several seminaries, including Union, where it is held. Within a few hours, I feel that I'm really attending two events. During the "morning" conference, speakers lecture on issues of social justice, particularly racism and homophobia. Often in academic jargon, they stress their differences with and from "Euro-American" society, or heterosexual society, or both. Even when I sympathize with their ideas, on subjects from the plight of illegal immigrants to the media depiction of African-Americans, it strikes me that the long speeches might have been given at a political science conference. Despite stunning advances over the past thirty years in human rights in general and women's in particular—especially in the world of religion—there's little sense of progress, much less celebration.

Since the first wave of female clergy and theologians of the 1970s, women not only preside in pulpits—their first dream—but wear the bishop's miter. Perhaps more significant, they now outnumber male professors in the seminaries, where much theology and policy are gestated. Women have arrived, yet they still face many challenges, including subtler forms of sexism. As women achieve leadership positions, for example, some men have withdrawn their involvement from institutions, leading to fears that religion will become a "pink collar" profession. If most of their difficulties have been imposed by a cruel history, however, it seems to me that some women in religion are themselves creating new problems.

Following the first morning's lectures, one theology professor paraphrases, but with far less economy, a slogan from my youth: "The personal is political." Another adds that "from a sociological perspective, God is a group, constructed by group decisions." Some greet these observations as original, even revolutionary, but I feel I've entered a 1970s time warp. I want to ask some questions. What about the other God—the one who's not constructed by group decisions? Do these bright women remember how their academic predecessors oversecularized and -politicized religion during the God-is-dead era, and helped empty America's mainstream sanctuaries? Just as the "excellent women" of the churches and temples of yore were restricted to "charity work" or teaching, couldn't women still get bogged down in religion's social and political dimensions—housework on a global scale? Raising my hand, I ask only why there has been so little reference to God or religion at this theology conference. Many scornful or pitying faces turn in my direction, and another professor rather grandly informs me that it goes without saying that the Spirit is in *everything* she does.

If the strength of the small-group phenomenon is democracy, its weakness is the potential for fragmentation. At lunch, after the divisive, hopeless tone of the past three hours, the tables are as segregated as Selma in 1960. Plopping my tray down on the nearest one, I listen to a half dozen strangers lament that the morning was so long on politics and short on religion. A divinity student wonders if she should drop out of school, because the lectures left her feeling "so stupid." A businesswoman and community leader remarks on the irony of the feminist complaint that in male institutions, a powerful elite with its own technical language patronizes and excludes others. A practical deacon wonders why so much precious time and energy are being spent on what St. Paul called "the foolishness of preaching to save them that believe."

By dessert, the accomplished women gathered at the table are giggling like schoolgirls behind Ms. Crabapple's back.

After lunch, the second, or "afternoon," conference commences. The morning lectures were a given, but now, we can choose among various workshops. Many of these, too, are political, from "Neither Charity Nor Empowerment: U.S. Women on Welfare" to "Anti-Racist Social Change as a Public Response to Intimate Violence." Choosing one that sounds theological in the usual sense of the term, I head off to "Jephthah's Daughter," a presentation of a new religious ritual to commemorate one of the nameless women of history and the Bible.

Because they continue to affect how women are treated in religion today, sacred texts are of great interest to feminists. Scholars' first concerns were with the actual nuts and bolts of biblical language. To make it "inclusive," they purged the unnecessary use of "he" and "his," substituting "they" and "their" or "she" and "her," and changing "men" and "mankind" to "humanity" and "people." Where God was concerned, the traditional "he" was judged as reflecting not the divine gender but the patriarchal power structure: What is important is male, and what isn't, female. Notwithstanding some largely unaesthetic attempts to recast God as "she," the consensus today is that what's needed isn't a deity in skirts but one whose complexity requires both male and female attributes and, above all, mystery.

Along with its language, feminist scholars address what Scripture does—and doesn't—say. Religious texts have frequently portrayed women as either feckless or sinful—mothers or whores. Often they're cast only in relation to men, particularly as the source of male obstacles or problems. Worse, women's own spiritual experiences have seldom been recorded. Thus, in addition to correcting erroneous portrayals and interpretation, scholars also try to re-create religion's past, supplying the lost women's half.

To help recover Jephthah's daughter, Rabbi Donna Berman and her colleagues have designed a multifaceted ceremony. Surrounded by incense, we sit on the floor atop a colorful cloth spread with fruit and nuts. First, Donna compares inventing a ritual to "making an airplane in the garage. You wonder, Will it fly?" Although she hopes that this one will become part of the Jewish calendar, it isn't just about injustice wreaked on Jewish women, she says: "In America, a woman is beaten every twelve seconds." When we each introduce ourselves, several participants mention their own or their mothers' experiences of violence.

First, we read from the Book of Judges, in which the warrior Jephthah swears that if God gives him victory, he'll sacrifice the first thing to walk out of the doors of his house. Seeing his only child come forth, he says, "Alas, my daughter! You have brought me very low, and you are my troubler; for I have opened my mouth to the Eternal, and I cannot go back on my word." Learning of her doom, the girl asks if, first, she might have two months to spend with her companions in the mountains. After her slaughter, the Bible says, "And it was a custom in Israel, that the daughters of Israel went yearly to lament the daughter of Jephthah the Gileadite four days in a year." Like the name of the human sacrifice, the details of this annual women's ritual were lost.

To commemorate Jephthah's daughter, we pray and sing, drink grape juice, and wash each other's hands. The time reserved for midrash, however, is my favorite part. In this group of scholarly Jewish and Christian women, provocative questions fly: Why is the focus on Jephthah's grief, instead of the girl's? Why is he later named in the Bible as one of the righteous? Why does this story end so differently from that of

Abraham and his son Isaac? What was going on in the community that caused this story to become part of Scripture? Could the girl's retreat with her companions be a reference to gayness?

Before leaving, we pair off to give and get a woman's blessing. I ask my partner for a traditional Hebrew one. As we smile across our different traditions and histories in a way that our mothers and grandmothers couldn't have imagined, it seems to me that Jephthah's daughter has raised plenty of political issues but addressed them in a uniquely religious way.

Attending this new ritual makes me think of Susan Schnur, one of the first women rabbis, who is deeply concerned with egalitarian, experiential religion. Now working on a doctoral degree in psychology, she has founded two congregations and serves as the editor of *Lilith,* a magazine for Jewish feminists; she has also written a series of "Hers" columns for *The New York Times* and, from a woman's perspective, translated Hebrew texts and invented new religious rituals. One day, she told me about how, in the course of helping some people through a bereavement, she helped turn a small group into a new synagogue. After she married a woman and a man who suffered from cancer, the young husband died. Susie conducted a shiva, or seven-day mourning ritual, for their estranged, secular families. "I told them, 'Take off your shoes, turn the lights low, and chant,' " she said. "I broke all the rules, but what did they know? Every night, there were a hundred people there who had felt marginal to religious life and were stunned that any of this could work for them. When the mourning was over, they said, 'What can we do?' " Unlike people in less privileged parts of the world, said Susie, "we aren't challenged by daily adversity to be spiritual. Then a friend gets cancer. Really understanding that everyone's going to die places you in a corrective reality that's very soothing. It's the way things are. To be okay with what's happening—that's what spirituality is all about."

To Susie, ritual, which always involves experience, often the small-group sort, is crucial to spiritual awareness. "What happens on Yom Kippur is that you sit there all day," she said. "Come the twenty-second or twenty-third hour, something will happen to you. But nobody knows how to tell people that anymore, or that in this faith, that's how you come upon enlightenment. It's the paradox of religious experience! Yes, you're bored through lots of it. You just sit. You tune out and get distracted, but the hours pass, and you are there. The sun starts going down, and you're in tune with how dark it is, and you're hungry and tired and have a caffeine headache and you've really paid dues in a way that we don't know how to speak about. Many people don't even know there's an alternative to a quick fix."

Lacking their own rituals, women must "build the plane in the garage." Describing a gathering convened by Wicca, a witchcraft group, in which five hundred women banged on drums, Susie expressed interest in "what of this stuff can be brought back into Judaism. Women in religion have forgotten how to yell and shout and sing and have fun and feel empowered." Recently, she took on a more temperate feminist renovation of one of Judaism's most sacred rituals: the Passover seder. Because Elijah is expected to usher in the messianic era, each family sets out a cup of wine for him on that special night. In her Haggadah, or version of the Exodus story that's read during the meal, Susie also emphasizes another of Passover's redemption themes, which concerns "schlepping through the desert, the journey as home, nurturance, water, births—women's stuff that just got overlaid by the rabbis." The Bible contains a short text about how

Miriam, a prophetess who was the sister of Moses and Aaron, sang and danced at the Red Sea; there's also some midrash, or rabbinic commentary, about Miriam's well drying up upon her death. To honor the contributions of this important but neglected woman, Susie made a Passover cup, filled with water, for Miriam. (Last year, at the seder of some friends, I noticed that the hostess had put out a cup for Miriam.)

By successfully combining the old and the new, Miriam's cup symbolizes the "new place" to which Susie thinks women are heading. "Figuring out compromises between feminism and our personal and religious inclinations is a hallmark of maturity," she said. "Going to an Orthodox synagogue and sitting in the balcony and having the men do it for me can be very appealing. We need to admit to some of these feelings, then make some compromises." Although much work still needs to be done, Susie is both grateful and hopeful: "In feminist terms, it ain't over, but ten years ago there weren't these books on women biblical figures or rewritten prayers."

On the women's conference's second morning, the best of the three political lectures is given by Maria Lugones, a gay Latina who is the director of Latin American and Caribbean Studies at the State University of New York at Binghamton. Questioning some ideas harbored in many religious breasts, she discusses efforts to "help" and "understand" those "less fortunate." Because the West regards itself as "the original," and the rest of the world as a "bad copy," she says, Westerners must get beyond their imaginary ideas about what others are like. To do so means replacing introspection, "which will show a 'good person,'" says Lugones, with reflection, which includes historical perspective. I enjoy her talk, but such is the morning conference's tone that when I see Lugones standing alone at a coffee hour, I don't approach her and tell her so. Social interaction seems impossible because I don't feel like myself; I feel like a white heterosexual Westerner.

By the third day, I play hooky from the morning conference. After scanning the afternoon workshops, I skip "Treason to Whiteness Is Loyalty to Humanity" and try the one that has the most "spiritual" title. Just as the morning sessions recall seventies politics, however, this workshop brings back that era's touchy-feely group psychology, spiked with consciousness-raising. Under a sugary, "supportive" façade, the leader is a bossy Big Nurse. I don't want to be harangued by political idealogues, but I don't want to sit in a circle and indulge in emotive chat, either.

Later, I find the right intellectual and spiritual balance in a workshop called "Embracing Differences: A First-Generation Recipe from the Apostle Paul." In his First Letter to the Corinthians, Paul said, "Let your women keep silence in the churches. . . . If they will learn anything, let them ask their husbands at home" (14:34–35). Choosing Christianity's leading misogynist for seemingly positive treatment at a feminist conference is right up the alley of Minka Sprague, a New Testament scholar at New York Theological Seminary, whose provocative preaching I've heard at the cathedral.

First, Minka offers some historical context. Predating all four Gospels, Paul's thirteen letters were written between 55 and 62 C.E. Scholars now think that seven—I Thessalonians, Galatians, I and II Corinthians, Romans, Philemon, and Philippians—are actually his, and the others were composed by followers. To a heterodox congregation made up of Jews, Romans, Greeks, and farflung provincial communities, Paul wrote: "In Christ there is neither Jew nor Greek, master nor slave, male nor female, but all of you are one in Christ Jesus" (Galatians 3:28). To Minka, his great theme is "a way to live in radical freedom in society while embracing differences. His message is 'Stand fast for freedom. For freedom Christ has freed you.' "

Because Paul's insistence on freedom clashes with the

misogyny in First Corinthians, Minka and other scholars think that the offensive remarks weren't his but were inserted into his text before the turn of the second century. Not only do the abrasive words suddenly pop out of Paul's discussion of something else altogether, but scribes down through the ages have preserved strange breaks around them. Minka is among those who think the offensive passages were added during or after the reign of the emperor Domitian, which extended from 81 to 96 C.E.; his demand to be worshiped set off the widespread persecution of Christians. In such troubled times, she argues, churches led by women or slaves made Christians too conspicuous: "After Domitian, sticking with the unadulterated Paul meant death."

After listening to Minka make her case, I've learned new things about Paul and the early church, and I'm even prepared to consider the possibility that he didn't write the nasty parts of First Corinthians. However, I'm not persuaded that the man or men who might have done so were thinking merely of avoiding lions. When Constantine made Christianity the state religion in 325, no one bothered to call off the misogyny.

The afternoon ends with Philippians 4:8–13: "Finally, brothers, fill your minds with everything that is true. . . . There is nothing that I cannot master with the help of the One who gives me strength." When we each offer a personal commentary on these words of Paul, one young woman quietly says that she is trying to come to terms with the death of her husband in the Oklahoma City bombing. One can almost hear the sound of her listeners' struggles falling into proper perspective.

Without mentioning the challenges faced by women in religion per se, Minka says, "In jail, where I also teach, a former drug dealer once told me, 'Fear is simply lack of faith.' We manifest fear when we seek authority outside ourselves. I

don't think *any* of this makes any sense if you don't know
what the business of faith is, which is stepping out not on
what you know, but on your belief that you have what you
need at that moment. That God will be with you. That the
angels won't let you fall."

Thus blessed and sent on my way, I walk home, thinking
about my accumulating experience with small groups. Although I have a weakness for professors and their opinions—
perhaps because of it—I'm coming to enjoy the democratic
kind of education that transpires in these informal circles.
The quality of the ideas varies, but there's usually a shining
moment that comes from someone's own experience. Perhaps
because the subject is religion—the meaning of life—rather
than economics or Shakespeare, these personal contributions
have a resonance that many intellectual constructs lack. At
this conference, certainly, my best times were had in the
meeting rooms, not the lecture halls, where even women academics acted like . . . academics.

One Sunday morning, I join an ongoing discussion that
goes right for religion's jugular: theology. An hour before
Eucharist, a group of people gather in the cathedral to talk
about "Weaving New Stories: A Way of Doing Theology."[3]
Surely some had risen early less from scholarly zeal than from
curiosity about the Very Reverend Harry Pritchett, the
cathedral's new dean, who will lead the sessions. The lean,
gray-haired priest in the preppy blue clerical shirt and black
penny loafers can't stand still, much less sit still; he's a theater-
lover, former army officer, Sewanee professor, and dedicated
runner. Rocking on his heels, pacing this way and that in the
Great Choir, he says, in a still-unfamiliar Alabama accent, that
whenever we "do theology," we're putting limits on the lim-
itless and describing the indescribable. Whatever we come up
with will be inadequate and flawed because, says Harry, "God

is a surprise." Nonetheless, we keep at it. We want to talk about "what's nearest and dearest to us" and most of all, he says, because our species is "driven to make meaning out of our experience, which is everything that happens to us, whether we're aware of it or not."

Unlike Jews, Christians of all stripes have a long tradition of talking in very specific terms about God: nature, qualities, motivation, plans for us—the whole nine yards. Leaving very little to the imagination, human or divine, many theologians have tried to render God as predictable as the rest of the clockwork Newtonian universe. Although a religion needs some "short-cut jargon" so its people can communicate, says Harry, formal theology doesn't do much for "the human need to be affected. As John Wesley said after he got off that bus in England, 'I don't know what happened, but somehow my heart was peculiarly warmed, and my whole life changed.' "

For a dean, Harry seems remarkably unconcerned about doubts and uncertainties. "Most thoughtful people aren't too interested in creeds today," he says. "Einstein said that the great question is 'Is the universe friendly or not?' There's a big difference between saying yes or no. Between saying 'There's no sense or meaning to life' and saying, 'There is some, but I haven't discovered it yet. I'm moving toward it.' " Rather than looking askance at millennial images of searching and jour-neying, Harry points out their ancient roots. "Gregory of Nyssa, a patristic father of the church, said, 'To be perfect is to be on your way,' " he says. "That's very true of folk today." These restless inquirers prefer to do their own theology. Of the three basic kinds—narrative, conceptual, and systematic—Harry feels that the first and oldest, storytelling, best suits us. As Moses did with his story of the burning bush, we can use narratives to talk about the things that happen to us and what they mean.

To illustrate narrative theology, the dean shares an essay written by a former parishioner (like many Southerners, Harry has a way with words and a wealth of both friends and stories). This one concerns a camping trip to "the piney woods" that this fellow and his eight-year-old son had taken with a group of other men and their boys. Feeling sheepish that his outdoor skills didn't match the other fathers', the man headed away from the campfire and its braggadocio to turn in early with his son. Snuggling into his sleeping bag, the boy suddenly burst out, "Dad, I want it always to be like this—you and me in the tent." Years later, the father lost this son to schizophrenia. Yet his sureness of the existence of love, says Harry, symbolized by a tent in the piney woods, allowed this man "to live with buoyancy in spite of tragedy."

Theology can be beautiful, but it makes me uneasy. It often seems to be elaborate justification for believing the unbelievable. But Harry discusses even the high-flown conceptual sort in a sensible way. What interests him about, say, the Trinity—one God who is Father, Son, and Holy Ghost—is "the experiences and stories that allow people to come up with something like that." In the Trinity he sees the reflection of three different kinds of human encounters with the divine. When we run headfirst into the way life really is, limitations and all, some of us decide to embrace it and call it Father. In the flesh, says Harry, here and now, somehow or other, we may meet the Son. That mysterious quality that holds, heals, and unifies us some call the Holy Spirit. Labeling these different yet related experiences "the Trinity" makes "biblical and intuitive sense," says Harry. "I believe *what it's about.*"

To help us figure out how to do our own theology, Harry shows us how he does his. He uses three types of stories. First are those of the "community past," taken from the Bible, the lives of the saints, and religion's whole history, which remind us that "we walk in a procession." Then come stories of the "community present," including the works of secular artists and writers. Last are our personal narratives. "My story has to get into it," says Harry, "but it's only about me, it's not theology. If it's just about me and the past—me and Jesus in the garden at sunrise with the dew on the roses and we know something nobody else does—it's still too limited. If it's only me and the present community, it becomes the Church of What's Happening Now. To get theology where the good new things break in, all three stories have to intersect. You can't force it. It's revelation."

Next, the dean shares a piece of narrative theology about facing adversity, which he developed along with a small group. Drawing from the community past, he recites a bit of Psalm 23: "Thou preparest a table for me in the presence of my enemies. . . . My cup runneth over." Introducing the community present, he tells us about a small parish in the contemporary South. Jim, the senior warden, was a staunch AA member and pillar of the church. Bill, the junior warden, quit his job as an aerospace engineer to work in the garden shop at Sears because he loved nature. Along with Tony and Ginny, who served on the vestry, they had recently participated in a workshop, led by writer Martin Bell, on how to think about religion in new ways. Among their eclectic exercises had been writing new lyrics for Leonard Cohen's song "Suzanne" in which the heroine becomes the church; translating the old Christian maxim "Take up your cross" for the era of social justice as "Lay on the barbed wire of history so that others can cross over safely"; and deconstructing *Requiem for a Heavyweight,* in which Anthony Quinn plays Rivera, a punch-drunk prizefighter who surprises everyone with his heroism.

Right around Easter, Jim dropped dead. Two weeks later,

so did Bill. Two weeks after that, Ginny and Tony's mentally ill son blew his brains out. The church leadership was wiped out, says Harry, "and so was I." The next Sunday, he looked at his brokenhearted congregation, reeling from funerals and grief, and said, "The best sermon is, 'We're here.'"

After practically crawling home from church with Allison, his wife, and their three children, Harry pushed open the rectory door to find a table prepared for them in the presence of the enemy Death. With the feast was a note: "Suzanne sends you tea and oranges, all the way from China. We love you." Above hung a mobile, made of barbed wire, whose decorations included a "Reverend Rivera."

In doing their theology, Harry's small group had identified an important experience: shared loss. Using stories—their own, the church's, artists'—they had figured out its meaning for them: Somehow, they were still together. They had translated their theology into signs and symbols: a banquet in the presence of the enemy. Making the crucial step, they used their theology to guide their behavior: Some way or other, they'd go on marching in that great procession. Paraphrasing "Suzanne," the dean says, "Just when you have no love to give her, there's a new revelation."

Thus far in my reporting, the biggest surprise has been the pleasure and rewards of joining others—strangers—to talk about what's most important in life. Without this stimulus, I think, it would be difficult to move past "there may be something." Perhaps it's possible to be spiritual on your own, but religion mandates community, and increasingly, religion is what interests me. In millennial congregations, what some regard as its most important function—determining right and wrong—is increasingly influenced by psychospirituality and democratization.

CHAPTER FOUR

GOOD AND EVIL

ONE OF MY FAVORITE PAINTINGS in the Metropolitan Museum is Sassetta's *St. Anthony*, which shows the desert father battling with a bright pink, horned Satan. Anthony's vision of evil as an external force—the devil— seems quaint to neoagnostics, whose minds are more accustomed to internal demons. In some congregations, however, sin and how to teach people about it are still conceived of along the lines of Sassetta's painting. Like hundreds of other conservative churches, the Abundant Life Christian Center, an Assembly of God ministry in Arvada, Colorado, a suburb of Denver, observes Halloween with a thirty-minute tour of Hell House: an "in your face, high-flyin', no-denyin', Satan-be-cryin', keep-ya-from-fryin', no holds barred, 'cutting-edge' evangelism tool of the '90s!"

Guided by a "demon," visitors move from room to room, in each of which actors portray different grisly scenarios. First, in a casket, there's a homosexual who has died of AIDS: "We've got your alternative lifestyle all right. In Hell!" In the next room, writhing in pain, there's a young woman undergoing an abortion: "Killing babies is a wonderful choice. After all, it's so-o-o-o convenient." After the drunken-driving room, starring a man who has killed his family, and the teen-suicide and drug-overdose rooms, comes hell itself. As souls wail in eternal torment amidst the reek of burning Limburger cheese, the devil gloats. Finally, in potpourri-scented heaven, God waits to proclaim his love. Of the 4,500 visitors to the show's first eight nights, 510 signed cards saying that they had asked Jesus Christ into their lives for the first time.[1]

For many, religion's main function is to preach right and wrong, and most Americans think something has gone wrong with the country since the good old days so often cited by conservative religion. After taking the nation's psychic pulse, an interdisciplinary team of Cornell professors concluded that "values commonly judged as 'good' seem in decline, including honesty, a sense of personal responsibility, and respect for others anchored in a sense of the dignity and worth of every individual."[2] The three elements that the scholars singled out, particularly the last, lie at the core of every religion's moral code. Perceiving a moral and cultural slippage that social-engineering schemes have failed to reverse, Americans are more concerned about ethics now than at any time over the past sixty years in which they've been polled on the subject.[3] Two thirds are dissatisfied with society's morals and think that religion can answer most contemporary problems. For the first time, a majority think that the quality of their children's lives will be worse than their own. Even among Wade Clark

Roof's baby boomers, 70 percent favor a return to "stricter standards."

Getting a society that is increasingly diverse culturally and religiously to agree on what's right and wrong presents major challenges, however. In millennial congregations, I learn, "sin" is often applied to structural evils, such as racism, political oppression, and pollution, that set off destructive chain reactions affecting multitudes, even generations. Religious conservatives, however, still see sin in personal terms, such as sexual license or drunkenness; for them, the moral crises of our age are abortion and homosexuality. The distinction between these two ethical visions, both religious, is an important one for me. Like many raised in the fifties or before, I was taught that God was terribly concerned about personal flaws and failings that seemed to me to be ineradicable and inevitable. The desire to dodge this Sisyphian task and the hard master who imposed it helped propel me out the church door.

Americans talk tough about the need for moral reformation, but our philosophical traditions militate against acting in concert. Along with respect for individual rights, a laissez-faire attitude about others' behavior, at least the private sort, is bred into the American bone. Most agree with Emerson that "good men must not obey the laws too well." Rather than looking to rigid religious or moral dictums, the majority is guided by broad principles, such as the Golden Rule and "Do the best you can."

The majority of Americans eschew black-white, either-or positions, and even a person who's adamant about one controversial issue, such as homosexuality, may not be about another. According to statistics gathered over considerable time, about 20 percent of Americans are totally opposed to abortion, and roughly the same number feel that it's permissible for any reason; the majority think it's justified under certain circumstances. Even regarding less politicized matters, such as premarital sex, about a third of the population think it's always wrong, while about a quarter feel it's never wrong; again, the largest group rests somewhere in between.[4]

One day, while talking about postmodern morality with an expert on that of the previous millennium, I get an important insight into these statistics. Rabbi Burton Visotzky, author of *The Genesis of Ethics* and a scholar who specializes in the rabbinic Judaism of the Greco-Roman world, says that morality and ethics concern principles that people decide are best for themselves and society. Religion asserts a divinely revealed set of rules.[5] While the two codes often overlap—don't murder or steal—they don't always. "God doesn't have to care a fig what humans decide is right," says Burt. "God can simply say, 'Thou shalt' or 'shalt not.' God can say to Abraham, 'Pick up the knife and kill your kid.' And it's not up to us to judge the command of the Creator, even though I find it morally abhorrent." When I express sympathy for Abraham, Burt reminds me that in Hebrew, "holy" is *kadosh,* which means "set apart"—"often literally apart, including some-one who hews to a different morality, marches to a different drummer. If you're following God's voice, you may not be much of a *mensch*—a nice human being—which is rough." For the rest of us, Burt says, the rabbis reasoned that the best plan is to be merciful and compassionate, as God is and we have the capacity to be.

As an institution that can ask someone to kill his child or to condone slavery, religion doesn't necessarily foster pure morality. "We've committed a lot of horrors in the name of religion," says Burt. "Because I'm very wary of commands of God that the rational person in me can't verify, I'd like morality always to be a controlling aspect of the way Jewish law is transmitted." Elaborating on this "push-pull," he says that religion's demands should lead to morality, and "when they don't, we should be very suspicious. That's how we stay on the straight and narrow, both in terms of what most people decide is moral and what godly people decide that God demands. Frankly, I'm not sure you can have one without the other."

For their code of right and wrong, fundamentalists look primarily to what they have decided that God demands. Although "fundamentalism" implies a heroic return to the basics of the good old days, the movement is a modern one that began around World War I among Christians reacting against scientific rationalism. At first, it was a rather intellectual phenomenon whose advocates, including Oxford and Cambridge scholars, argued that the fundamental principles of their faith were the best antidotes to modern secularism and ambiguity. Over time, particularly among rural American WASPs, a peculiar fundamentalist subculture evolved. According to its rigid theology, the Bible had to be accepted as objectively true, and salvation was exclusively restricted to right-minded Christians. The fundamentalists also emphasized personal piety ("They don't smoke or dance or chew, or go with girls who do" went the joke) and, increasingly, conservative politics, which by the mid-1950s was perceived as the antidote to godless Communism.

The accelerated growth of this explosive combination of fundamentalist theology and conservative politics, known as the religious right, dates to the social upheavals of the sixties era. The Supreme Court's decisions against prayer and Bible-reading in public schools and the spread of sex education attracted fundamentalists to Barry Goldwater's Republican Party, and their numbers soon climbed. When President Jimmy Carter's White House conference on the family, which included gays and feminists, failed to agree about what a family *is,* fundamentalists, who were already heavily Republican, saw a unique opportunity: The Democrats were challenging traditional Christian "family values," a term that rapidly became shorthand for opposition to abortion and homosexuality.

Despite the media attention they attract, research over the past twenty years shows that the number of fundamentalist American Christians isn't nearly as large as is often assumed, hasn't increased, and seems to be slightly declining; surveys indicate they represent around 15 percent of the population. The common misperception of the movement's size owes much to the combination of its stridency and the mistaken tendency to lump traditional, fervent, "born-again" evangelical Christians together and assume that all are fundamentalists. Similarly, the religious right turns out to be a noisy minority.[6] Even at the time of the 1994 Republican landslide, only about 18 percent of the population considered themselves members of this movement. The strongest identifications were reported by Republicans, the elderly, Southerners, women, and people who hadn't attended college; contrary to the popular impression, blacks were almost twice as likely (30 percent) as whites (17 percent) to describe themselves as members of the religious right.

Fundamentalism began within Christianity, but it's not restricted to that faith. Discussing the spread of this modern religious and political phenomenon, Harvey Cox says, "Fundamentalist Jews? Hindus? That used to be an oxymoron, but they exist now." No matter what core faith they derive from, he says, all fundamentalists have certain things in common: possession of "the only way," dedication to spiritual revival in an evil world, and witch-hunting. Most important, they respond to a rapidly changing world by attempting to create old-fashioned, black-and-white certainty. As Cox puts it, "fundamentalists are the people who try to put on the brakes by taking a particular part of the tradition"—scriptural inerrancy, say, or the land of Israel—"hauling it up into the present, and making it the capstone around which everything else gets organized." This kind of certainty and simplicity became more attractive as so-called civil religions, such as socialism and science, failed to fulfill their promise, leaving societies without a sense of coherence and the big picture, prey to uncertainty and worry. "Fundamentalist offshoots of the great traditions speak to that modern sense of anxiety," says Cox. "In their frantic effort to oppose modernity, however, fundamentalists have inadvertently embraced its fatal flaw—literalism—which makes them prosaic and shrill."

Fundamentalists could be defined as people who prefer answers, even if they might be wrong, to questions. They want rules for behavior—others' as well as their own—that come straight from God or God's exclusive representative. ("My opinion is," wrote Thomas Jefferson, "that there would never have been an infidel if there had never been a priest.") Like most aspects of personality, this predilection can be attributed to nature or nurture. Modern society's angst notwithstanding, sophisticated research conducted with identical twins at the University of Minnesota shows that people who exhibit a highly genetically determined trait that psychologists call "traditionalism" are naturally inclined toward hierarchy and judgmental, black-and-white thinking. Those endowed with a less strongly heritable trait called "absorption" easily tune out pedestrian reality and focus intently; they're also inclined to be imaginative. Percentages of both kinds of individuals help explain the percentages of fundamentalists and mystics not only in the general population but within each denomination—even within each church or temple.

As for the effect of nurture on a person's religious style, one of the strongest predictors of a preference for straight-and-narrow religion is education. No longer the province of the rural and uneducated, fundamentalism has an increasingly Middle American profile. Nonetheless, among Roof's middle-aged subjects, 40 percent of those with postgraduate degrees thought of Jesus more as a great teacher than as a divine savior, for example, but only 10 percent of high school graduates regarded him that way. Concerning ethical issues, from sexuality to urban problems, the more educated were likelier to offer social or scientific rather than individual or supernatural explanations. Interestingly, Roof found that compared with the more educated and more skeptical Americans, the traditional believers, who regard religion as a "shelter" in an evil world and morality as living for others, require much less in the way of excitement and ego gratification—and are happier.[7]

One little-remarked influence on spiritual style, I suspect, is that for some, religious submission has a sexual frisson. On the radio one day, I hear a reporter describe her travels in the Muslim world. To her surprise, she found that many women liked the status quo. One wife pointed out that she was pleased the reporter had spoken with her husband that day, because the company of a Western woman would excite him, and the wife would reap the rewards that evening. I suspect that many more men than would admit to it are also enthralled by orthodoxy's demands of trying to please and serve an exacting master, such as the one who demanded that Abraham cut off the end of his penis or requires celibacy in exchange for ravishing the soul as if it were a bride. Like an obsessed lover, the zealot has one libidinal focus and makes a single choice that obviates all others. One needn't be a flagellating, fasting fanatic to take pleasure in the roles of submission and dominance, as well as the freedom from uncertainty and ambivalence they bring.

While the religious right, focusing on abortion and homosexuality, has laid noisy claim to America's high moral ground, others have been quietly refining a different ethical vision for a millennial civilization that will depend on interconnectedness and understanding. For a week in September 1997, a huge ferryboat circuited the sewage-clogged, chemically poisoned Black Sea, one of the Earth's sickest bodies of water, carrying an unusual group of passengers. Mingling with the three hundred scientists and politicians were Jewish, Muslim, Hindu, and Christian clergy, most notably Patriarch Bartholomew I of Constantinople, the leader of the 170 million members of the Eastern Orthodox Church. Twenty-five years earlier, the Anglican Church pronounced that abusing the environment constituted a sin of blasphemy. But this very public personal demonstration by the head of a faith known more for mysticism than activism attracted particular attention. Unlike most Christian churches since the Enlightenment, the Orthodox had never forgotten that, as it recently stated, "evil is not only a matter for human beings but affects the entire Creation."

Like an increasing number of problems in an ever smaller, less boundaried world, restoring the health of the environment requires not only politics, economics, and science, but religion, which has a unique potential to effect the necessary global change of heart. According to what I've come to think of as "ecomorality," the do's and don'ts of personal piety are less compelling than systemic well-being, whether of the planet or community.

One Sunday about a year before Patriarch Bartholomew took his toxic cruise, I listened to the renowned Harvard sociobiologist E. O. Wilson preach a sermon at the cathedral in New York. As the home base of the National Religious Partnership for the Environment, this church has long fostered connections between science and religion. Winningly birdlike in a vast red liturgical robe, the professor sounded the millennial theme of relationship, specifically as it pertains to biodiversity. We face a pivotal moment in history, he said, a time when forests shrink, the ozone layer thins, and farmers and developers burn 5 percent of the Earth's landscape each year. Already, three quarters of Hawaii's birds are gone, as are a fifth of the world's.

The loss of tropical forests is Wilson's particular concern. Although they cover only 6 percent of the planet's land, they harbor half of its species, including the plants that yield 40 percent of all prescription drugs. Beyond such obvious practical considerations, he said, when we lose nature, we also lose vast amounts of information and an enormous source of psychological health and aesthetic pleasure. "We're the first creature to become a geophysical force that actually changes the atmosphere and climate—a human superorganism," said Wilson. "We could be recorded as the most destructive generation in history. As we enter the century of the environment, we need a global ethics that transcends nation and denomination, so that we can carry as much life as possible through the bottleneck of the next hundred years."

Just a few weeks after E. O. Wilson spoke about the environment, Muhammad Yunus, the founder of a revolutionary bank for the impoverished in Bangladesh, the world's poorest country, preached on economic ecomorality. Situated in the shadow of Everest, Bangladesh is the size of Florida but is home to the equivalent of half America's population. During the terrible famine of the early 1970s, Yunus, a university professor, quickly shifted his focus from global, to national, to individual solutions. "Could I help even one person for one day in some way?" he asked. "Was there *anything* to be done?"

Deciding to try to learn from the people rather than operate from books, he visited a village and met a poor woman who supported herself by making and selling lentil soup. Despite her industry, her take-home was two pennies a day. Because she had no money of her own to buy ingredients, she was forced to borrow the requisite tiny amounts at high interest, which ate up most of her profits. Surveying the village, Yunus found forty-two others in similar predicaments. Loans of only a few dollars would allow them to be self-supporting. Amazed that it was possible to provide "so much happiness to so many for so little," he approached some banks. None would lend to the poor—they had no collateral. "The more you have," said Yunus, "the more you can borrow, and the less you have, the less you can borrow."

Determined not only to help the poor but to teach the banks a lesson, Yunus lent the villagers the money they needed. "They all paid me back," he said, "but the banks still didn't care." By 1983, the bank that Yunus started for the poor was officially recognized. Now in 36,000 villages, it lends millions in tiny amounts, often to women. A customer's first loan is usually ten or fifteen dollars. "The big problem," said Yunus, "is overcoming the poor's fear of borrowing. But they gain great confidence when they're able to pay back their loans."

Today, only a third of Bangladesh's population remains abjectly poor, and Professor Yunus has a different view of economics. "Poverty is created not by the poor," he said, "but by concepts and institutions. The basic responsibility of any society is to ensure human dignity to all its members. Being human should be enough collateral. We must change our institutions and create a poverty-free world, which is possible." He concluded by saying that he dreams of the day "when our children or grandchildren have to visit a museum to see the misery and indignity of poverty." If he makes any distinction between the spiritual and material impact of his work on his neighbors' lives, like Jesus, Yunus didn't say. In an unusual gesture during a liturgy, the cathedral's congregation rose to applaud a Muslim who, like the Hindu Gandhi, exemplifies modern "Christian charity."

Ecomorality isn't restricted to the environment or economics. On a hot spring day in 1997, a crowd made up of Asian monks, Prada-clad uptown Buddhists, and students mills around outside the cathedral's Synod House, hoping for a glimpse of the Dalai Lama, who has joined some Nobel laureates in a protest against the sale of arms to dictators. Just before the press conference, I penetrate the Buddhist security, i.e., smiling college kids, and take a seat. The attractive, mostly young crowd of all races argues that Buddhism is The Gap religion. The two young black men to my right are so enthusiastic about His Excellency's imminent arrival that my chair vibrates. When I request some compassion, they cheerfully comply. On my left are two blond college girls from Boston, wearing Tibetan dresses. They belong to Students for a Free Tibet, a cause that, like Vietnam in the sixties, is very hip on campus. One earnestly tells me, "We always try to be in His Excellency's presence, because he's so strong. Without it, we'd get burned out in the cause."

Of the Nobelists who speak first, my favorite is Oscar Arias, the peacemaking president of Costa Rica. Considering that 1.3 billion people on the planet earn less than a dollar a day, he says, spending money on arms is doubly obscene. "Like the drug and slave trades," he says, "it traffics in death. War and the preparation for war are the greatest obstacles to human progress. Imagine if the $800 billion spent each year on arms went to humanity instead. It could give the whole world basic decency. We don't need military security. We need 'human security'—freedom from fear and misery. The poor are crying out for schools and doctors, not tanks and generals."

When the Dalai Lama takes the stage, he gets a warm but dignified reception. The first thing I notice about this surprisingly robust man in maroon robes is his grin, which reminds me of President Eisenhower's. Its infectious warmth is coupled with a C'mon-we-can-do-it quality. Whether bodhisattva or four-star general, cheerfulness, confidence, and capability make for an irresistible leader. First, the Dalai Lama apologizes for his "poor English, which always was poor, and now, like me, is older, too." (His English is excellent.) He's cheered that not only Nobelists but so many of the young are enthusiastic about curbing weapons of mass destruction. We must mobilize, he says, to decrease violence, not only among nations, but within families and between individuals, because "peace gives us happiness. What's the use of anger? Hate? We'll always have problems in the self, family, and world, but we must not use violence to try to solve them." If Wilson sees the twenty-first century as the age of the environment, and Yunus looks for the elimination of poverty, the Dalai Lama hopes for an era of "dialogue," he says. "Please try to make an effort. If we all do, there's a real possibility to transform humanity."

If ecomorality is about transforming the external world, "psychomorality" concerns transforming the internal one. Its motivation, as Psalm 51 phrases it, is "Create in me a clean heart, O God, and renew a right spirit within me." One April evening, I go to B'nai Jeshurun, to hear Rabbi Nilton Bonder discuss his recent book *The Kabbalah of Envy*.[8] He begins with a rabbinic saying that a person is revealed by how he handles money, food, and anger: down-to-earth gauges related to our "animal parts" and survival. Like the rabbis of old, Rabbi Bonder is particularly concerned with anger. To him, its "deepest" form isn't revealed in obvious manifestations, from a shouted epithet to a punch, but more subtly, as envy.

One day, says Rabbi Bonder, God tells Moses that if he wishes, he will never have to die. Nonetheless, God adds, Joshua must go on to become Israel's new leader. Moses accepts. After a while, however, he returns before God, saying "Let me die." Describing envy's peculiar destructiveness, Rabbi Bonder says, "When you're jealous, you want something someone else has. When you're envious, you just don't want him to have it. Your only pleasure is in depriving another of it." Only consider the man, he says, who was told by an angel that he could have anything he wished, with the caveat that his enemy would get double. After some thought, the man said, "Blind me in one eye." The point of such stories, says the rabbi, is to remind us that "we have a lot of violence in our lives, without realizing it as such."

Where the particular violence of envy is concerned, pretending that we don't feel this universal emotion only compounds its dangers. Effortlessly adopting psychomoral language, Rabbi Bonder says, "It's better to own your envy, not only so you can fix it, but because looking at it tells you about who you are and what enslaves you." In hard times, he says, "you may have ten friends who will help you. But if you win the lottery, will you even have five who will be happy for you? Stick with them, because they're real friends." Invoking the Yiddish antonym for envy, Rabbi Bonder says, "To be with someone in his happiness is to *fargint*—to open up and embrace, rather than contract. Maybe this *fargint* is the cornerstone of the messianic era."

According to the principles of psychomorality, nonviolence means more than "Thou shalt not kill" or even "covet." It also means "Thou shalt not manipulate." Because it's wrong to shame someone, Rabbi Bonder says, "the rabbis were even concerned about blushing." Expanding on this sophisticated moral sensibility, he could be addressing every spouse in America: "The rabbis said that we're not ready to see or hear everything. Sometimes we have to cover our eyes or stop our ears. We also have to forget certain things, so we won't be violent." Reiterating this hard truth, he says, "It's *violent* to remember things you should forget. We need to be sensitive about when to speak up or be silent, to remember or forget."

In the rabbis' centuries of talk about ways to avoid conflict, Rabbi Bonder discerns what he calls a "technology of peace." Employing it effectively begins with life's everyday encounters. "We have a lot of violence in our lives that we don't acknowledge," he reiterates. "Let's say you lend something to someone who once refused to lend something to you. But if you say, 'Okay, I'll do it, because I'm not stingy like you,' you're creating violence. We say to another, 'Do this favor for me—it's easy.' But maybe it's not for the other person! The law tells us that we can't assess the cost of something to someone else—it's violent." Stopping for another story, Rabbi Bonder tells of a Hasid who complains to his rebbe that wherever he goes, people step on his toes. "The rebbe says, 'You don't give people room, so they have nowhere to step but on your toes.' We can do the same thing in social situations, where we hog the limelight, refusing to give others some space."

If psychomorality has obvious applications in our personal lives, it's not restricted to them. Rabbi Bonder cites some Yiddish wisdom that underlies Martin Buber's philosophy: "If I am I because you are you, then I'm not I, and you're not you, and we can't talk. But if I know who I am, I don't need 'the other' to be the opposite." Turning to the Mideast, the rabbi says, "Enemies are important people, because they can show and tell us things about ourselves that friends can't or won't. In the next life, your enemy will be your *hevruta*—your study partner—because he can teach you the most. Jews and Palestinians—why are they afraid of each other? Make a list. There's a lot of information there. If we mend our relationship with our enemies, we can learn."

Citing what he calls "a real developmental progression," Rabbi Bonder quotes the kabbalah as saying " 'Hate yourself as you would hate others.' From hating in yourself what you hate in others, you move to 'Don't do to them what you wouldn't have them do to you,' to loving your neighbor as yourself, and finally, to a simultaneous loving of self and other, so that the other is internalized. In four steps, you move from hate to taking the other inside. Hate and anger are a virtual reality that we can render unreal."

Sharing a midrash that epitomizes the millennial psycho- and ecomoral sensibility, Rabbi Bonder describes a man who asks his rabbi a deep question: How can we pray for someone to change without interfering with his free will? Beginning at square one, the rebbe of yore reasons thus: What is God? The totality of souls. Because whatever exists as a whole also exists as a part, in each soul, all are contained. Therefore, if a man changes and grows, he also transforms his neighbor— "the he in me, and the me in he." Because we're all part of what was once a great single reality before the differentiations of Creation, this rebbe decides, "you're not interfering with someone *when you change the you in him.*" Moving from our own species to the rest, Rabbi Bonder asks: "Why save the whales? Not because they're cute, but because there's a me in the whale that goes when he goes, severing a connection."

After days of dazzling blue skies and snowy vistas, Ash Wednesday is gray, heavy, rainy—February at its gloomiest. In the somber cathedral, the priest marks my forehead with ashes and intones in a James Earl Jones voice, "Remember, man, that thou art dust and into dust thou shalt return." Despite all our fitness regimens, therapy, insurance, and improvement schemes, how weak we are, how flawed and disappointing! As St. Paul wrote, "For the good that I would do I do not; but the evil which I would not, that I do."

In my childhood, Ash Wednesday was a grim day on which Father Cassidy reminded us of our many sins and Jesus' lack of same, and we resolved to balance the scales by giving up candy for forty days. I realize that times have changed as soon as I take a seat in the back of St. Martin's Chapel as Susan Harriss, clericals brightened with grass-green sweater, meets with a group of children from the Cathedral School, where she serves as chaplain. As the kids file in and take their seats, a guitarist plays a song called "Don't Let the Light Go Out!" The words may be symbolic, but the children are utterly focused on whose turn it is to set the altar's candles ablaze with the special stick.

When they settle down, Susan asks the kids if they've ever been "so mad or sad that they threw themselves right down in the dirt—even a mud puddle." Many hands go up. Long ago, she says, when people were upset over something they had done and afraid that God was angry about it, they wondered what they should do. Have the children any ideas about that? "They could have killed themselves," offers one boy. "Oh, I hope not!" says Susan. A girl suggests hiding, but Susan answers, "That didn't work so well for Adam and Eve." Instead, she says, the people put on sackcloth—"like their worst clothes"—smeared themselves with ashes, and just sat there. Why would they do that? she wonders aloud. "So they wouldn't look like themselves," offers one clever student. When another says, "To show how sorry they were," Susan nods. "We all make lots of mistakes—hitting, saying mean words, even head-butting," she says, eliciting nods and giggles. "Ashes are more than just saying you're sorry, but *showing* that you are and seeking forgiveness."

Although the Cathedral School is Episcopalian, it welcomes children of all faiths. Susan tells the class that while she'll discuss the meaning of Ash Wednesday, she won't mark their foreheads, which can be done only with their parents. She explains that this is the first of forty special days that Christians set aside to think about their behavior and resolve to do better, a period the church calls Lent. When people get a smear of ashes on their foreheads, they don't just do it for God or others, but for themselves, too, says Susan, because "making mistakes usually means you're not too happy. Now, think of something you did or said today or yesterday that wasn't so good, then ask God to erase it." The children are delighted with this idea. I wish it felt that simple to me. At the end of the service, which they have clearly enjoyed, Susan asks the students to sit up straight with their backs against their chairs for a minute of quiet thought. When she says, "Let us bless the Lord," they chime in, "Thanks be to God!"

Most of the children file out, but one boy stays behind. Recently, he has been kicking the peacocks that wander the cathedral close and hitting other children. Susan suspects that someone is picking on him. She asks if he has ever seen those Russian dolls that open up to reveal smaller ones. He nods. "When there's a chain of hurting others because you're hurt," says Susan, "the littlest one"—a doll, a bird, a smaller child— "gets hurt the most." Before lashing out in pain or anger, she says, "it's good to try to stop and just *think* for a minute."

When the boy smiles and hurries back to class, Susan says that when he sees her during the day, he often makes the open-palmed gesture of prayer and meditation that she calls the "listening position" in chapel. At first she thought the boy meant to ridicule her, but it doesn't seem that way anymore. In the empty chapel, quiet but for the birds beyond the stained-glass windows chirping resolutely in the rain, we two mothers sit for a few minutes, struck by childhood's often overlooked heaviness. Susan recalls that when she asked, "When did the people who receive ashes make their mistakes?" one boy had thought that "maybe it was when they were children." One of the kids had even suggested suicide as a response to guilt.

When I was a child, a sin was "an offense against God," much as a crime was an offense against the law. In the psychomoral era, " 'sin' is a way of identifying that something is wrong," says Susan. "We all make mistakes. Some of them, even when made in love, like choosing the wrong person or marrying too young, end up in abortion or divorce. But I don't think the church ought to be holding people in those marriages or pregnancies to compensate for mistakes. Our actions have enough consequences that we don't need to talk about hell. Who needs hell? There has to be a way to stop the suffering so that growth can continue." Susan sighs and grins. "I love the psalm that says, 'Oh that my ways were made so straight, that I might keep your commandments.' That just makes me weep, because it speaks of the modern mind so perfectly."

Susan remembers a teacher in seminary who said to her class, "I know you don't believe in original sin, but take the subway to Times Square at five P.M., and by the time you get to the top of the stairs, you will know that something is wrong with the world. That 'something' is original sin." To Susan, sin is "that something wrong with the world that, like an illness, makes us feel spiritually sick. There's so much distress that you or I have nothing to do with that just . . . rises up, or is the condition that we find ourselves in." As wives, mothers, and daughters, we commiserate over how, in a family, one problem can lead to another until just figuring out where to start the repairs is a daunting prospect. "*That's* what sin is like," says Susan. "It's a condition of entrapment, in which we do things that we don't really intend. So much in the world is imperfect, incomplete, unfulfilled." Slipping between psycho- and ecomoral perspectives, she says that in seminary during the politicized seventies, "the worst thing you could do was quote Jesus as saying 'Blessed are the poor in spirit,' instead of 'Blessed are the poor.' Everyone said, 'He meant the poor who are physically hungry.' But I think he meant spiritually hungry. To me, the spirit is your whole self, and to be 'poor in spirit' means to feel crushed. To know your need of God. Blessed are you when you're crushed."

Considering his ministries of the environment and healing, it's not surprising that Canon Jeff Golliher is fluent in the languages of eco- and psychomorality. One weekday Eucharist, he begins his sermon by saying he has just returned from an interfaith conference in Istanbul. Clearly jet-lagged, he plucks a nice phrase from one of the day's readings about being borne up "by the wings of eagles," wanders here and there with it, then suddenly snaps back into focus. At the meeting in Turkey, he says, there was much talk about how to resolve problems in a multicultural world. "We must understand that we can never know the whole story about any issue," says Jeff. "We should 'rest in God,' and almost not really even know what we think. Otherwise it's so easy to polarize into 'right' and 'wrong.' " I have to smile at the thought of what a fundamentalist would make of such a statement.

To illustrate the difference between his "both/and" way of moral thinking and that of "either/or" religion, Jeff brings up sexuality. Distinctions about whether it's in or out of marriage, hetero or homo, "may seem to be lending clarity to behavior," he says, "but they really aren't. Such rules are more simpleminded than clarifying, because our lives are so complex. And complex is the way God created things to be—intrinsically good and not to be diminished for the sake of black-or-white distinctions. We don't need divisive objectivity, we need subjective connectedness."

Blending eco- and psychomoral themes, Jeff says that to him, "God or the Holy Spirit are just words for a living presence outside ourselves, and 'religious experience,' like healing and ecology, are about this greater whole and how to live within it. The way we've treated the Earth—almost as an obstacle—is an extension of the way we regard our own bodies." Although we talk as if "the environment" or "the body" can be observed disconnectedly, he says, that's both conceptually and experientially wrong. "Ecology and healing restore the right context by reminding us that we're *part of* creation, with all that implies. We're part of a living, holy universe, not a dead 'it' that's just there for us to use for ourselves. That's a simple statement, but also quite amazing, especially considering the opposite way in which the system of the past several hundred years has been moving."

Turning to a classic psychomoral analogy, Jeff says that not supporting ecology "is like the decision to stay in a bad marriage because you worry that you can't support yourself or fear that you'll lose your sense of who you are. Your identity is defined by the relationship, but you're dying in it—that's everyday life in America." Learning to see clearly, rather than in narcissistic and materialistic terms, is hard, he says, "but according to the great religions, that's really it. Religion has always said that the way the world works is not God's way. To be part of creation and God, as opposed to 'the world,' is to not be self- or object-identified."

Later, I ask Jeff about an ancient moral construct that's discussed far less often in millennial sanctuaries than in traditional, conservative ones. "I have to admit that I don't like to talk about evil at all," he says. "It's not that I don't think about it a lot or haven't had experiences of it. But it's best not to put a lot of energy into talking about evil, because that gives it power. What evil wants is your attention. The goal of spiritual practice is to *try* to keep yourself filled up with light." When I observe that both psychotherapists and the church fathers maintain that evil is simply the absence of good, Jeff grins. "There's a very practical reason for that stance," he says. "Neither one wants to give evil the attention."

As vocal critics point out, eco- and psychomoral attitudes about good and evil have their flaws, notably the potential for subjectivity and self-indulgence. By stressing sins of omission over sins of commission, however, they place a healthy emphasis on moving forward, beyond the self and toward the common good. As I recall from the confessional, focusing on personal failings and flaws can encourage narcissism and navel-gazing in a different guise.

At the millennium, religion must speak of right and wrong, old and new, mystery and science, and body and soul. Its efforts to integrate these elements are epitomized by the popular phenomenon of healing.

CHAPTER FIVE

BODY AND SOUL

I will be glad and rejoice in thy mercy:
for thou hast considered my trouble;
thou hast known my soul in adversities.

—PSALM 31

THE FIRST HEALING SERVICE I attend is a "laying on of hands" held in one of the cathedral's small chapels on a snowy night. After a brief prayer, Canon Jeff Golliher invites us to approach the altar. The deep, cold quiet is punctuated with the popping of snaps and sliding of zippers as fifteen people loosen their coats. If any are physically ill, it isn't immediately apparent. Perhaps most, like me, are suffering from what's easiest to call stress.

A pretty Caribbean woman and her teenaged daughter go first. When they return to their seats, the daughter, seemingly overwhelmed or exhausted, first rests her head on her mother's shoulder, then in her lap. Next comes a middle-aged professional couple. Encouraging her doubtful partner, the woman whispers, "This stuff is better than acupuncture."

When it's my turn, I'm a bit skittish, uncertain about what's supposed to happen. When Jeff puts his hands on my back, I feel physically energized and, as if from an invisible hook in my sternum, somewhat lifted up and forward. Psychologically, I feel a sense of well-being. These sensations might be a response to the ritual's novelty and trusting contact with a kindly "stranger"—in our culture, an unusual event. When each of us has had a turn, there's a brief prayer, and we walk out laughing and talking. As if speaking for everyone, Canon Susan Harriss, who has clearly had a hard day, says she feels "so relaxed now."

It may sound experimental or somehow suspect, but healing is as ancient as religion itself. In Christianity, it goes straight back to Jesus, who was probably best known for that skill during his lifetime. Not until the Enlightenment, when Western medicine conceptualized the body as a machine, did religion withdraw from the blood-and-guts side of ministry. After hundreds of years, however, healing has returned to mainline religion, just as spirituality is penetrating mainstream medicine. In a nationwide Gallup study conducted in 1996 for the Harvard Medical School's Mind/Body Institute at Deaconess Hospital, a surprising 30 percent of Americans report they've experienced a "remarkable healing" of a physical or psychological problem. Most credit either a "higher power," such as God, or the action of prayer, whether their own or others'. Interestingly, many respondents say these perceptions of healing changed not only their religious lives but also their health habits, such as diet, and increased their interest in alternative medicine.[1]

One evening, I attend a healing service at Ansche Chesed, a big nineteenth-century New York synagogue that anticipated millennial religion back in the 1970s. By then, some of the idealistic young West Siders who helped produce the sixties had started families and begun to reconsider religion. The late political activist Paul Cowan, with Rachel Cowan, Michael Strassfeld, and Burt Visotzky, now distinguished rabbis, and other kindred spirits began to build a new kind of egalitarian, participatory synagogue. Unmoved by rationalistic Reform Judaism, they turned to tradition—Hebrew and prayer shawls, davening and keeping kosher—to recover a long-submerged Jewish spirituality. Determined to "do Judaism" themselves, they went without a cantor, and for years, refused to hire a rabbi. Nearly thirty years later, the erstwhile seminarians, graduate students, and hippies are mostly gray-haired professors and professionals. Joined by younger congregants, they still hew to the same ideals, particularly an experiential spirituality and the vision of a religious community as a democratic "culture of learning," much of it embodied in small groups.

In all religions, healing is involved with nature. Tonight's service at Ansche Chesed coincides with Tu B'Shvat, or the festival of trees. After a quieting-down song led by Debbie Freedman, a well-known musician in Jewish religious circles, Rabbi Michael Strassfeld gives us some orientation; a leader in the Jewish "renewal," or spirituality, movement, and an expert on Jewish music, Michael is also the coauthor of *The Jewish Catalog,* a religious version of the *Whole Earth* sort. First, he explains the special nature of the mini-seder, distributed in tidy individual plastic bags, that we're about to enjoy in honor of Tu B'Shvat. As we munch on fruits and nuts, he says that they offer an opportunity to reconsider ourselves and our relationship to creation. Like some of us, the nuts are "physical" types: hard-shelled on the outside, hiding the softer, spiritual part—even God's presence—within. Like olives and dates, "emotional" types are the reverse. Some, symbolized by strawberries and grapes, are "cerebral," or soft through and through. The most spiritual creations are invisible. All, says the rabbi, are good.

Gently, the teaching and music, food and prayer, do their work of reminding us that we're more than our bodies and minds, and especially, more than our problems. In this large group of perhaps sixty people, some are clearly ill and frail. Come what may—and eventually must—like nature itself, we will all somehow go on in God, who, as the prayer says, "keeps faith with those who sleep in the dust." No matter what its vicissitudes, we're reminded that we have been fortunate to receive the unearned gift of life. Toward the end, Rabbi Strassfeld adds a healing ritual's crucial element of respect for the individual to its subtle stress on the universality of the human condition. With a glance at each person, he offers a silent invitation to name oneself or others in need of succor. To all the Jewish names, my father's Irish one is added. On a page, this sounds like a small thing, but in a room full of others struggling in one way or another with sickness, it's deeply moving. Before leaving, we sing, swaying together: "May the source of strength / Who blessed the ones before us / Help us find the courage / To make our lives a blessing / And let us say, Amen."

Although there are healings in the Hebrew Bible—the prophet Elisha even raises a boy from the dead—such services are new in American Judaism. One afternoon, tall, scholarly Rabbi Strassfeld, who reminds me of Abraham Lincoln, describes the effort of devising a ritual that taps into the ubiquitous millennial New Age holism and love of nature while retaining his religion's mythic majesty and tradition. To him, healing is just one part of the larger movement toward spirituality, which is particularly attractive to a people "who bought into secularism, reason, and science, especially medicine, more than others. Now, we're engaged in a real search, because rationalism, even halakah, isn't enough anymore. To become more observant of the law, which is always Judaism's goal, Jews today must feel joyful, not guilty, about Judaism, and have the sense that they're moving toward something deeper. They want spiritual practice that gives a sense of the holy, which in turn leads to the desire to behave in ethical and moral ways."

In contrast to the dramatic Bible-thumping "faith healers" of yore, with their whiff of charlatanism and promises of instant cures, the understated new breed to which Michael and Jeff belong espouses a broader, more realistic, primarily psychospiritual aim: a coming to terms with the way things are. In religion, a healing "should take us beyond ourselves, not make us more narcissistic," Michael says. "The goal is spiritual, not physical, although that kind of healing sometimes happens too. The services aren't support groups but opportunities to be in touch with mystery, tradition, music. Often, it's hard for people who are ill in some way to find a place where they can just *be*. If you ask people why they come, many say, 'It just feels good to be here.' "

Months later, I have another kind of healing experience that surprises me. Stuck in the city on a humid August weekend, I realize that although I've worked hard all month, I have little to show for it. Moreover, strenuous recent efforts on my family's behalf have failed to please either the younger or older members. In short, I feel awful: hot and tired, oppressed and depressed, anxious and angry. With nothing to lose—at least I can be alone in church—I decide to go to the cathedral's Sunday Eucharist and stay for the healing service that follows.

In one of the small chapels, with a direct approach very different from Jeff's reticence, Lanice Cutrona, a white-robed healing minister, motions me into a chair near the altar.

An obstetrics nurse whose stature and gravitas evoke one of Michelangelo's Delphic sibyls, she flat-out asks me what's wrong. Shocked into responding in kind, I say that I have a big, demanding family and a worried mind. Standing behind me, Lanice puts her hands on my rigid trapezius muscles and, in a strong African-American voice, starts to pray aloud. Because I immediately begin to cry, all I can remember of what she says is that if I "keep Jesus in mind," he'll "uphold" me.

Although I don't have it, I can recognize unalloyed faith, and like physical courage, it always undoes me. If I were an actress and had to cry on demand, I would only have to think of the dying words of the wounded Stonewall Jackson, who had both: "Let us cross over the river and rest under the shade of the trees." Wiping my eyes with the hem of my fortunately longish cotton dress, for no reason that I could explain, I feel infinitely better, if embarrassed. The next day, I work productively for the first time in weeks.

Much of healing's popularity derives from its fusion of two contemporary enthusiasms: spirituality and science. Its comeback has been accelerated by research showing that many, even most, visits to doctors' offices concern stress-related problems: headaches, backaches, depression, fatigue, high blood pressure, insomnia, digestive complaints, and other "mind-body" ailments that often resist standard treatments. Psychoneuroimmunologists have learned that experience affects the endocrine, immune, and nervous systems. Focusing on a larger picture, researchers who study how people's lives affect their health have found that those who lack supportive relationships have a higher incidence of untimely death from all illnesses.[2] Their social aspect probably helps explain why simply attending religious services of any sort has a healing effect.[3] In one large, solid, federally funded survey, for example, researchers at Duke University's medical school found that among nearly two thousand older people, both healthy and infirm, those who visited a church or temple weekly were much less likely to have high blood levels of interleukin-6; this biochemical produced by the immune system is associated with many diseases, including cancer, and even with difficulties in managing routine tasks. In attempting to explain their results, Dr. Harold Koenig said, "Perhaps religious participation enhances immune functioning by as yet unknown mechanisms, such as through feelings of belonging, togetherness, even perhaps the experience of worship and adoration."[4]

Whether or not there is a God who answers them, prayers may indeed promote healing. For that matter, in the Harvard-Deaconess study, a third of those who felt they had experienced a "remarkable" benefit attributed it not to God per se, but to their own prayers or those of others. A feeling of efficacy promotes mental and physical health. No one knows whether teaching patients to visualize healthy cells eating up tumors helps kill cancer. Like healing services and prayer, however, such take-charge strategies can reduce anxiety, pain, and hopelessness, and improve the ability to cope. Now that the Harvard, Johns Hopkins, and George Washington University medical schools and others offer courses on spirituality and health, medicine will undoubtedly probe further into healing's uncharted territory, even its fringes. Already, some studies—say, of whether very sick people who are prayed for without their knowledge do better than those who aren't prayed for—seem to push the limits of science and spirituality. When prayers become coins that pay for "results," religion becomes a slot-machine.

The best evidence for prayer's positive effects on health comes from considerable research on meditation. Meditation has measurable physiological effects, such as reducing heart, respiratory, and brain-wave rates. Perhaps by stimulating certain immune and endocrine responses, this practice can also aid the ill. At Harvard's Deaconess Hospital, Dr. Herbert Benson and his colleagues have helped thousands of patients cope with cancer, infertility, pain, hypertension, cardiac rehabilitation, AIDS, insomnia, and menopause by teaching them the meditative "relaxation response": sitting quietly for at least twenty minutes and repeating a word or short phrase with each breath, gently returning to it when distracted. While some experience dramatic cures, many report improvement of one sort or another, from lessened symptoms to better mood.[5] The "medical" forms of meditation are usually identified with Asian practices, such as *zazen* and yoga, but other religions have similar traditions. In the Second Temple period (fourth century B.C.E. to first century C.E.), some Jews may have assumed a special crouching prayer posture and focused on their breathing while repeating a mystical term. Roman Catholic and Orthodox Christians in particular have always stressed meditative prayer, from the mantra-like rosary to the repetition of ejaculations, or short pious phrases.

If I were conducting research on how spiritual practices affect well-being, I'd focus on memory. It's always involved in healing. Whether conducted in a church or synagogue or on a massage table, such an experience reminds the participant of something else: a vital reality whose importance has been forgotten. Just recalling it is restorative, moving the person closer to being, if not physically well, then well-balanced. The memory could concern a painful incident that went unmourned and got "stored" in some dim corner of the mind, or even in a sore back or stiff neck, where it awaits release. The healing recollection might be of a better time, which puts a current rough patch in perspective. It might be a sudden remembering of God, or of one's true self.

From science's perspective, without memory, there is no

self. Without its mortar to join up our different states of being, we'd have no sense of identity. We'd be unable to connect the sad "me" of an hour or a month ago with the cheerful one now, much less the infant and child we once were with today's adult. What scientists have articulated only recently, religious thinkers understood many centuries ago. Psychologists call one's habitual ways of being, which are the components of personality, "states." Buddha called them *skandas,* or "skeins," whose loops make up the self. Contemplating the longing of his loosely coiled, state-shifting human identity for the sole changeless repository of all reality, Augustine articulated the fact that to feel whole, we need to feel remembered, contained, or as psychoanalysts say, "held"—by big mind, God, or "object."

Modern religious thinkers, too, speak of the intimate connection between the sacred and memory. To Abraham Joshua Heschel, the individual's task is to be a "reminder of God."[6] In *Omnipotence and Other Theological Mistakes,* the academic philosopher Charles Hartshorne, a specialist in metaphysics, disputes predestination by arguing that because the future doesn't yet exist, and because even God can't "know" what does not exist, God, like us, has free will and the ability to change in response to events. This flexibility in turn accounts for the evolution of the divine character in relationship to creation, as charted in the Bible. Just as Heschel's human being is charged to be a reminder of God, the task of Hartshorne's God is to remember everything that has ever happened—one way to think of eternal life.[7]

In the Hungarian Pastry Shop one morning, I try to get Jeff Golliher to explain what happens in healing. This is a challenge, because one of his virtues is a habit of stopping before saying too much. After struggling with language's limits where what Augustine called "subtle realities" are concerned, I say, I inevitably fall back on scientific analogies. To me, healing feels like plugging into a vast electrical circuit to which all things are somehow connected. "That's exactly what it is," Jeff says. "It's feeling that the environment isn't separate from you. That realization moves you behind one mind-set right there, without even thinking about it. It just happens. What does an experience like that mean about our assumptions about the way the world is? That's where the transformation comes in."

This sense of reconnecting to a larger reality, which Zen practitioners call big mind and New Agers describe as "holistic," is the least common denominator of healings. As both priest and anthropologist, Jeff disputes the widely accepted idea that Christians have Christian experiences, say, and Hindus have Hindu ones. A Central American shaman performing a healing "might call upon of the living presence of what is, and becoming part of that, which would require from us a complete restructuring of experience," he says. "But whether a healing is performed in a church or a rain forest, the reality entered into reveals that we and the world are alive in a way that our habits of thinking and feeling don't allow us to recognize or be open to. Healing puts us back into the world and the hands of God, which are interrelated. Part of our problem is thinking that we can and should control everything, including other people. In the end, that means lying to yourself about who you are and what you're feeling. Healing means remembering that God is in control."

Circling back to my what-happens question, Jeff says that whether what occurs in healings is spiritual, psychological, or physiological, or any different from the neural firings evoked by art or music, "is a good question, but not one that interests me. Who knows exactly what happens? It's up to God.

Healing 'works' not in the pragmatic sense we usually mean, but in how the universe moves. As a result, people are relieved of a lot of suffering."

People suffer a lot. Our species' nervous system is exquisitely attuned to danger and loss. This orientation has been a great evolutionary advantage. On the savannah or in the forest, survival depends on rapid flight-or-fight decisions. Our sensitivity to pain, and even to the possibility of it, is less adaptive in the urbanized world of corporate struggles and the battle of the sexes. When stress responses meant to last seconds or minutes persist for weeks or months, the result is anxiety—the emotional equivalent of the common cold—and depression, which afflicts one in ten Americans.

Then, of course, there's death—not just the event but our awareness of it. Suddenly, a third of Americans are middle-aged. Their parents are becoming frail and dying. They themselves confront not only reading glasses and Retin A but high cholesterol and breast or prostate cancer. The culture's phenomenal interest in healing and alternative medicine is partly a reaction to seventy-five million bodies simultaneously manifesting mortality.

One Wednesday, I bring a neoagnostic friend who's undergoing chemotherapy to Jeff's noontime healing service. First, the Eucharist unfolds with that grand simplicity that is the work of centuries. Then, as we kneel at the altar rail, Jeff moves down the row, dabs each brow with holy oil and then, placing his hands on each head, prays with quiet intensity. When the service is over, people smile but move briskly to the doors, busy urbanites due back at work. Walking the length of the darkened cathedral toward the bright afternoon outside, my friend and I reminisce about our childhood religions. Although she has drifted from her long-ago lukewarm Protestantism, she wants to "do everything possible to make this disease feel unwelcome." For her, this means not only the best high-tech medical care but Buddhist meditation and vespers at the cathedral, long walks by the river, a vegetarian diet, and yoga. As part of the massive overhaul of her priorities set in motion by her diagnosis, she has resigned from a high-profile job in the fast lane—"the stress is what made me sick"—to spend more time with her family and in the country. A few years ago, cancer was an illness to be attacked by oncologists. At the millennium, it's often the point of embarkation for a spiritual voyage.

As my friend's complex experience suggests, healing is not just about curing sickness; it's also about righting something that's gone wrong or is out of balance. One day at General Seminary, Elisabeth Koening relates the recent explosion of interest in spirituality to social, as well as individual, suffering. Along with appalling destruction and devastation, including two world wars, the Holocaust, nuclear weapons, and continuing genocide, she says, the twentieth century has brought the quieter, peculiarly modern scourge of dehumanization. Since the Industrial Revolution, an insidious sense of individual worthlessness has been abetted by the increasing emphasis on technology. "People are trying to retrieve their sense of self-worth," says Elisabeth. "Not only because they're hungry for it, but because, despite the cultural messages, they intuit that life has profound meaning. As Julian of Norwich says, we have to be very careful about 'spying into God's privities'—there are certain things we're not given to know. But other periods of great spiritual awakening have also been accompanied by a social upheaval that devalued and denigrated what it means to be human." In short, the spirituality surge suggests to Elisabeth that "perhaps God is doing a new thing among human beings at this point in time."

Jeff, too, sees the cultural as well as personal dimension of healing. After hundreds of years of vesting authority in experts and institutions, "a whole way of life is being questioned," he says. "Healing isn't just about health or religion, but about being alive. We might not think in those terms, which seem so abstract to us. Instead, we wonder, What's the point of this culture? Of my life? How come I feel bad? Our disorientation and malaise point to the problem of finding wholeness and seeing life as interconnected. People are looking for a way to be different. The world is being reorganized. During this time of transformation, it makes sense that both doctors and clergy would have new insights about how to live."

Institutions that have long ignored the spirit and focused on the flesh, like medicine, or idealized the spirit and denigrated its husk, like the church, have much to gain from embracing the contagious holistic assertion that bodies aren't just something we have but part of who we are. The old Western body-versus-spirit dualism has caused one sort of trouble, but Jeff stresses that the untempered New Age approach can create another kind. In all the great traditions, he says, "the first teaching is to say, 'Your body is good, but it's not all that you are.' Through meditation, as you realize that you are more than you see, you learn that the soul or spirit is *bigger* than the body. That can seem like you're separating them, but it's actually recognizing a part-whole relationship. The body is smaller than the spirit, but they're related. After what looks like asking you to think dualistically, then religion can and should talk to you about wholeness and integration. But the New Age makes that integration step one by identifying the soul *with* the body. As a result, people can get confused and narcissistic."

Long ago, Gregory of Nyssa said that the ladder of spirituality has three rungs: first comes the fear of God, then hope of divine reward, and finally friendship. Perhaps some people are inspired to ascend by good fortune and freedom from adversity, but from Buddha to Moses to Jesus, I can't think of any. Our society rejects the idea of the transformative power of hardship and suffering as masochism, denial, or superstition, if not downright delusion, yet the association is time-honored. An eminent, worldly psychiatrist once surprised me by recounting a story about the Buddha that he sometimes tells depressed patients. When a young woman who was deranged by grief over her baby's death was dragged into his presence, Buddha told her to visit every house in the village and bring him a grain of mustard from each one that was untouched by such loss. As always happens in healings, by the time the woman had made the rounds, she had remembered something important, which restored her right mind. Then the doctor told me another story, this one about two women in his circle. On receiving a diagnosis of breast cancer, one committed suicide and the other—his mother—started a support group and counseling program for other women suffering from the disease. Particularly in the depressed, said the psychiatrist, "an essential spiritual dimension is often missing."

Common neoagnostic wisdom has it that religion papers over life's viscissitudes with fantasy or denial. Yet it's often spiritual people who cope best and most straightforwardly with the Buddhist list of things that can't be helped—old age, sickness, death, decay. Like the Dalai Lama and Martin Luther King, they're the ones who can face darkness, yet maintain a lightness of heart. Before his conversion, Apollo of Scetis, one of the early church's *abbas,* had murdered a pregnant woman and cut her abdomen open simply to satisfy his curiosity about what her baby looked like. Later in life, he said, "Only the great lovers of God and others can look steadily at real human sin and not despair."

For fifty years after his ordeal in Auschwitz, the writer and activist Elie Wiesel practiced Judaism although he could no longer believe in God. His eloquent efforts to prevent violence and hatred brought him the Nobel Prize. In 1997, he published a letter commemorating Rosh Hashanah that began, "Master of the Universe, let us make up." He continued, "In my testimony, I have written harsh words, burning words, about your role in our tragedy. I would not repeat them today." In spite of all that had happened, he wished reconciliation, because "it is unbearable to be divorced from you so long."[8]

Not long after he had been subjected to charges of sexual abuse, which were later proved false and retracted, Joseph Cardinal Bernadin, the popular Catholic archbishop of Chicago, was told he had fatal cancer. On hearing the diagnosis, the cardinal wrote: "God was teaching me just how little control we really have and how important it is to trust in him." He wrote candidly about the great emotional and physical pain he had suffered, including moments of sadness and doubt. Nonetheless, the man who signed all his letters as "Joseph, your brother" spent his last days helping others at death's door; at least one had been consigned to death row. When he died in November 1996, this true "prince of the church" appeared on the cover of *Time* and was mourned by many Americans of all faiths for his compassion, honesty, courage, and faith.

One sunny afternoon at the cathedral I talk about the relationship between spirituality and suffering with Dean Harry Pritchett. "It's not that pain is good," he says, "but that it's real. There's something wrought into life's fabric that means we have to face pain in order to move through to the other side." The intuition that Harry expresses in Christian terms pervades all religions. "You don't have Easter morning till after Good Friday, and life is full of both."

After thinking hard about why he "right away likes some people and not others," Harry says, "Those I'm drawn to know about suffering and about their own corruption. In classic theological terms, about death and sin. People who are mature, centered, and joyful don't deny pain, or that they mess up. Religion's answers don't make any sense unless those questions about suffering and fallibility are asked." In my neoagnostic milieu, I say, most people wouldn't think of directing their existential questions to religion. How can someone who may not even know what it is start doing his own theology? "It's not in any book," says Harry. "Sometimes, someone has to tell you, or show you, what most matters."

Like the rabbis, Harry teaches with stories. He tells me about a man who was dying of AIDS early in the plague, when no one understood what it was or how it was spread; along with their other torments, many victims were objects of dread and disgust. Listening to this sick man describe his terrible experience, the priest started weeping. "And *he* kept telling me it was going to be all right," says Harry. "There's no way to affirm that except by faith. That man became my pastor and gave me the word I needed. 'It's going to be all right' became something I find myself saying a lot. Pain makes some people cynical, small, turned inward, but it takes others, like Jonah, into life at its depths."

To my surprise, Harry says he used to answer questions about death more easily, "yet what I believe now is probably deeper and firmer. It's close to knowing that the universe is friendly." He tells me another story. On the night he died, his father, who wasn't religious, looked up at Harry's church-going mother and said, "I'll be leaving you soon." She said, "I know. But I won't be far behind you." And the dying man said, "God, we'll have us a rendezvous!" To Harry, what Christians call the communion of saints is "kind of about a rendezvous of souls. When my mother died, I remembered what my father had said, and I just felt utter joy and relief. Some would call it sentimentality, or wishful thinking, or preciousness about family, but there's a truth to it."

After our chat, Harry sends me a xeroxed page from *Markings,* the memoir of Dag Hammarskjöld. The hugely respected former secretary general of the United Nations wrote: "I don't know Who—or what—put the question, I don't know when it was put. I don't even remember answering. But at some moment, I did answer Yes to Someone—or Something—and from that hour I was certain that existence is meaningful and that, therefore, my life, in self-surrender, had a goal. From that moment I have known what it means 'not to look back' and 'to take no thought for the morrow.' "

After reporting on millennial religion for a while, I began to realize that like many privileged persons in this privileged society, almost subconsciously I cherish two illusions. The first is that it's "normal" for life to be good, or at least okay, unless one happens to be among "those less fortunate." The second, complementary idea is that I'm in control of my life: ready and able to subject any problems that might arise to a lethal bombardment of competence, my own or hired experts'. As I attended different religious services, I began to acknowledge these assumptions, and then watch them begin to crumble.

At the cathedral, just after the Eucharist's sermon and creed, the priest reads aloud the names of the sick, troubled, and recently deceased. The congregants can also offer names, which creates a soft communal sigh. Next comes a series of general invocations for divine help—for bishops, the aged, firemen, addicts, the abused, the president, the confused, AIDS victims. Last, the people pray for themselves, that they may be delivered from "all danger, violence, oppression, and degradation," and end their lives "in faith and hope, without suffering and without reproach."

At first these so-called Prayers of the People didn't affect me. They seemed rote and generic, mouthed along with strangers. Over time, however, the recitation, offered while standing shoulder to shoulder, rich and poor, black and white, young and old, male and female, happy and sad, brought home a hard fact: We're all in the same leaky boat. One or maybe more of the predicaments mentioned in the prayers usually applies to me or to someone I know. If that isn't the case one Sunday, it will be on another. Whether I'm too fretful or too complacent about how my own life is going, the others' voices and sheer animal presence during these prayers is a powerful corrective that restores perspective on the human condition.

One Friday morning, my oldest child called from college to say that he had just been diagnosed with an aggressive form of cancer. Immediately, I flew to his rural town for his first surgery, which had to be done right away. Staying with him while he recovered from these nasty preliminary procedures, I thought of something Jeff had said at a weekday Eucharist. Concerned about someone going through a hellish divorce, he talked about how we survive hard times. In a crisis, we focus on the difficulty, he said, in his Southern, just-wondering way, "but there's always something else that's going on, too. Something invisible that has to do with holding on to what's important and letting go of what's not?"

A vigorous young male on painkillers, my son insisted that on Saturday, sleet notwithstanding, we go out for lunch and to a movie. Hungry, cold, and tired, we arrived back at his distinctly bachelorish apartment at seven, only to find a nearly bare cupboard. For dinner, we had vodka and scones. Later, as I settled down to sleep on a nest of couch pillows and quilts on the floor, I realized it was one of the best days I'd ever spent, because I knew what was important and let everything else go. Even in this brush with death there was something else going on, too. In the church, bread and wine are power-ful symbols; my theology honors vodka and scones.

When my child got cancer, I saw life as religion sees it. As I once heard a Buddhist monk say, "We have this idea that 'everything's gonna work out.' But it won't." Before she died, Jackie Kennedy is said to have remarked that she hadn't had much time for priests before, but they were "awfully good about dying." Did she mean that religion is just another opiate? A soothing form of denial? There's truth to the no-atheists-in-foxholes position, but for me, I found, it was no longer the whole truth.

Returning home on Sunday to arrange appointments for my child's further treatment at Memorial Sloan-Kettering, I walked into an air terminal that was eerily empty on this holi-day afternoon. As the only other person there came toward me, I recognized Minka Sprague, the biblical scholar and then one of the cathedral's deacons. As inevitably happens in healings, she remembered something for me: Appearances notwithstanding, I had what I needed at this minute. "We just get some puzzle pieces," said Minka, "but God has the pic-ture on the box." I wasn't sure she was right, but it sounded good anyway.

At the cathedral's Wednesday Eucharist, about fifteen peo-ple were in the little chapel. Jeff asked me to read the Prayers of the People. My voice quavered and cracked. When the time came to exchange the "sign of peace"—for me, usually a brisk handshake with my immediate neighbors only—I turned to Susan Harriss, who had quietly moved up beside me, and started to cry for real. If I had been in any other pub-lic place, strangers would have averted their eyes, or perhaps got up and left. A Latino grandmother walked back to my row and squeezed my hand. A white middle-aged man in worker's garb turned to smile and nod okay. Another priest came over to ask what was wrong. "Oh, no," she said. "Oh, no." She has a son the same age.

For several minutes, we all just sat there with the kind of event that makes plain just how much control over life we really have. No one offered any maxims or suggestions or explanations or words of cheer. No one told me that it was God's will or that God would fix it. From the woman who had converted from Judaism to the elderly black man who seemed a little confused, they just kept company with me and hard reality. They did all that anyone could do, and it was just enough. Turning back to the altar, Jeff said, "Sometimes, a lot is going on," and continued the liturgy. Later, it struck me that that perturbed Eucharist probably resembled the first ones, held long before Christianity became a state religion run from Rome. Without much fuss, a few people from various backgrounds summoned up a strange "kingdom" based on love of God and the stranger and the sharing of bread and life as it really is.

On the day before my son's second, very serious, operation, I knelt again in the chapel at the cathedral and prayed. As naturally as breathing, I silently poured out my heart amidst the familiar religious symbols, sounds, and smells of my childhood. Finally backed against the wall, I responded from instinct, looked homeward, and found wholeheartedness. I gave no thought to whether I "believed" in God, or just who that might be, or whether I was really a Christian. I was pleading for my child, of course, but there was something more. I was groping toward a different reality, in which life is not an accident and dark threads are part of a bright fabric. Whatever happened, I would trust in a benignity and design vast beyond my imagining that could somehow give meaning to—redeem—what seemed like chaos. No matter how bloodied and bowed, I understood, like the Psalmist, that somehow or other, I would not be crushed: "For he shall give his angels charge over thee, to keep thee in all thy ways. They shall bear thee up in their hands, lest thou dash thy foot against a stone." This peculiar optimism in the midst of my misery was a shock. I recognized that Mozartian sense of ultimate all-rightness no matter what that's said to pervade the great religions. Finally driven out of my mind, I encountered something that is aware but not cognitive: the soul.

On the way out, I turned to the person beside me, who was an African-American man I'd never seen before, and asked if he would remember my child in his prayers. He said he would, and went on his way. In a moment, he was back. "What is your son's name?" he said. What enabled two strangers of different races and genders to get right to the heart of the human condition? Under our feet was the shelter for homeless men and the soup kitchen. Down the aisle, people were lighting candles for loved ones lost to AIDS. We were surrounded by reminders that when it comes to what really matters, we're much more like everyone else than we care to admit, and that while we're not in control of life and are not exceptions to its hard rules, we're not alone, either. Like Minka, that stranger was one of the many angels, as I understand the term, sent to bear me up.

The next morning, in what was surely the worst hour of my life, I waited with my son in the pre-op area just outside the surgery. Suddenly, Susan Harriss appeared. While I wept in the bathroom, she anointed my unchurched child and, as he put it, "whispered some nice things about Jesus." Then, to while away some of the time before we'd know anything, she took me across the street to a luncheonette for a milkshake. Hours later, we learned that the operation had been successful. My child would recover and is expected to remain well.

Once, a great rabbi taught the people that they should put God's words across their hearts. Finally, a student said, excuse me, but don't you mean *in* our hearts? No, said the rebbe, you aren't ready for that. Lay them across, and when your hearts break, God's words will fall in.

CHAPTER SIX

PLURALISM: SOMETHING FOR EVERYONE

The various modes of worship, which prevailed
in the Roman world, were all considered by the
people equally true; by the philosopher, as equally
false; and by the magistrate, as equally useful. And
thus toleration produced not only mutual indul-
gence, but even religious accord.

—EDWARD GIBBON,
The Decline and Fall of the Roman Empire

IN THE BEAVERKILL, which is the Northeast's premier trout-fishing region, Dai Bosatsu Zendo sits amidst fourteen hundred acres of Catskills forest like an apparition in a Kurosawa dream. In too many minds, New York City, which lies more than a hundred miles south, obscures the reality that much of the big rural state still looks like a Thomas Cole landscape. Nestled into a hillside above a private lake, the large building with its characteristic hipped roof includes two meditation halls, quarters for the hundreds of people who come here each year for retreats, and rooms for the twelve to fifteen monks and residents who live here. Eido Shimano-roshi, the monastery's Japanese abbot, divides his time between Dai Bosatsu and Shobo-ji, the parent *zendo* in Manhattan.

Since attending the *sesshin,* or Zen retreat, in California, I've done *zazen* several times a week. Following my son's illness, meditation seems more essential, and I've come here for a refresher course. In a sunlit white-carpeted room furnished Japanese-style with cushions and a low table, I meet with Jiro/Andy Afable, DBZ's head monk. A strapping man of Filipino-Japanese ancestry, he radiates, in his early fifties, that young silverback quality that keeps primate populations, particularly largely male ones like this, running smoothly. Born in the Philippines, he came to America at twenty-two to attend the Iowa Writer's Workshop. Next he taught literature at Howard University for six years, then renovated houses and started a cabinet-making business. His immersion in Zen was abrupt. After reading about it, he sat on a phone book to meditate, and "knew that was it." Eventually, he studied with Eido-roshi and was ordained in the Rinzai tradition. For the past five years, he, his wife, and their small daughter have lived in DBZ's gatehouse. A good mechanic, Jiro's "work practice" includes keeping the monastery's motley motor pool running.

First, I try to wheedle from Jiro some tip or trick that will enable me to maintain an empty mind for more than a nanosecond or two. Unphased, he takes me back over the basics. "The Zen state is a trancelike condition that can be learned," he says. "The directions are very simple. You sit in a certain posture, watch your breath, and focus on your exhalations. Over time, your mind gets more and more focused on the breath. It's a condition of awareness that has no subject or judgments. Everything is coming to you fresh. In the broadest sense of the word, that's pleasure."

Elaborating on Zen's peculiar pleasures, Jiro singles out a "giving up of the effort to achieve anything. A dropping away of concerns. It's not indifference, but Buddhist detachment. Things are coming in, but somehow, because you're not judging them, there's a feeling of stillness and peace. A sense of completion. Nothing is missing. That, to me, is the Buddha's experience." When I repeat Huston Smith's assertion that all the great religions agree on the fact that everything is going to be all right, Jiro says softly, "Yeah. That's the Buddha's great message. Although he went through an ascetic phase, in the classic image, he has that contented look on his face. There's no sense of giving up or renunciation. That's Buddha's universal appeal—his well-being. As a friend says, she likes Zen 'because there's no angst.' "

Not that Jiro maintains that his religion is for everybody. "What we do in the *zendo* is important," he says, "but not for people who aren't looking for it. There's a famous Zen calligraphy that's translated as 'the great question.' In some translations, it's 'the great doubt.' That's one of the keys to Zen." Jiro is surprised by the speed with which dharma, or Buddhist teaching, has bloomed in America. Already there are different models, from the traditional Japanese sort, like Eido-roshi's, to the more American, such as Kwong-roshi's, to the truly homegrown. American spirituality's experimentation and proliferation speak of richness to Jiro, but also "restlessness, unwillingness to take a clear direction, and straddling the fence." The unwary "can be suckered into some guru thing," he says, while the intellectually picky shop around for the perfect master and resist commitment to a particular practice. When I ask if having a teacher is important, Jiro indulges in one of the long pauses common in conversations with Zen folk. What's the hurry? Finally he says, "I don't know!" He is easily amused—another Zen trait—and his mobile face takes on a roguish, wild quality. "I've never told anyone that he or she needs a teacher," he says. "If a person doesn't feel the need for guidance . . ."

As I sit on my cushion in the warm sunlight, it strikes me

that this is truly a millennial moment: an Irish-American woman studying Zen with a Japanese-Filipino man, both of whom were born Catholic on different sides of the world. Until thirty years ago, discriminatory immigration laws restricted Americans' familiarity with Buddhism, Hinduism, and Islam to an elite of wandering intellectuals, such as Emerson: "I am the doubter and the doubt / And I the hymn the Brahmin sings." Righting this injustice, in 1965, President John F. Kennedy signed a new immigration act that brought waves of people from Asia, Africa, the Pacific nations, and the Middle East to American shores. According to the U.S. Census Bureau, by 2050, white people of European ancestry, who account for nearly three quarters of the population today, will constitute barely half; most of the growth will occur among Latinos and Asians.[1]

Along with their different cuisines and music, languages and customs, America's new cultures have brought "new" religions. Although some sources report higher figures, particularly regarding Islam, Gallup surveys show that Islam, Buddhism, and Hinduism are each claimed by about 1 percent of Americans (some perspective: 2 percent profess Judaism; 1 percent, Eastern Orthodox Christianity; 2 percent are Mormons).[2] Virtually every large American city includes Buddhist, Hindu, and Muslim communities and sanctuaries. In their rural suburb, my elderly parents are cared for by a Hindu doctor, whom my mother describes simply as "a saint"—quite a statement for someone who was forbidden in youth even to enter a Protestant church. Although such everyday interactions with professionals, merchants, PTA parents, and neighbors of very different faiths go largely unremarked, "it's a strikingly new thing in our time," says Diana Eck, professor of comparative religion and Indian studies at Harvard.[3] With members of Harvard's Pluralism Project, she has found that Los Angeles, with its Thai, Korean, Sri Lankan, Vietnamese, Zen, Chinese, and Japanese communities, is now the world's most complex Buddhist city. In New York City's Flushing, Sikh *gurdwaras,* Hindu temples, and Korean and Chinese Buddhist temples nestle against churches and mosques. Since the 1980s, Hindu temples that rival South India's dazzle Pittsburgh, Houston, Nashville, and Atlanta. Since building the first one in Cedar Rapids, Iowa, in 1934, American Muslims have erected more than fifteen hundred mosques and Islamic centers. Many other sanctuaries are nearly invisible, occupying former offices, theaters, and fraternal lodges, yet they too are changing what Eck calls America's religious landscape. "What's new isn't just religious diversity," she says, "but the fact that virtually all people, not just missionaries and travelers, must deal with it."

The increasing interrelatedness and interdependence of Americans of different faiths means that indifference, even the polite sort, is no longer enough. Eck offers a historical analogy: "There was a time when Christians really had to come to terms with science. They couldn't just say anymore, 'Oh, we won't pay any attention to science.' Similarly, we now know that other religions as sincere as ours—and part of our elbow-to-elbow daily lives—have their approaches to theology and the big questions of our time, too. Simply to ignore this is no longer intellectually respectable."

Always an American ideal, religious tolerance is increasing.[4] Nearly half of the middle-aged now consider all faiths equally good and true.[5] Openness to "new" religions seems even more marked in the younger generation: Nearly 30 percent of teenagers express not just tolerance toward, but interest in learning about, Buddhism and Islam, and 44 percent express the same attitude toward Native American spirituality.[6] Nonetheless, there are still terrible instances of prejudice. In 1995, the infamous bombing in Oklahoma City was first falsely blamed on "Islamic terrorists," and over two hundred acts of violence were directed against mosques and Muslims nationwide. Such ignorance and hatred are not only dangerous, says Eck, but deprive us of the joint resources to address social problems, particularly urban ones: "No one group can handle things that don't stop at the borders of family or community. We're no longer metaphorical round-the-world neighbors, but next-door neighbors. We have to know one another better so we don't fear and do violence to one another."

In America's more diverse religious landscape, says Eck, "what grounds us spiritually isn't necessarily confined to membership in our own birth tradition. As a Christian, I find much spiritual sustenance in the Hindu and Buddhist traditions. If I go as a guest to a mosque at the close of the day during Ramadan, I find the evening prayers a profoundly religious experience. It's not something alien just because I'm not a Muslim." She advocates a widespread understanding of Americans' non-Christian religions, particularly Islam, that's based on neither a shallow relativism nor an outmoded triumphalism, but on a "pluralist" view that approaches differences as grounds for dialogue. "Because the one we call God is too vast to be fully comprehended by any human construct," she says, "all the great traditions are necessarily partial and incomplete." In her view, "a *credo* isn't 'I believe this list of propositions in an intellectual sense,' but 'I give my heart to this.' It doesn't mean that nothing else could possibly be true or that the one we call God has nothing to do with other families of faith." Eck hopes that as our religious landscape continues to change, Americans will increasingly "recognize God in other faiths, precisely because we have experienced God's presence in our own."

. . .

The most dramatic response to America's new religions is conversion. While the number of citizens of European descent who embrace Buddhism, Hinduism, and Islam is still small, it's increasing.[7] One day I go to the Mosque of Islamic Brotherhood, which belongs to the Sunni branch of Islam. Begun in the late 1960s in the basement of a Harlem housing project, the mosque moved to its present home in a tenement building on West 113th Street in 1980. There I meet with Imam Talib 'Abdur-Rashid, a robust African-American who began life as a Christian in the segregated South. After courteously shaking my hand—later, he'll explain that Muslim men don't touch women outside their families, and demonstrates the preferred salaam—the imam shows me where to leave my shoes and leads the way to his office. There, he offers herbal tea and a brief primer on Islam.

"All people around the earth have a conception of a supreme being who is the creator of heaven and earth and reigns over all," he says. "That's Allah. People call him by different names, such as Almighty God or Yahweh. Islam teaches that Allah has ninety-nine names. I use my terms, but Allah is not some localized deity—the god of the Muslims. There's only one God, and Muslims call him Allah." He explains that the teachings of the Qur'an, Islam's revealed text, are supplemented by the Sunna, or example set by the prophet Muhammad. The faith's five major tenets are belief in one God and in Muhammad as his prophet; prayer of worship five times each day; generous almsgiving; a monthlong annual fast, called Ramadan; and, if possible, a pilgrimage to Mecca. In classic millennial language, the imam describes Islam as "experiential spirituality. It's both belief and lifestyle, as opposed to just belief. Human nature is to be complacent, but Islam draws us into movement."

Activism is in Imam 'Abdur-Rashid's heritage. In their native North Carolina, his parents were friends with early figures in the civil rights movement. When the family moved to New York City, they settled in a neighborhood then mostly populated by Irish Catholics, German Lutherans, and other first-generation Americans. Although his family was mainly Methodist and Baptist, friends invited the boy to the Lutheran church, where he became the first African-American member and eventually taught Sunday school. At eighteen, he became spiritually restless. "It was the sixties," he recalls, "and the pastor's answers—he was a very old gentleman—seemed kind of tired to me. The new guy fresh from seminary who replaced him gave the same answers. So, without really deciding to, I found myself drifting away from the church a little at a time."

Imam 'Abdur-Rashid came of age at a historic moment, particularly for a young African-American man. "It was the height of the civil rights and antiwar movements," he recalls, "and I was right in the middle of it. On trips back to North Carolina in adolescence, I encountered segregated movie theaters, but because I now lived in New York, I could see racism was learned behavior. All that affected me deeply. I tried to deal with it as it came to me, and act according to how people behaved, not how they looked." At Syracuse University, he began his own study of comparative religion—except for Islam, which was still unfamiliar in America. "The more I read," he says, "the more I saw that religion was essentially the same. Even the prayers. It opened my mind about other people's traditions."

It was through his involvement with the black theater of the sixties that the young man first learned about Islam. While preparing for a role as a member of the Nation of Islam, he read a little booklet on mainstream Islam and "a light went off in my mind," he says. "Wow! I thought. I like this! This is what I've been looking for." A fellow actor took him to the mosque he now leads. Of Shaykh 'Allama Al-Hajj K. Ahmad Tawfiq, the black American imam who founded it, he says, "My teacher thought in very universal terms on the one hand, yet was very dedicated to the uplifting of black people on the other. I attended a service, and I've been here ever since."

Imam 'Abdur-Rashid's wider ministry includes educating Americans of all faiths about the stereotypes that surround Islam. Although there are more Asian and African-American than Arabic Muslims in the United States, Islam's identification in the popular mind with inflammatory politics here and in the Middle East has helped make it "our most misunderstood religion," says the imam. "People associate it with foreign terrorists or angry African-Americans and Nation of Islam–type stuff, which is pseudo-Islam. In fact, Islam is a simple way of life centered on one's relationship with the Most High—a universal faith embraced by people of all ethnicities and classes." One reason he's a board member of the city clergy's Partnership of Faith, he says, is that "between being isolated by others and isolating ourselves, there are a lot of areas in society where people don't see organized Muslim participation."

Discussing the commonest misperception about Islam in this country, Imam 'Abdur-Rashid compares the position of the Nation of Islam in American Islam to that of Iran's Shiites within the global body of Muslims, "except that the Nation is even further out. The language can sound the same—Allah, Muhammad—but their teaching is so totally different that most Muslims don't consider them to be Muslim in who they mean by Allah or what his message is. They may be Muslims in their intention, and some grow out of it into Islam." Regarding Minister Louis Farrakhan, the imam says, "Muslims are either negative about him or have mixed feelings, because people respect his lifting up his voice on behalf of oppressed people. On the other hand, he has misrepresented our religion. Minister Farrakhan is not the leader of Muslims in America, and his thinking and teaching, and even his perspective on race relations and oppression, is not a Qur'anically based understanding."

Active lobbying by the well-organized American Muslim Council, in Washington, D.C., and an increased interest in Islam among native-born Americans are slowly changing the stereotypical picture of Islam and those who profess it. Especially in New York, Chicago, and California, says Imam 'Abdur-Rashid, "Americans of European descent and Latinos are becoming Muslims left and right, converting from Christianity and Judaism. At the presidential inauguration, there's a Muslim up there with the other clergy. People aren't going to be able to avoid the fact that Islam isn't some evil foreign entity that's encroaching on American life, but a positive and established part of it. If not now, then later, someone in their family is going to become Muslim."

Just as Buddhism particularly attracts Americans interested in contemplative spiritual experience, Islam seems to speak especially to activists. "You can't be a Muslim and sit on your hands while the world is going to hell," says Imam 'Abdur-Rashid. "There's a verse in the Qur'an in which Allah says, 'And why *shouldn't* you fight on behalf of those who are oppressed?' Now that people are beginning to liberate themselves around the world, they're seeking to recapture what they were about before they were squashed down by Western imperialism. Part of that is Islam. When so-called minorities in America who associate Christianity with slavery and colonialism look for a religion of liberation that encourages you to struggle against oppression, they run smack-dab into Islam."

Part of the "calcification" that Imam 'Abdur-Rashid sees in mainstream American religion derives from its leadership's lack of concern about social injustice. "The civil rights movement in America wasn't led and powered by just anybody," he says, "but by religious people. Dr. King wasn't just *any guy.* He was intensely religious. That movement pricked the moral conscience of the nation. When its leaders became fat and complacent, the movement faded, and also the consciousness of the American public. That's what we're witnessing today." Observing how easily people become detached from dry, rhetorical religion, Imam 'Abdur-Rashid says, "Spiritual life can become, as my teacher said, like a frozen lake, with people skating on the surface. They don't know that if they would just cut a hole and look, there's a whole world beneath." Confronted with opaque, frozen religion, some people simply stop practicing, while others turn against it. Islam finds many of its converts among a third group, says the imam, "who decide, 'Let me go find another religion.' "

Already, Imam 'Abdur-Rashid sees Islam in America entering a second phase of development. Some Muslims feel the religion is still in a "Mecca phase," named for Islam's first ten years, when an oppressed minority concentrated on faith and conversion. Others, including him, sense a "Medina phase," which recalls a later era, when Muslims were an established faith community in the midst of Christians and Jews. "A return to fundamentals may be all right if there's a guiding vision that says, 'We've lost focus, and we need to pull in a little so that we can reach back out,' " he says. "But those of us who have moved into a Medina phase don't want to be isolated, because the times demand just the opposite. We're approaching the millennium, which is a time to be reaching out."

Subtler than conversion, another effect of America's increasing pluralism is far more widespread. Like the imam's and Jiro's, my religious life has been changed by a new tradition, but in a way that's much more difficult to describe. As I reacknowledge my Christian roots, I'm also moving deeper into Zen meditation. Tolerant researchers refer to this combining of beliefs or practices from more than one tradition as religious layering or blending, and point out its benefits of richness, personalization, and freedom from dogmatism. Critics charge that "designer religion" loses in depth what it gains in breadth and particularly fails to challenge the individual with established religion's outward focus on the commonweal.

The histories of Buddhism and monotheism demonstrate that choosing elements from one tradition and combining them with those from another, along with fresh ideas, to make a "new" religion is hardly unprecedented. What's different about spiritual synthesis at the millennium is that it has become much more rapid, individualized, and complex, in that there are many more toolboxes to be drawn from. Just as the new global information culture supplies us with world news, scholarship, and music, it brings us the world's religions. Confronted by multiple systems that have stood the test of time, we find it hard to maintain the conviction that any one faith has a monopoly on truth—an idea that's also challenged by other disciplines, from history to feminism to science. In this milieu, most religious Americans will respond with increased tolerance, but remain in their own tradition. Some, like Jiro and Imam 'Abdur-Rashid, will adopt a new one. Many will attempt to combine elements from more than one faith. Despite nay-sayers' attempts to lump them together, these spiritual eclectics fall into two groups: people who try to fashion their own one-man-band religion and those who primarily identify with one tradition but add to it. To me, the first group risks shallowness on the one hand and exhaustion and isolation on the other. While the second group also faces challenges, I feel they have much to gain.

Christian Zen practitioners, say, or Jewish yogis attempt to satisfy a hunger for personal spiritual practice in a country where religion has long stressed its social, humanitarian dimensions. The medical professionals who repackage meditation as stress-reduction or relaxation therapy know that using yoga or *zazen* to "come to rest and *just be* before heading off to the next thing can be a vital source of renewal," says Diana Eck. "It's extremely important because we get so preoccupied. Millions of people take pills or suffer from chronic sleep disorders. They're aware that they're incredibly anxious, or that the minute they sit still, they get depressed. Today doctors in white coats teach what used to be the province of swamis in orange robes." Although the *vipassana* meditation that this Methodist practices is called Buddhist, "it's really a form of breath-centered meditation that goes beyond labels," she says. "I don't do it for hours, but I need to meditate for ten to twenty minutes daily."

Layering complements the pychospiritual perspective that Americans increasingly apply to their religious lives. As they continue to question the go-for-it frontier mentality, says Eck, "people want to investigate the terrain inside—not just what we do, but our motivations and habits of mind—which is tremendously fertile ground for us. More and more people are discovering that terrain, which Freud and Buddha talk about in different languages." Indeed, to Eck, the ubiquitous term "spirituality" is religion's equivalent of psychology's "inner journey." Discussing the New Age, whose manifestations often have Asian overtones, she says that although the term "carries the connotation of a market-basket approach to spirituality, something much more is going on. It's almost as if secularism has lost its juice and has no vivifying energy for people. Imperceptibly, a new, more Eastern worldview has slid under Western culture and provided a new source of life-giving energy."

Zen has done just that for me. It also makes my religious life more complicated. My experience during my son's illness revealed the unexpected depth of my roots. My evolving religious style is Christian, even "Catholic," in the sense of emphasizing liturgy over sermons, as the Protestant church I like best does. Yet if I go to Shabbat on Saturday, I don't go to the cathedral on Sunday, and in terms of actual practice, I spend the most time on *zazen*.

Once, I thought one could just be a Christian or Jew who, say, did Buddhist meditation. It's not that simple, for me, at least. I suspect it's impossible to borrow a religious practice without absorbing some of its view of reality, too—the point, after all. In churches and synagogues, there are usually too many words for my liking. They often feel more like distractions than prayers. Yet in Zen, ultimately there's Nothing, and I'm tuned for Something. For me, Judaism and Christianity can feel like too much, and Zen, not enough. And is big mind the same as Paul Tillich's "ground of being" or Dietrich Bonhoeffer's "beyond in the midst of our life"? Does Nothing ultimately become Something? Is the goal to blend the self into a larger reality, or form a highly individual relationship with it? At times, I envy the people I meet who've been able to make a wholehearted conversion.

When I confess to Huston Smith that I sense God in non-theistic Zen, yet can't recite the creed in church, I'm steeled to hear something along the lines of "neither fish nor fowl nor good red herring." But he smiles kindly and says that although America's increasing religious pluralism raises the specter of McReligion, "it's also an opportunity. Relinquishing the complacent assumption that all truth lies in one historical channel is a good thing. The danger is do-it-yourself religion. While that isn't bad, and is probably better than nothing, it doesn't have much transformative power."

One reason I'm drawn to Christianity is the Gospels' relentless stress on others' welfare—something that, if left to follow my own inclinations, I'd often overlook. I smile ruefully when Smith says, "If you were wise enough to know which religious components you need, you'd be at the end of the journey, not the beginning."

As we've talked, I've tried to guess Smith's religion, and bet aloud on Buddhism. He smiles. "I succeed in alienating everybody! The conservatives, because I think that God reveals him-, her-, itself, in all the great eight traditions that I've studied and don't prioritize. I don't say he didn't reveal himself more fully in one, but that from my experience, I don't see anything that enables me to say that he did so. I alienate the liberals, because I have a very strong doctrine of revelation. I think these traditions were revealed by God, although you can also say, 'Ultimate reality disclosed itself through these traditions.' They're not carbon copies—they had to communicate to different people and levels of understanding—but they reveal the same reality. The universal message of religion is that a happy ending blossoms out of adversity necessarily struggled with and triumphed over. We're in good hands, and in gratitude for that, it would be well if we bore one another's burdens."

To my surprise, Smith elaborates further with illustrations from Christianity, "not that it's better, but it's my own." Immediately, this apologia resonates with me. The stress test of my son's illness showed me that trying to dismiss Christianity would be like trying to dissociate myself from my family. Neither institution is perfect, but both are part of who I am, and must be engaged. To Smith, the religion's "ecumenical creedal truths"—the bane of neoagnostics—are what supply Christianity's power and vitality, and, he says, "I don't know any other institution in history that has empowered people more. I think early Christianity created a divine Gestalt that had tremendous force. The power is still there, but the mainline churches have revised Christianity so much! The Jesus Seminar, with its admittedly secular historical methods, stands in judgment on the Gospels, whereas I go to school to them and try to get my head inside them, where Christianity's power lay." Observing that Wittgenstein pronounced the *Confessions* the greatest book ever written, Smith says, "Augustine forged the mind of the Western world for a thousand years! The roomy magnificence of his vision of reality is awesome. I don't think that spiritually we know anything that Augustine or Thomas Aquinas—or the Buddha and Shankara—didn't know."

In Smith's view, "If one is really interested in transformation—and if you're not, why are you interested in religion?—situate yourself in one of the eight great enduring traditions. They have proven themselves over the centuries to have nurtured the human spirit in masses of people. It may be the one you're born into, maybe not, depending on the kind of nurturance it gave you." Smith got the best sort, but like me, many of his students have been "wounded Christians" reared on moralism and dogmatism. "Once one is established in a tradition," he says, "one can pivot, like a basketball player. With one foot planted *there,* I see no danger in moving the other foot around. That's the way it is in my case."

Outlining his spiritual schedule, which always includes church on Sunday, Smith says he begins each day with yoga, then goes on to the Islamic prayer, which he does five times daily. He also reads a chapter from "one of the revealed texts"—usually the Bible, but sometimes the Upanishads or another work. The fourth and earthiest element is composting, "which grounds me in ecology, which is a very important issue today," he says. "You can see how eclectic this regimen is. Many would think it a mishmash, but it doesn't feel that way to me."

At the millennium, Smith urges "a reappropriation of our respective traditions, which I call humanity's wisdom traditions." We should focus on their view of the nature of reality, he says, "the biggest picture there is, and the attendant ideas about how human life may best be made to comport with that picture. I see nothing in modernity or postmodernity that rivals their profundity on those fronts. That they converge in what they say is a kind of independent verification."

Just as her new religions change America, she changes them. At first, newcomers often immerse themselves in their old-country tradition—a refuge in which they can feel at home in a strange culture. "I doubt that my grandparents were any more religious than I am," says Eck, "but the Swedish church mattered immensely to them. As immigrants they moved to communities where there was a good Swedish Lutheran church." Newcomers also understand that in lightning-paced America their hallowed traditions will be preserved or lost within a couple of generations. As Eck observes, most of the Hindu temple builders in America are professionals, "doctors and engineers, who would never be so involved in religion back in, say, Madras."

To prosper, even ancient traditions must adapt to new environments. The Reform and Conservative Judaism that predominate here, for example, are nearly unknown in Israel. "What's interesting about this country is its dynamism," says Eck. "As they take root in our soil, what will Islam and Hinduism become? Something will change, and has to."

Primarily interested in "ongoing change—what develops, what it becomes," Eck's Harvard team has already recorded some pragmatic alterations in America's new religions, such as a pattern of weekend observance. Other changes have more theological implications. As Hindus, for example, find themselves asked about their faith, Eck sees a kind of simplification taking place in their responses. "What do Hindus believe?" she says. "That's a hard question to answer. Most people don't want to hear an hour lecture, they want a few sentences. Pretty soon, those sentences become almost a catechism— and there is one published in California, as well as a so-called Ten Commandments of Hinduism. Whatever scholars may think of these developments, they're happening." Fundamentalists pine for the good old days when their tradition flourished in its original, pure form, but as a historian, Eck stresses that "a religion never was 'as it was.' The most dangerous people are those who want to keep it as they imagine it was sometime back when. Just think of how Christianity has changed here. The Puritans who started it off in New England would be astonished over what it looks like today."

So many of the Americans who have embraced Buddhism are Jewish that they've gotten a nickname: "Ju-Bu's" (this non pejorative abbreviation is widely used, even by rabbis). One day at Dai Bosatsu, I talk with Ippo/Marc Hendler, an intense, dark-eyed, fortyish resident. Although he had a Jewish upbringing and a bar mitzvah, Ippo recalls, he was a philosophical child, full of questions, who "couldn't believe in a deity or 'the chosen people.' Then I found out the rabbis didn't even believe, and became antireligious." At thirty-three, participation in a twelve-step program interested him in moving beyond the form of "higher power" spirituality he encountered there. He started reading, and when his father died, Ippo finally "looked in the phone book under 'Zen,' " he says. "I saw that life is suffering. Just a mindless pursuit of things that don't make you happy. The eightfold path is a way to cease the grasping that causes suffering. I just sit here and do nothing and have a few minutes' relief."

After five years of rigorous practice, Ippo has changed.

"I've become calmer," he says. "I suffer less. After *zazen,* something that seemed like a big issue—being angry at someone, say—just recedes." Regarding the existential issues that have absorbed him from youth, he brings up an experience in the zendo, "when the entire question of meaning—or right and wrong, good and evil, and other self-created judgments— itself became meaningless. Acceptance of the *unknowable* nature of existence produced a profound—and momentary— sense of relief and liberation." Although Zen appeals to him because it's "so rational—you have to find things out yourself," Ippo laments the common misperception that Buddhism is "a nihilistic religion. There's a faith element, too. We believe that we can experience what the Buddhist patriarchs did, which is confirmed by our little 'ah-ha's!' "

Noirish testimonies like Ippo's are powerful wake-up calls for mainstream clergy, Christian and Jewish, who are both sympathetic to and frustrated by accusations that they somehow represent spirituality's opposite. Aware that the Judeo-Christian tradition no longer enjoys a monopoly in America, those who work in the neoagnostic milieu are rising to the challenge by changing the ways in which they present their faiths. In particular, many try to recapture and stress their own traditions' long-neglected mysticism.

In his office at B'nai Jeshurun, Rabbi Marcelo Bronstein supplies some historical and intellectual context for a discussion of Ju-Bu's. From Marcelo's perspective, the Enlightenment value system that shaped Judaism, along with the rest of Western culture, collapsed under the weight of the Holocaust. "The rationalism that created politics, existentialism, and great art and literature also produced this catastrophe," he says, "so people are cynical about it, and materialism as well. One response is fundamentalism. The other is to try to find meanings in the particular that can jump to a more universalist approach to humanity."

As a rabbi living in a bastion of neoagnosticism, Marcelo has thought a lot about why Ju-Bu's look so far afield for meaningful particularity. "I could say to my teachers, 'Halakah! Jewish law! That's what we do! The rationalism in our critics' stance on the Bible? That's great.' But now, so what? If there's no meaning or personal involvement—no spark— law is not enough." Yet neither is science: "We don't go to our texts for *how* the world was created and all that. For that, we go to Darwin. But the question of '*Why* was the world created?' Oh, yes! We're still people of the book. What we want now is to own the book again by making it part of our Jewish lives, not just a page that we study, understand, and rationalize. We were intellectualizing, as if transformation would come just by knowing more. Now, we look at how knowledge relates to your soul and brings you to a different level of consciousness, concerns, and behavior in the world."

To that end, B'nai Jeshurun's rabbis support the new Jewish renewal movement. "It's about this word 'spirituality,' " says Marcelo. "About a group of people keeping its commitment to halakah, but also trying to get back to Judaism's experience and feeling as well." Through the medieval era, mystical practices—studying in silence, contemplating the different permutations of the letters of the name of God, breathing exercises—were part of mainstream Judaism; after the Enlightenment, this tradition was abandoned outside Hasidism. Now, scholars and activists in Jewish renewal are working to recover this esoteric knowledge; the surge in interest in kabbalah is one result. Touching on Judaism's genius for keeping its feet on the ground even when its head is in the clouds over Sinai, Marcelo says that the Jewish mystics "give us a wonderful example. Many were also very involved in the law. It's as if in the morning they wrote about the most boring, concrete details of life and behavior, and at night they had these mystical, esoteric encounters. But there was no schism in their minds, because they were more sophisticated than we. They were living on the Earth with the laws of nature, and at the same time in another reality."

Among those promoting Jewish renewal are former Ju-Bu's, who return to shul still wearing their new spiritual layer. Although they're willing to give the faith of their fathers a second chance, "they don't want to lose what they found," says Marcelo. "They raise the question of whether we have room for mindfulness, silence, and inwardness in our tradition, as well as passion for social justice and human rights. We need to unbury the Jewish names and approaches to these practices. They're there." Marcelo learned to meditate several years ago during a Jewish retreat in Jerusalem; now he teaches a meditation workshop at B'nai Jeshurun called "Increasing *Kavannah*"—Hebrew for "attention," "concentration," "focusing energy on one place."

Whenever I attend Shabbat, I say, I hum for the rest of the day. "*That's* owning the experience," says Marcelo. "And at BJ, we do it in the middle of the city, as part of mainstream religion. It could and should happen, but at the intersection of rationalism, law, intuition, mystery, enlightenment, and a deep respect for the search for meaning. We're not a retreat center. We believe that the two-thousand-year-old institution called synagogue can be the most exciting place on Earth. People can come here and share their lives and the meaning of life—its real questions, pains, and joys. Here you can be reminded of what's important, not just what's urgent."

Rather than ministering to a mainstream Jewish congregation, like Rabbi Bronstein, Jonathan Omer-Man is a kind of missionary to neoagnostics. In Los Angeles, he encounters many caught in reaction against the rationalistic Judaism of their youth, unaware of the faith's mystical tradition that has long been nearly inaccessible to all but the initiated few. Recently an angry critic informed the rabbi that the Course in Miracles, espoused by Shirley MacLaine, is "the height of spirituality, while Judaism is about the feeding patterns of my aunts and uncles," he says. "There was almost a complete separation between the soaring soul and the neurotic, dysfunctional family." Although Judaism is not a mystical religion, he says, "it can have a place for a mystic. This may not seem exciting, but Jewish mysticism is simply a place where you can be a mystic and Jewish. The truth is, in any religion, mysticism is for the minority." While discussing Ju-Bu's, Rabbi Omer-Man says, "I hope they are wrong in thinking their birth religion has nothing to offer them. My life's work is to try to relegitimize a contemplative Judaism that isn't necessarily Orthodox."

Thomas Merton once compared the great traditions to spokes on a wheel that all lead to the same hub. To Rabbi Omer-Man, the religions differ outwardly in specific, broadly intelligible ways: Torah and New Testament, *zazen* and Eucharist. Because Buddhism, a nontheistic religion, "leads you to a place of knowledge of the divine without there being God," he says, "an enlightened Jew doesn't look like an enlightened Buddhist. Or a Sufi. There are many different paths to God, just as there are many ways of cooking." On each religion's esoteric level, however, "it's all one. But before you reach that place, you must go on the path of separateness. That's why the Christian mystic and the Jewish mystic might have a great deal in common, whereas other Christians and Jews don't."

Like Jiro, Rabbi Omer-Man has reservations about America's eclecticism and fast-forward pace where religion is concerned. "You can only get to the esoteric through the exoteric," he says. "You can't get to Jewish mysticism without Judaism." Although trying to present it afresh to neoagnostics is hard work, he says, "I'll affirm again and again that there is a mystery, that it informs my life, even though sometimes it disappears, and that Judaism is a path to it. I'm willing to share the journey with others and engage in dialogue, and whatever they choose I respect."

More and more people—particularly the well-educated—choose to explore the mystery on one of the many paths of the New Age.

CHAPTER SEVEN

A NEW AGE

BREATHING IN the blossom-scented air of a mountain-top garden high above Berkeley, I find it hard to believe this lush Eden is really a Lutheran seminary. Aside from its almost excessive natural beauty, the former estate, built to rival William Randolph Hearst's San Simeon, has a Roaring Twenties, oh-you-kid ambiance that would scandalize, at least subliminally, the sober Lutherans of Lake Wobegon. But I've come to California to learn more about the New Age, and this seems like an appropriately lyrical place to begin.

After giving birth to the cultural phenomenon called the sixties, California has fostered its less political, more spiritual successor. The New Age can be as silly as believing that hunks of quartz heal, as dangerous as the Heaven's Gate cult, or as benign and sensible as the local health food store and hospice.

It can seem as old as Stonehenge or as new as the latest variation on Scientology. It can look spiritual or assume secular camouflage as "personal growth" or green activism. Less a religion than a sensibility, the New Age's diverse phenomena are unified by the thread of mysticism, or the cultivation of the sacred through contemplation and emotion rather than belief or reason.

By definition, New Agers resist categorization and quantification. According to the Princeton Religion Research Center, about 2 percent of the population—approximately the same percentage as that of Episcopalians or Jews—believe in a cosmic force rather than a personal God.[1] Wade Clark Roof describes about 10 percent of the middle-aged as "new seekers." Even more turned off by habit, rules, dogma, and bureaucracy than other Americans, this small but significant group of spiritual-not-religious people find meaning in the heightened personal experiences of an inner journey. They regard all religions as true. They envision the soul as evolving toward union with—or perhaps being already part of— the divine, which is right here, not up there. Free spirits, they're more likely to be female than male and tend to be single, politically liberal, and working in an altruistic field such as teaching or counseling. Sometimes-zany beliefs notwithstanding, the New Age is largely a movement of well-educated white-collar professionals whose spirituality must accommodate science, nature, and psychology.[2]

Like America's newly imported religions, the New Age affects vastly more people than the number who profess it. Since the scholarly Joseph Campbell took to public television to urge the middle class, "Follow your bliss," tabloids and talk-show hosts have taken up the cry. Oceanic or tinkling, New Age music mellows shoppers in malls and patients in dental chairs. It's not surprising that "channelers," or spiritual mediums, crystal healers, and aromatherapists abound in the city; after all, most things do. But the general store near my country house in one of the state's poorest counties, which used to carry doughnuts, cold cuts, and insect repellents, is now run by a homegrown utopian religious group that sells only pricey "pure" food. Used to adjusting their emotions with Bud and Colt 45, customers are now offered homeopathic remedies. However unlikely the locale, American homes increasingly harbor a herbal elixir or bit of crystal, a feng shui guide or a UFO novel, a tape of lapping waves or some tranquilizing incense.

None of the ironies of being a Protestant minister and scholar in the Garden of Earthly Delights are lost on Ted Peters, a professor of theology here at Pacific Lutheran Seminary and at the Graduate Theological Union in Berkeley. Since his days as a young inner-city pastor, he has been interested in society's religious dimensions that aren't recognized as such. One of his beats is science, and another is the New Age, whose roots and flowerings he has studied for many years here and in Europe and India.[3] Unlike most of his peers in religious academe, Peters takes the movement very seriously as a cultural gauge and, despite significant criticisms, finds much in it to inspire and admire.

As a historian, Peters stresses that despite its label, the New Age isn't so much new as renovated. The single greatest influence upon it has been the theosophy movement, whose guiding light was Madame Helena Blavatsky. "An adventurous Victorian hippie," says Peters, she lived at a time when the British Empire was much taken with India, just as flower children would be a hundred years later. After careers as a circus equestrienne, piano teacher, and snake charmer, Madame B. traveled in the Middle East and America, where she became a famous medium. When she moved to India, her theology of theosophy, or "God wisdom," crystallized around the teachings of Asian spirit-masters who channeled their insights through her. Primarily influenced by Hinduism, theosophy emphasizes monism, or the unity of all that exists; karma, or destiny as a matter of moral cause and effect; and reincarnation. Its language and symbols often have a Buddhist cast, but the constructs of the self and the sacred resemble Hinduism's atman and Brahman. (The influential God-within theology of Ralph Waldo Emerson is also strongly flavored with Hinduism, which, like Madame B., the nineteenth-century transcendentalist studied.)

Like theosophy's, the New Age's viewpoint is Eastern, says Peters, but it's Western, too. Through it runs a deep streak of gnosticism—the belief in a changeless, universal, elusive, yet redemptive spiritual knowledge of reality that's pitted against an evil force. Utopianism, too, colors the New Age, particularly the theosophical idea that the cosmic consciousness to which we all belong is evolving toward a kind of heaven on Earth, which Madame Blavatsky called "the new civilization." Interestingly, early theosophists believed that California would have a special role in the species' spiritual evolution.

Upbeat and inclusive, nondogmatic and experiential, the New Age is particularly appealing to a society whose national virtue is independence and whose citizens almost automatically prefer their own intuitions to any authority's dictums. "Americans are radically individualistic," says Peters. "Our whole educational system is aimed at fostering that." Although the New Age is also very popular in Germany, its character there is shaped by a nationalistic idealism: a mystical belief that important philosophical constructs live through *das Volk.* "It's the idea that the person is part of a spirit, or *Geist,* that's bigger than the individual," says Peters. " 'Our hearts beat with one beat, our blood flows in one stream . . .' " Considering this monistic cultural priming, Peters wasn't surprised that while he was in India researching the New Age, two out of three of the foreigners in the ashrams were Germans.

Like many high-minded individuals and movements throughout American history, the New Age expresses not just reverence for nature but a strong sense of being part of it. The nation's first utopian communes began as religious groups, says Peters, "often eschatological or millennial, who believed that God, nature, and people all went together. In the sixties, the hippies got rid of God but kept the belonging to nature and community parts, which the New Age also lifts up."

Transcendentalism and utopianism, individualism and love of nature, have been part of the American scene for a long time. Two newer influences, however, help explain the New Age blossoming of the late twentieth century. One is psychology. Previous religions, says Peters, have found the self to be a problem. The New Age, however, incorporates psychology's notion of the self and its belief in self-development as cure. Hybrid of the monistic East and the individualistic West, of selfless religion and self-oriented psychology, the New Age "me" aspires to be both universal and particular. " 'I'm God, you're God, we're all God, and the more we each affirm the self, the more divinity comes to expression,' " says Peters. "Although that's not just sheer selfishness, in the history of culture, it's the height of self-assertion."

If the soft science of psychology is one major catalyst of the eclectic New Age, hard science is another. The most striking example is medicine. Referring to holistic health as the "New Age leaven," Peters traces its origins back to J. C. Smuts, a South African Renaissance man who proposed that nature is constantly creating new wholes, which are always greater than the sum of their parts—a key concept in healing and ecology.[4] The movement's popularity among nurses as well as patients has helped both the medical establishment and the New Age "kind of legitimize each other," says Peters. Turning to a more colorful cross-fertilization between spirituality and science, or at least science fiction, Peters says that as a serious, long-term student of UFOs and the groups they attract, he's struck by the way in which religious ideas are now being blended with the technical ones that formerly predominated. "Most people believe that science yields Truth, as opposed to religion, which they see as superstitious dogma. On the other hand, our species has these deep religious, transcendent impulses. If you can't believe in God, it's nice to know about outer space. Its physical infinity communicates to us what Olympus did to the Greeks."

Combining spirituality and technology, a UFO group called the Aetherius Society (after a space being of that name) prays to a battery. After they fill it with spiritual energy, this power is transmitted to UFOs that orbit Earth, beaming down a force that protects our planet from World War III. Just as a battery looks more scientific than a cross or scroll, UFO mythology taps into other Western enthusiasms, particularly the concept of evolutionary progress. Like E.T., says Peters, "these intelligent beings on other planets are more biologically evolved and technologically advanced than we are, and their message is holy. They're celestial saviors who are coming to give us something we can't get on our own—world peace—as well as the reincarnation type of thing involved when you move from one world to another."

More *haimish* and pastoral than many religious academics, Peters is particularly perturbed by mainline Protestantism's unwillingness to learn from the New Age—and more traditional, yet spiritually minded, religions. With considerable amusement, he recalls a nun who told him that the Catholic college where she taught had started offering courses on Christian spirituality: "When I asked what *that* was, she said, 'It's the stuff we've always done, but now the Protestants are interested, so we're teaching classes.' The bequeathal of Catholicism's sense of spirituality to its people needs to be thought about very seriously. Not only has it been kept alive, but it has also been reenergized by the New Age and anger at the established dogmatic part of the church."

Painfully aware that the New Age fills a vacuum created by the miscalculations of institutional religion, Peters, like Huston Smith, traces a disastrous decline from the World War II era, when Protestant churches tried to become secular "and gave up miracles and that supernatural stuff. Just when pastors learned to golf and church colleges stopped requiring chapel, the people started becoming religious again," he says. "The New Age gets some of them, but it's not sheep-stealing." Other dissatisfied Christians find their way to the new evangelical megachurches. Despite their theological conservatism, Peters allows that "they know how to meet human needs. Parents with troubled kids, addicts . . . there's a little group for whatever is bothering you existentially." The megachurches, with their souped-up music, slide shows, and dramatic presentations, also address one of mainline religion's worst problems: "Sheer boredom," says Peters. "One thing about the New Age—it's not boring."

Like other astute observers of America's alternative religious scene, Peters has noticed the disproportionate numbers of participants who were born Catholics or Jews. "The Catholics often say that they went to church school and became used to spiritual practice," he says. "As they grew up, they didn't like dogmatism or authoritarianism and became secular. Then, when they reach their thirties or forties, they get these spiritual impulses again. Even if they call themselves

Buddhists, what they're practicing is transmuted Catholicism. It's very observable." I shift a bit in my chair.

The New Age has more strengths than either traditional religion or neoagnostics might like to admit, but it's not without serious weaknesses. Along with some obvious silliness and shallowness, Peters singles out the movement's "think happy" naivety about human nature and the world's very apparent evil, issues he feels are addressed much more realistically by the great traditions. He also notes the potential for abuse by unchallenged "spiritual masters." Then too, he says, as a "shoppers' religion of mom-and-pop operations," the New Age has a disturbingly rootless quality.

As I take leave, Peters reiterates that the New Age is "a culture, not a cult," and that despite some of its nuttier manifestations, it is an important cultural and religious development that should be taken far more seriously by intellectuals in general and theologians and clergy in particular. He commends the New Age particularly for its healthy holism, which has soothed many souls wounded by harsh, punitive religions, and for its opposition to materialism. "The mainline churches didn't have a clue," he says, "and don't right to the present, about what's going on in our society." To his pastoral duties, Peters has added discussions of the New Age with clergy in the trenches: "I tell them that this is going on among their people, and that they need to be alert to it and to say something that's nondefensive and engaging about it. Even at the Graduate Theological Union, the bulletin boards are full of it, but the students and teachers won't discuss it. It just baffles me! The New Age is where the excitement is, but nobody in the profession of religious studies is willing to talk about it."

The great revelation of the Esalen Institute's legendary al fresco baths, where nude "seminarians" soak in the sulfurous waters of natural hot springs, is that although almost no one has a perfect body, everyone's has something really nice about it. Chubby women with graceful waists and curvy behinds, balding men with strong legs and proud shoulders—these are real bodies as they appear in art museums rather than underwear ads. With the middle-aging of the baby boomers, there are even fewer ideal bodies than on my first visit to Big Sur's warm, fuzzy think tank almost fifteen years ago. We're no longer young, but here we still act like kids at the park sprinkler, naked and smiling. Part of our benign intoxication derives from the most beautiful piece of real estate in America. In front of us, the Pacific presents Hokusai waves and cavorting seals. Behind us, the cliffs throb with wildflowers, and above are the lush acres that produce much of the institute's delicious food.

Esalen evokes Paradise not merely in its gardens and nudity but in its atmosphere of newness and experimentation. Incubator of the human-potential movement and many other strands of the vast sixties cultural revolution, Esalen remains a showcase for esoteric ideas—some flaky, others profound—as they emerge from the academic, cultural, and social avant garde and head into either the mainstream or oblivion. Its eclectic catalog lists many courses that fuse several of the New Age's leading enthusiasms: spirituality, nature, science, and especially psychology and holistic health. Along with titles such as "A Potter's View of the Universe" and "Is It Love or Is It Addiction?" are many classes geared to nurses, counselors, and body workers that are accredited by governmental and professional agencies. Over the years, highly respected figures in many disciplines, from neuroscientist George Solomon to mythologist Joseph Campbell, have taught at Esalen. My own visits here have been for the purpose of interviewing various significant alternative voices for responsible, sometimes downright stodgy, national magazines.

My first trip to Esalen was part of my reporting for a science story about drugs. Thinking that some information about altered states produced without chemicals would add to the article, I hoped to interview Michael Harner, an anthropologist who is a pioneer in research on shamanism, who was giving a workshop here. Once practiced nearly worldwide, shamanism is related to animism, or the belief that there's a spirit or force in every living and inanimate thing. In the tribal societies where the practice endures, the shaman, who is a kind of medium and healer, enters a trance and mediates with the spirit world on another's behalf. One way in which the shaman cultivates the proper state in which to do this work is through a loud, monotonous form of drumming that's meant to drive the listener deep inside himself, into a kind of waking dream.

Initially, Harner was neither friendly nor forthcoming, and only grudgingly admitted me to a drumming session. In a large meeting room that held perhaps twenty-five people, many of whom seemed to be health care workers or therapists of some kind, Harner outlined a meditative visualization technique that we were to employ once the drumming began. Then he set to his loud task. Despite feeling unwelcome, dubious, and awfully silly, I proceeded to have an experience that did indeed resemble a dream in its magical realism. Because I was awake, however, I could participate in this drama transacted between my ears and even ask questions of the various characters. A psychologist might say the exercise provided a format for looking at life from different, more imaginative points of view; a psychoanalyst might talk about the subconscious. Whatever its source, the drum ritual helped give me some fresh insight into a particularly stubborn problem that was bothering me at the time.

Not so long ago, it would have seemed bizarre—even

"heathenish"—for an educated Western urbanite to borrow a tool now mostly used by the indigenous peoples of Siberia and Latin America. In today's atmosphere of religious pluralism, such experimentation has become commonplace. Shamanism is still less familiar to Americans than Hinduism and Buddhism, but like yoga and mindfulness, its practical applications, too, will be culled, repackaged as "nonsectarian" or "New Age," and taught at the local community center or health club.

When the sixties, to say nothing of the New Age, were still a gleam in America's eye, Michael Murphy, the charismatic prototype for one of the brothers in John Steinbeck's *East of Eden,* had already been east to India. After studying religion and meditation at the ashram of Sri Aurobindo, a respected sage, he returned home and developed a piece of family property into Esalen. Dating the millennial sensibility to that tumultuous era, he remembers that "suddenly, there were paperbacks of the Upanishads at the corner store. For the first time, Americans were hearing about sitting in the lotus position and meditating. That's an experience you don't necessarily get on your knees in a Presbyterian church for a few minutes once a week, after being blasted by a stern minister calling you to a conventional morality!"

As America opened to the East's "cosmic consciousness," both Buddhist and Hindu, it also began to rediscover its own native shamanism and the mystical strains within Judaism and Christianity. Innovative psychologists such as Esalen luminaries Fritz Perls ("I do my thing, and you do your thing"), Abraham Maslow, and Will Schutz began developing what Murphy calls "the yoga of emotions." Before long, "Gestalt," "peak experience," and "encounter group" were part of the American vocabulary. In 1962, Esalen was America's only "growth center." Five years later, there were two hundred such places. Soon, similar courses were offered at the YMCA, says Murphy, "or even in the church basement. The sudden infusion of new ideas made a hole in the dyke, which led to a flood that went all over the place."

In time, the flood reached the former U.S.S.R., where Esalen ran an intensive exchange program that helped to foster *glasnost*. Murphy is proudest of such intellectual enterprises, yet the greatest popular success of this former Stanford fraternity man and gifted athlete is a sports book that, twenty-five years after its first printing, became a best-seller and the plot of a future Clint Eastwood film. Considering its author's ideology, some of the accolades accorded to *Golf in the Kingdom*—"the bible of Republican mysticism"—are nothing short of stunning.[5] To slip the teachings of Sri Aurobindo—the oneness of mind and body, say, or evolution as spiritual as well as biological—onto America's playing fields, the breezy, preppy Murphy democratized them: C'mon, let's *all* have the esoteric experiences that religions call "mystical."

Unlike prima donna gurus and stodgy theologians, Murphy can deliver *dokusan* on a sailboat or a golf course and have *kensho* at a Forty-niners game. The first time I met him was at a dinner party just after the team had won the Super Bowl. The ardent hometown fan professed that a certain higher, Californian consciousness raised Joe Montana and his glorious ten above their crass competition. Then Murphy, a serious runner, went on to speculate about the neurophysiology behind the sport's well-documented "high." (Murphy isn't the only satori seeker in sneakers. One day, he interrupted our phone conversation to greet a houseguest: "Here's Richard Baker–roshi [heir to Shunryu Suzuki and one of America's few Zen masters]! He's just come in from running, and he has no pants on! No, lo and behold, he does have on a pair of shorts under that T-shirt, thank God!" When I said that I had recently returned from *sesshin,* Murphy put the roshi on the line. He wisely advised that to sustain my Zen practice, I should find a group to sit with once a week and go on a retreat once or twice a year.)

There are plenty of religious terms for suddenly sensing the all-pervasive yet usually concealed wonder of things, from Zen's *kensho* to Judaism's *zohar.* Murphy's mission, however, is to demystify mysticism by including the experiences of suburban jocks as well as monks and saints. Since his special vision of sporting spirituality infiltrated the mainstream, "hundreds if not thousands of people have told me about their mystical experiences on the golf course," he says. "One lady wrote to me that she was going back to the clubhouse late one summer day as the sun was setting—*now get this*—and the light of the sun was replaced by another light and the whole world looked like *God's negligée.* She wasn't trying to tell me she'd had a mystical experience, but what I call a metanormal, as opposed to paranormal, one." In a very different kind of book nearly eight hundred pages long, called *The Future of the Body,* Murphy examines mysticism, everyday as well as esoteric, democratically redefining it as "functioning in some way markedly superior to the norm, in which it naturally occurs to you that you've touched something greater than the ordinary self. It's the kind of experience that forces you to see the immanence of the secret splendor."[6]

To develop a vocabulary for the extraordinary in everyday life, Murphy, like William James, "collects specimens of human experience to see what patterns they make." He has concluded that everyone has self-transcendent experiences, but for most, they don't happen in a formal religious context. While people within religion are biased toward more cognitive, *kensho*-type illuminations, he says, "an athlete 'in the zone'—we have such poor language for these things—also has a sense of awe or the numinous or something else." Catherine of Siena experiences grace in one way and Tiger Woods, another. For most Americans, however, epiphanies are likelier to come from golf or gardening than from ascetic rigors. Listening to Murphy, I recall that even that proto-Puritan Augustine considered the marriage bed to be the closest thing to heaven on Earth.

In developing his idiosyncratic theology, Murphy looked not only to Asia, but also to Europe, particularly to the works of Hegel and the German idealists. Like Sri Aurobindo and the Jesuit anthropologist Teilhard de Chardin, these nineteenth-century intellectuals theorized that the divine is somehow involved in evolution, so that the universe *is* the process of the divine revealing itself over time. According to a complementary premise called panentheism, says Murphy, the ultimate reality that had been implicit in the Big Bang is becoming more and more explicit. Slipping easily from New Age to age-old vocabulary, he evokes the catechism of our youth when he says, "The divine is both immanent—present here now—and transcendent—more than just present here now." By birth half Catholic and half Episcopalian, Murphy cheerfully falls back on what he calls the "language of grace" when describing how people experience this mysterious panentheistic presence. A spiritual energy that's free for the asking, he says, "grace is a *fact,* which operates because the universe itself—and all of us—is a progressive manifestation of the divine nature."

Like Billy Graham or Thich Nhat Hanh, the popular Vietnamese Buddhist teacher, Murphy knows that "a weekend, even a month, at a place like Esalen opens you up to new ways, but when you go home, you're swallowed up by your old conditioning. That's one of the problems with American

Christianity, where the pattern is that you get a little buzz on Sunday that wears off by Tuesday." To address the problem, Murphy is now developing a form of mind–body–spirit fitness, called integral long-term practice, that could be maintained in local communities. "The overriding concept is that all our parts can be sanctified or enlightened or develop," he says, "because the divine wants to manifest in each of them. Like a *zendo*, our centers would offer physical and psychological training, but they'd be centered in spiritual practice."

Esalen is often accused of promulgating navel-gazing, as is the New Age in general. Far from being self-obsessed, Murphy points out, most of its participants are teachers, counselors, nurses, and "people who serve others and are seeking some replenishment and renewal. Even Jesus went into the wilderness for forty days! Calling this stuff 'narcissistic' is a stupefyingly bum rap and one of the ways that the cultural guardians serve homeostasis." Like many a Californian, Murphy believes that some people, particularly in the East, tend to blur the New Age's "fuzzy thinking and true silliness, like UFOs and crystals" with its profound insights. "From New York," he says, "everyone in the movement looks like an Eskimo. If you know Eskimos, you know there are different kinds. Despite some of the foolishness and excesses, the New Age is a very real positive influence that's now all over America. After the Reformation and the Enlightenment, along with the rest of society, including medicine, religion lost touch with the body and the sacramental. Esalen helped turn that around."

Like many neoagnostics, I resist association with the New Age. Yet my aches and pains are addressed by my Sufi chiropractor—a convert from Catholicism—and when I'm out of sorts, I light up my peaceful incense. I'm soft on monism, think green, combine Eastern and Western notions, and add on to rather than subtract from my Rube Goldberg spiritual structure. Where one New Age contribution is concerned—the positive, holistic attitude toward the body—I'm an overt enthusiast. Before I leave California, I talk about healing with one of the chief architects of Esalen's philosophy of the body and health, Don Hanlon Johnson.[7]

Dispatching me on my first trip here, a worldly Time Inc. editor said, "Not even a bishop can be pompous when he's naked in a hot tub." In several visits since, I've yet to take the waters with a bishop, but I once shared one of the small stone baths with a Franciscan, a Benedictine, and a Dominican, convened for a seminar on spirituality and the body arranged by Don. Although Esalen is best known for such experimental education programs, arguably its most revolutionary element is its least obviously intellectual. Thirty years ago, its renowned massage school anticipated the millennial understanding of "spirituality" as a soul not ethereal but incarnate.

My most vivid personal experience here occurred while doing a magazine story on the "mind-body connection" just beginning to be talked about within the mainstream health care system. After giving me a spectacular outdoor massage, Deane Juhan, a specialist in the Trager technique, asked what I thought. When I said that my sense of being made of meat had changed to one of being made of sunlight, air, and vaulted arches, he smiled happily at this "textbook description."

Just as body work at Esalen is about more than meat, once otherworldly spirituality—New Age and traditional—has come back down to Earth with a thump. As the number of support groups run by churches and temples suggests, these days, it's associated less with ascetic practice than with grappling with gritty "real-world" problems, from addiction and depression to divorce and cancer. Most important, millennial spirituality is less something to believe than something to *do*. As Buddhists have known for twenty-five hundred years, the simplest way to produce direct religious experience—the sine qua non of today's spirituality—is to involve the body in practice.

A former Jesuit whose wiry frame and intense, reformer's mien call to mind Donatello's *John the Baptist,* Don Hanlon Johnson was a chaplain at Yale during the Vietnam War. Disenchanted with the hyperintellectual Society of Jesus of the day, he pursued his vision of the body "as an important path to meaning," discovered Rolfing, and changed vocations. Over two sunny days at Esalen, we share a soak and some conversation about somatics, or the modern body-work movement.

Well before the sixties, an esoteric group of American and European dancers and physiologists, including Moshe Feldenkrais and former science professor Ida Rolf, reacted against modern medicine's biomechanical model of the body. To these iconoclasts, the body was "a source of wisdom and idiosyncracy," says Don. "Esalen's contribution to the birth of somatics was to invite here all these teachers, who didn't know about—or hated—each other. Suddenly, they were all in the dining hall together." Hundreds of teachers and tens of thousands of students later, somatics, once the mysterious province of a few impresarios and a clientele drawn largely from the arts and academe, is now as mainstream as the mall, where chiropractors, shiatsu practitioners, rehabilitation therapists, and masseurs hang their shingles.

Like the ancient Asian psychophysical traditions, somatics is "primarily about reinstating the individual's deep bodily connections with the structure of the material world," says Don. "In all traditions except the Western medical one, the first step in healing is to reestablish the proper relationship of the cosmos and get connected again." Like Canon Jeff Golliher and Rabbi Michael Strassfeld, Don sees America's ubiquitous new holistic sensibility partly as testimony to the widespread agreement that there's "something very wrong about the degradation of the Earth, women, minority cultures, and the body."

After describing the cathedral's laying-on-of-hands service, I ask Don what he thinks happens in such rituals. Healing practices are "radically simple," he says. "Breath. Being with someone. The basic element is touch—using it to awaken and support the body's self-healing capacities. Even when you're sick, not all of you is sick, or you'd be dead! When someone touches you with a great deal of care and sensitivity, it gives you a sense of your own capacities, liveliness, and vitality, which might have become marginalized for you."

By way of illustration, Don describes his own most satisfying experience as a hands-on body worker. His patient was an all-state high school basketball champion who developed a very painful knee disease. Because the operation that could correct the problem would rule out basketball, he says, "the doctors said, 'Before we do the surgery, go visit this quack. It can't hurt.' " After two sessions, she was playing ball again, and soon Don was treating many of her friends. "Teenagers are so worried about their bodies," he says. "They were so grateful for careful touch, humor, engagement. I didn't have any easy answers for their problems, but just worked with them and *liked* them. Again, the fundamental thing that happened was that some inner light was rekindled."

Offering another personal example of the internal process that lies at the heart of healing, Don says that his small son had been sick virtually all winter with pneumonia and bronchitis. Finally, after being cared for by a skillful homeopath, the child began to recover, "and the betterness is so clear to me," he says. "As his core spirit gradually comes out—his joy, vitality, strength, ingenuity, resilience—the cough becomes more detached as a symptom. It's getting less and less important and drifting off. The focus of healing is on the internal genius, health, and beauty of the person. On top of that, there are special things to be done to help body parts get better and so on. Without the basic assumption that the person's own capacities have to be brought to the fore, however, not much healing is going to happen." Because it can interfere with self-healing, "a diagnosis can be deadly, particularly the terminal one," says Don. "What *that* does to people!"

Sometimes healing extends beyond the small realm of practitioner and client to involve others. Don describes a colleague who is formally trained in body work as well as social work yet also relies on African healing methods learned from her grandmother. While working with a family in which one member had murdered another, "she saw that unless they could tap into compassion, there was no hope for them," he says. "Her healing ministry became doing whatever she had to do to elicit in them that depth in the person where forgiveness lies." This healer, who can also treat bursitis and arthritis, touched her clients and helped them touch each other; she also cleaned their house and helped some of them find jobs. "This woman is technically very skilled," says Don, "but the heart of her very complicated ministry is this other thing."

Going beyond the interpersonal to the cultural dimension, one of Don's projects is a center for victims of political torture, who have come to the Bay Area from various nations. For them, part of healing is spiritual practice, he says, "but not a single common one. Any religion that works for everybody has to be low-level and unsatisfying." Rather than attempting to find some *über*-spirituality, the center tries to give each tradition an equal place at the table, which allows dialogue and collaboration. "We've had a Muslim and a Holocaust survivor who couldn't have talked theology," says Don, "but were able to discuss their healing practices."

Like his friend Michael Murphy's, Don's eclectic approach to healing and spirituality is deeply informed by his own religious heritage, particularly "this weird strain in Catholicism concerning the mystical transformation of the body." More than a hundred people reported witnessing levitations by Joseph of Copertino, a seventeenth-century Franciscan. Some saints were said to give off the "odor of sanctity," and others (like modern Tibetan monks who've been subjects in Herbert Benson's scientific experiments) to give off ovenlike heat. Such unusual physical properties are hardly exclusive to Catholic saints. The Bible records that after Moses talked to God on Sinai, his face shone so brightly that he had to veil it. Pilgrims to the nineteenth-century Russian Orthodox St. Seraphim, who once stood motionless for a thousand nights while reciting the Jesus prayer, said that looking at him was like focusing on a face in the middle of the noon sun. In the Jesuits, Don recalls, "how you held yourself was incredibly important. The body wasn't just this thing you slough off, but was going to be with you forever. By making it part of ordinary daily reality, the Reformation did something healthy, but also trivialized the body—took away the juice. For Ida Rolf, what was at stake in your posture was enlightenment, but for the Jesuits, it was salvation!"

One difference Don sees between healings conducted in medical and spiritual settings concerns the people involved. Not everyone who would take part in the laying-on-of-hands in a church would go to a massage therapist, and vice versa. As a teacher, he prefers to work with students who have deeply felt spiritual and humane convictions, even if they lack physiological knowledge and technique, rather than the reverse. "There's a whole generation of Americans now who have been raised without values," says Don. "They can get very good at touching and method and being present in an emotional way, but they lack profound spirituality—the depth, sensitivity, visions, memories." Over the years, his favorite students have been nuns, whom he describes as "a very misunderstood and underappreciated movement. Nuns and nurses are two very revolutionary groups! Even the less skilled nun is sensitive to an individual's profound self-healing capacities, because she doesn't just see a sickness, but a whole person, set in a context of love, compassion, spirituality, and eternity." As to whether healers tap some agency beyond themselves, Don says, "I really don't know, and I don't know if it would make a lot of difference."

With its panoply of religions and tradition of open-mindedness, California is a tolerant place. But even there, it's not every day that one hears a rabbi say, "Some of my closest friends are Cistercian nuns." As Jonathan Omer-Man and I talk about interfaith services, I confess that they don't seem particularly nourishing to me. On the other hand, I've been surprised by how much my thinking about one religion has been expanded by talking with people who practice another. Of such exchanges, the rabbi says simply, "I can't do without it. Some of those with whom I feel quite bored and have nothing in common are rabbis, even though on certain levels my identity and practice really resemble theirs. In other areas where our minds and souls fly, then I'm with my Cistercian nuns. And they have their problems with the Catholic hierarchy!" In the end, he says, "those who have gone through the exoteric to the esoteric aren't bothered about their differences. The nuns and I would never have an interfaith ceremony, but beyond their Eucharist and my Torah, there's a level at which we know the same things."

The new conversations between Jews and Christians are important not only for them, but as a model of the attitude that must obtain in the future toward other, less familiar traditions in America's rapidly changing religious picture.

CHAPTER EIGHT

BEYOND
TOLERANCE

ONE MORNING, I drive about two hours upstate along the Hudson River to the community of Mother of Perpetual Help. On four hundred acres of some of the most beautiful real estate in the Northeast, a group of Redemptoristine nuns devote their lives to contemplative prayer. Unlike the more familiar sisters who teach or work in parishes, they are cloistered, or committed to a life of religious seclusion. In part, they're supported by the Redemptorist priests, a missionary order that maintains a large seminary on the same property; in the Catholic scheme of things, contemplatives' prayer is a kind of spiritual fuel for the church's work in "the world." Like the fathers' massive fortress, the sisters' yellow brick convent was built in an era when many more Catholic men and women—often teenaged boys and girls—

chose religious vocations than do now. On weekends, the seminary buzzes with activity as a retreat center for Catholic laypeople, but both buildings are far too large for their permanent residents. The old convent is to be razed and replaced by a new one about a third of its size.

The architect chosen to build the nuns' new monastery, which includes a chapel, is my friend Stephen Katz, who's a religious Jew. He and the women he now refers to as "my sisters" have invited me to a meeting at which they'll review preliminary designs. By day's end, Steve hopes the nuns will express a preference for one of the schemes and indicate ways in which it doesn't quite suit.

At the millennium, envisioning a monastery for contemplative nuns is a formidable challenge. Some concerns are purely practical: For an aging group, for example, the comfort and care of the elderly warrant particular attention. Other issues are more difficult to address. Will the contemplative life take a different, decentralized form, as it already has in some places? In traditional monasteries, how will the balance shift between the cloister and the world? While trying to preserve the best of their tradition, Steve has challenged the nuns on some anachronisms and suggested some careful innovations.

In the fifty years since some of the older sisters here "entered," the cloister has already changed in ways that were inconceivable then. From the Middle Ages until the monastic reforms inaugurated in the 1960s by the Second Vatican Council, contemplative nuns almost never left the convent property, or "enclosure," and received visitors only rarely. Iron grilles, screens, or other barriers separated them even from their parents, whose deathbeds and funerals they couldn't attend. Today, the Redemptoristines can visit their families and travel occasionally to conferences and other communities.

They drive to town for shopping and medical care. Several times a year, they invite the local community to services in their chapel. Each month, they host a group of "lay associates" who are committed to a deeper prayer life in the world. While the nuns don't regard themselves as cut off from it, their vocation requires a certain distance from its distractions.

In the visitors' parlor, where the sisters meet "civilians" like me, I'm welcomed by Sister Paula, the prioress, a slender, blue-eyed woman with short gray hair whose calm mien suggests both sweetness and authority. She makes it plain that like other millennial Americans, the sisters are stimulated by looking at their tradition through the filter of another. When I ask what it's like for Catholic nuns to collaborate on so intimate a project with a Jewish male architect, she says, "Stephen is very nice to work with. It's easy for us to think we need a room for this and a room for that, and having to explain things to him makes us think." Describing the experience of another community of nuns who also happen to be working with a Jewish architect, Paula says, "He even talked to them about using the chapel for many purposes—something they would never have thought of themselves."

Regarding the practical considerations of building a cloister in the year 2000—including the iffy future of the traditional contemplative life—Paula has no illusions. One source of future vitality, she thinks, might be mergers of convents, even those of different orders. Far from nursing nostalgia, this pragmatic prioress says that once established in a more efficient home, "maybe we can spare two people to send to Puerto Rico, where they've been asking for us." Where aesthetics are concerned, the nuns seem to have Shaker leanings. "Our current building is . . . not beautiful inside," says Paula. "We want our new one to be simple, but beautiful. We'd like a little more space in our own rooms, where we spend a lot of time in personal prayer. We'd like light, and to see more of the outdoors."

When Steve arrives with Carl, the project's construction manager, we're invited into the cloister's "semiprivate" terrain. In the nuns' large recreation room, Paula introduces Sisters Mary Jane and Mary Ann, the other two members of the building committee, and Father Jerry, a Redemptorist. The sisters are clearly fond of Steve, whom they of course call Stephen. Young, handsome Carl, with his brawny shoulders and long black ponytail, gets many indulgent smiles.

After hanging up the large architectural drawings, Steve walks the nuns through the three sets of plans. Conceptually, they differ mostly in the degree to which they either compress or pull apart the building's main components of private, semiprivate, and public space. After many tape-recorded discussions with the sisters about the requirements of their way of life, Steve has designed a few elements that appear in all three schemes. Formerly, the nuns spent much time in the chapel, praying and chanting "in choir." They slept in small, anonymous rooms known as cells. Modern contemplatives, however, organize much of their own spiritual lives, which invariably means more prayer in private. Accordingly, Steve has designed larger rooms, whose L-shape can accommodate each sister's needs for prayer, rest, and relaxation. As he says, "They're not really bedrooms anymore, but private spaces." Because the rooms on the ground floor have direct access to the outdoors, he says, "they're almost like small hermitages." When he adds in a teasing tone, "All you need is a hot plate," the nuns smile. "A *few* more things," says Mary Jane.

Watching my friend and his sisters, I'm impressed by his combination of professional authority and sensitivity to his clients' rather special needs. Steve is very fond of these women, and particularly admires their simplicity and directness, their lack of pretension. He wants their new home to have certain features that they might not think to ask for, such as an open stair in a center hall, rather than an institutional-style enclosed staircase. "It's your home," he says firmly, "and a stair with landings is gracious and inviting." Privately, I've been rooting for a fireplace in the living room and a serious reduction in fluorescent lighting, and am pleased when the former appears in all three sets of drawings.

Finally, the discussion moves to the chapel, which Steve calls "the most special place." There's a big difference between a shul, which traditionally accommodated study as well as prayer, and a Catholic church, whose congregation believes that God is physically present in the consecrated bread of the Blessed Sacrament. Yet Steve has the sense of the sacred that religious people of all traditions share, as well as an interest in and respect for the ways in which it's expressed outside his own faith. He delights in the arcana associated with this commission, such as whether the sink in the sacristy, where the vessels used in the Eucharist are washed, must drain directly into the ground rather than into the sewer. To express the chapel's unique function, he says, it will have a special shape amidst the monastery's bold planes and sharp angles: a quarter circle. Although it's too soon to discuss the minutiae of the design, he asks for the nuns' opinions on the curved form and a few other features.

The first is light. The nuns want to draw nature into their new home, but Steve says, "I've been in churches that have a lot of glass, and I think it's a mistake. Especially putting a window wall behind the altar. There's glare, so that sometimes, you can't even really see it. For what I understand to be the most inward-looking space, there would be too much going on outside. Please correct me if I'm wrong?" The nuns agree. To incorporate nature in an appropriate manner, says

Steve, he'd like to frame certain small views—one of the great maples outside, perhaps—with windows. Most of all, however, he'll depend on diffused natural light. He explains how, back in his studio, he'll use a model of the monastery and a lamp to simulate the sun's arc over the building, coming up with a window scheme in which "the light will change in good ways throughout the day."

Next, Steve brings up the location of the altar. He'd prefer to put it in the center of the chapel's curve, which would create an expansive feeling for those at prayer. However, he allows that it could also go in the quadrant's apex, which would foster more of a focused-in quality. When Father Jerry says he favors the latter arrangement, Sister Mary Ann smiles and says tartly, "That's because everyone would be looking at you!" Steve wonders aloud about his placement of the tabernacle, or small cabinet that houses the Blessed Sacrament. Not even the majority of Christians share the Catholic belief in the "real presence," yet Steve understands what it means both to the chapel and to the nuns, and discusses it respectfully and comfortably.

By lunchtime, the building committee has decided that the first design, which is secretly Steve's favorite, is best. After a festive meal of chicken fillets—ham had been ruled out at the last minute—Steve meets with the full community, who also prefer Plan A's "character." There's some discussion about whether the high-ceilinged living room is homey enough and about how "the public" will enter the chapel on special occasions. Hearing this term, which the kind sisters unaccountably use a lot, I pantomime a boogeyman face, and they laugh good-naturedly.

As the shadows lengthen, Steve and I face a long drive back to what I'm already thinking of as "the world." Tomorrow, the nuns will begin a ten-day retreat of even more intense prayer and solitude. "Please ask for divine guidance and inspiration," says Steve. "I'm sure we'll get some."

On our way home, Steve and I talk about how seeing God in new places makes life richer, and sometimes more confusing. When he talks about how his experience with the nuns has changed his religious perspective, Steve uses the word "complicated" a lot. In his youth, he was taught that there was a huge difference between Judaism and Catholicism. Yet now, he says, "I'm more struck by the similarities in the imagery, practice, even the liturgy. Instead of a great gulf or break, I see an overlapping, a layering of the two traditions." Most complicated of all, he says, is his new level of comfort regarding Jesus. "It's not that I believe in his divinity," he says. "But I feel at ease about Jesus now and respect his importance to Christians. It really complicates my life as a Jew." In his version of what happens to me in *zendo* and church, Steve finds himself thinking about Judaism when he's in the chapel and Christianity when he's in shul: "Sometimes I have these fantasies . . ."

As Steve's remarks and his latest commission make plain, the relationship between the two faiths we were born into has changed in ways unimaginable when we were children. Just as he recalls growing up with an attitude about Jesus, I can remember prayers in church "for the conversion of the Jews." Our grandparents would have been shocked that both Steve and I would "marry out" and surprised by our friendship. In their stratified social worlds, there was little opportunity for the neighborliness that's the first step beyond religious tolerance. Even in today's multicultural America, suspicion of "the other" can have disastrous consequences. A few years ago, a deep racial and religious chasm opened in a Brooklyn neighborhood when a Hasidic driver accidentally ran over and killed an African-American child. This death provoked the murderous Crown Heights rioting, which included a fatal assault on a Jewish rabbinical student. The tragedy spoke to the very real dangers of stereotyping people who seem "different." Like many New Yorkers, I'm curious about the Hasidim, whose headquarters are here. I'm both fascinated by their dedication to a totally religious, insular way of life and uncertain about how they regard us "outsiders."

One Sunday afternoon following a busy week, I'm almost looking forward to a long flight from New York to Seattle. Contemplating the quiet, child-free, uninterrupted hours ahead, I decide I'll nap and read one of the addictive nautical novels of Patrick O'Brian. Naturally, the only baby on the crowded plane is seated right next to me. At first, I assume that his very young, very pretty mother is some sort of neo-hippie. Her long, loose dress is vaguely gypsyish and a "mad hatter" of dark velvet is pulled down over her hair. When she finally settles into her seat, removes her hat, and quickly whips on a loose turban, I realize that she's not a bohemian, but a Hasid. Like the black suits, broad-brimmed hats, and beards of the Jewish sect's men, her dramatically modest, if exotic, garb reminds her and the rest of us that she may be living in American society, but she's not of it.

Aware of the gulf between us, this young woman and I are a bit wary of each other. Just as I covertly glance at her headgear, she casts a startled look at my pre-dinner martini. But the chubby, gurgling baby, whose all-American nickname, Yankee, is short for Yankel, is a great icebreaker, and is soon perched on my knee so his mother can eat her kosher meal in peace. Explaining that she and her son are going to spend Passover with her father, stepmother, and numerous siblings, my seatmate goes on to tell me the story of her life. With almost every sentence, she dispels some idea that I have about what such very different people are like.

Although she's barely twenty, my companion has been married for two years. When she speaks of her spouse, who will join her later in the week, she glows. "People think that we don't know our husbands before marriage," she says, "but *we* dated." When I ask how long the courtship was, she says proudly, "Two weeks. Once we went to the Museum of Natural History and once we had tea." Modest but not prudish, the young wife confides that she's just recovering from a bout of cystitis brought on by what gynecologists call the "honeymoon syndrome." She knows, however, that not all marriages are so happy, even Hasidic ones. When her father, a secular Jew, embraced ultraorthodoxy, her mother, unwilling to do likewise, found herself divorced and has since suffered from serious bouts of depression that sometimes require hospitalization.

This Hasidic family saga begins to seem like a TV miniseries as my new friend describes her large stepfamily. Her father and his new wife had eight children, including a baby who's Yankee's age, but have recently lost one. When my face falls, she shakes her head and amplifies. A few years ago, her father and stepmother had been scandalized to learn in the newspaper that a Jewish orphan had been put up for adoption in their city. The couple called the local welfare agency and asked to be contacted the next time such a child needed a home. One day, they got a call. There was a baby who needed a home, but he wasn't Jewish exactly. In fact, he was an Indian. The Hasids took the child, raising him in tandem with a son of the same age. Two years later, some relatives traced the little boy to his adoptive home and demanded that he be restored to his own tribe. Before regretfully relinquishing him, the Hasids invited the child's family to spend a few days in their home to get acquainted with the small Yiddish-speaking Indian.

By the time we reach Seattle, I have a different view of a

people who seemed mysteriously monolithic and extremely "other" only hours before. When I mention that my husband is half Jewish, and that I know such marriages as ours and his parents' are lamented by Orthodox Jews, my good neighbor immediately pats my arm and says, "Not in your case."

If neighborliness is the foundation of religious tolerance, moving to the next stage requires gaining deeper understanding. To achieve that means seeing your own tradition from another's perspective. Shortly before the rededication of its original synagogue building, which has finally been renovated, B'nai Jeshurun sponsors an evening discussion called "What Makes a Space Sacred?" held at St. Paul and St. Andrew's, whose sanctuary it has shared. First, Rabbi Marcelo Bronstein directs our attention to a xeroxed portion of the Torah, which is always part of Jewish study. While on the road, we read, Jacob falls asleep with only a rock for a pillow. In his slumber, he sees a ladder connecting heaven and Earth, trodden by angels; he also receives reassurances from God about the eternal covenant with Israel. Waking up, the patriarch says, "Why, YHWH is in this place, and I, I did not know it. . . . This is none other than a house of God, and that is the gate of heaven!"

When Rabbi Rolando Matalon asks us what made that inauspicious spot so holy, we answer: Jacob's experience. Adding one of the little touches that enliven Jewish exegesis, Roly points out that the text says the angels move not only down but *up* the ladder, implying an element of exchange between heaven and earth at this sacred place. To him, Marcelo says, the text means that "now that I know I can find holiness, I shouldn't just fall asleep, because holiness happens when the God inside me and outside me get together. That's why a synagogue has to be built on a place that has a dream."

Having grown up in the religious tradition of Amiens Cathedral, Byzantine mosaics, and Tiepolo ceilings, I'm taken aback by the discussion that follows. There's a consensus that a place of dreams doesn't require the kind of splendor or ostentation that characterizes many churches—such as the nearby cathedral. "A synagogue is adorned because it attends to the community's most basic needs—food, jobs, mates, hope, consolation," says Roly. "It becomes holy through function. How will people feel coming into the new BJ? Our tremendous growth in five years has happened in a simple—and shared—place. In making the new building, we had to struggle to be both beautiful and modest."

When the *hevruta* partners begin our discussions, I'm still smarting a bit from the criticism of Christian churches' "ostentation." My partner is curious: How *can* such splendor be defended, particularly amidst urban poverty? When Constantine turned Christianity into a state religion, I say, it acquired many imperial trappings, aesthetic and otherwise, that would have appalled its ascetic early fathers, to say nothing of its blue-collar Jewish founder. Yet some good things have resulted, particularly glorious art, which the poor, who are often starved for beauty and tranquillity as well as food and clothes, can enjoy for free. When my partner nods, I immediately feel less defensive. We don't have to agree about whether shuls or churches are "better," or come up with some syncretic formulation that satisfies no one. We only have to understand and respect each other's point of view.

In figuring out how to hallow the sanctuary they share, the congregants of B'nai Jeshurun and St. Paul and St. Andrew's have had many such conversations, and have moved beyond neighborliness toward understanding. Even after the synagogue's rededication, the Jews of BJ will continue to hold many services in the much larger church and preserve their special bond with the Christians. One morning, I visit with the Reverend James Karpen, St. Paul and St. Andrew's pastor. A laid-back fellow with a graying ponytail, he looks like the classic Upper West Side academic liberal that he turns out to be. Along with his ministry here, he's a chaplain at Columbia and a doctoral candidate at Union Seminary, where he studies Jewish and Christian ethics. Asked what he considers the major feature of millennial religion, like his rabbi colleagues, Pastor Karpen immediately says, "Taking experience more seriously. People are realizing more and more that God isn't just a good idea, but a reality." Given that understanding, he says simply, "I think it's important what I do."

Back in 1984, when Pastor Karpen first entered the hundred-year-old Methodist church, which had been a bustling landmark until the "white flight" of the fifties, he found thirty-five old folks and Columbia kids in a space that seats eleven hundred. "God," he prayed, "what have you gotten me into?" His growing congregation now numbers several hundred people from diverse Christian backgrounds; socially, they resemble BJ's congregation. Their similarity is even "partly theological," he says, "in that both congregations want reconciliation with all people. That distances both the Christians and Jews here from some of their own elsewhere."

Considering Christianity's historically triumphalist position in American culture, Pastor Karpen is in an interesting position. His church offers standing room only—at synagogue services. Like many mainline clergy, he's frustrated by his religion's ossified image, particularly among neoagnostics. "It's not as hip to be Christian as to be something else," he says. "That's because, largely based on poor early experience or misinformation, many people have their minds made up about what Christianity is." Making matters worse, he says, are aggressive evangelicals, whose ways suggest that Christians are "narrow-minded and go around trying to convert everyone." The pastor stops to paint a wonderful scene. Because sharing a roof with other congregations is not only ecumenical but economical, the St. Paul and St. Andrew's building is also used by two other groups: Ethiopian evangelicals and gay Hispanics. "Just once, we had all four groups in the same room," he says. "It was a disaster. The evangelicals were trying to convert the Jews, the gays were outraging the evangelicals, and the Methodists were running around trying to make everything better!"

The most striking thing about Pastor Karpen's remarks about Jews and Christians and their differences is his easy, unself-conscious tone. It's the way we'd all sound in a world of true religious tolerance. Speaking of the ardor of B'nai Jeshurun's services, he says, "They have a Pentecostal quality of being spirit-filled and attentive. They've borrowed a lot of good stuff from the Orthodox and Hasids." Recently, he spent five hours with BJ on Rosh Hashanah, "which is a long time for a Methodist." After a while, he says, "I lost all sense of time and was just *there*. I love Shabbat and feel like I'm in the presence of God, but I don't feel Jewish." At first, he says, the two congregations worried that they would lose their separate identities and turn into the " 'West Side religion.' But our experience has been that sharing helps the Jews get into being Jewish and the Christians into being Christian. Learning about and experiencing another tradition makes you more aware of your own."

When Pastor Karpen made his pilgrimage to the Holy Land, he did so in the company of seventy Jews from B'nai Jeshurun. Although he had to seek out the Christian sites on his own, he says that he "got a better sense of Jesus, having gone with Jews." The one Christian shrine the BJ group visited was the teeming Jerusalem church built atop the supposed site of the crucifixion. In this spiritual equivalent of Rockefeller Center, the pastor recalls, "Roly said to me, 'This

isn't what it's really about, is it?' 'Not for me,' I said. Then
Roly said he felt the same way at the Western Wall."

The most obvious indication of moving beyond tolerance is
intermarriage. In my youth, I had two Jewish friends whose
parents disowned them for wedding Christians. At the millennium, about half of Jews "marry out." In such mixed
unions, if both spouses are secular, they often tacitly avoid addressing religion. If one—much less both—is committed to a
particular tradition, life becomes more complex.

One Saturday evening, I cross Central Park to an elegant
East Side club where a bride from a prominent WASP clan
and a groom descended from an old Jewish Baghdad family
are to be married by Rabbi Susan Schnur. In the gleaming
library room where the ceremony takes place, the plain white
cotton *chuppah,* suspended from four wooden poles held
by friends, adds a pleasant note of simpler, ancient times on
far-off deserts. All the proprieties are observed, yet the atmosphere is subtly charged with a Montague-Capulet tension.
Earlier in the week, the disapproval of the groom's parents on
religious grounds had caused the wedding to be temporarily
called off.

Even without the extra frisson, this ceremony would be a
dramatic, highly personalized occasion, from the handmade
paper embedded with flowers on which the nuptial contract
is inscribed in calligraphy, to the bride's retro-Dior peach satin
gown. One look at the chic guests confirms that like the bride
and groom, they expect the best in spiritual experience, as in
wine or clothes. An accomplished singer and small ensemble
perform music, some solemn, some not. Hebrew prayers create a sense of tradition, leavened by the more personal blessings offered by chosen relatives and friends. When making his
vows, the groom adds his own touches, declaring that he

wants to be his wife's "lush-life man." Often throughout the ceremony, the couple's expressiveness runs over into spontaneous kisses and hand-holding.

The beautiful ceremony is a classical millennial mix of old and new. Susie's English homily is studded with Hebrew: Tonight under the *chuppah,* she says, the couple are *kadosh*— set apart, special, not like others. Yet her remarks are also very personal and strongly colored by psychology. While stressing that marriage goes "beyond love," Susie also describes it in the adventurous language of self-development: a "wild work" filled with rewards and challenges that's conducted by the "dearest friends." When it's time to break the wineglass— traditionally the groom's prerogative—the couple stomp on it together.

Both an effect and a cause of America's religious tolerance, mixed marriages, once rare, are increasing, including those involving Buddhists, Muslims, and Hindus. In my own circle, the most striking example is a practicing Protestant and a secular Jew who were married in a Hindu ceremony. Just because what was unusual is now more common doesn't mean it's easy. Looking at this couple, I'm full of questions. They must be deeply committed—just getting to the *chuppah* has been fraught with obstacles. But with respect to religion, where will they go from here? Will one or both drop out? Will their life together incorporate bits of both their traditions? Will the bride convert? How will they raise their children? "Expose" them to both faiths? Just one? Avoid the whole painful issue? Religious decisions about children pose important questions beyond the theological: What does this choice say about me? My family? Will I end up somehow marginalized in my own home?

After the wedding, Susie and I talk a little about interfaith unions. The questions they raise are so difficult, she thinks, because marriage isn't just about ideology, like being a Democrat or a Republican, but about who a person *is*. Couples such as Julia and Jamil confront issues of identity involving not just church and synagogue but parents and grandparents, ethnicity and class, history and experience—all the elements of what Susie calls the "great contemporary struggle to have a *self*. It's very moving to see how lost wedding couples are, confronting the existential terror of pairing up. The process of preparing means thinking about things like Who am I? What do I care about? Who do I love, and why?"

Similar questions that seem to be about religion but are deeply entangled with identity surface again in new parents. Particularly for neoagnostics, deciding which "values" they want their children to have means deciding for themselves, as well. "It's a belated time for adults to begin to do their own work," says Susie, "but we use our kids to teach us our best lessons." Because parents want to do right by their offspring, she believes that religious literacy will be "the big thing for the next decade." This is particularly important for Judaism, because it's a minority religion that has a very high intermarriage rate, requires some knowledge of Hebrew, and, says Susie, "hasn't done a good job of marketing itself." Adding to the complexity, she says, is the idea that "to be a Jew, you have to be the real McCoy, with two Jewish parents. But today so many kids are 'half.' They face a whole different set of issues, because for them, religion becomes a choice."

As I know from my own marriage, deciding "what to do about the children" isn't easy. Although my father-in-law had a bar mitzvah, he became secular and married an Anglican. The only teaching about Judaism that he offered Mike, my husband, was that anti-Semitism is bad and swimming at the YMCA was forbidden. Educated in private schools in a Nordic midwestern culture, Mike grew up with a Jewish name and a Jewish nose, but with no knowledge of Jewish religion. On the other hand, he isn't really comfortable with any other kind. For complex reasons more emotional and experiential than rational or intellectual, when pushed, he "feels Jewish," just as I "feel Christian." Although he sometimes talks about investigating one of the synagogues in walking distance of our house, he hasn't. One immediate obstacle is that as a sophisticated adult, he's uncomfortable with the idea of not knowing any Hebrew or Scripture; he's used to being on the fast track. Because he likes good music, a thoughtful sermon, and the way liturgy can lift one out of one's petty concerns, Mike sometimes accompanies me to the cathedral. But he doesn't really "get" Christianity: "Why do they make such a big thing about Jesus?"

For neoagnostics, inchoate feelings of religious identity often surface in situations that call for standing up against intolerance. In a rural restaurant, Mike was ready to come to blows over comments occasioned by his surname on the reservation list. Trying to lend an ecumenical air to our holidays, one Christmas Eve we went to a Jewish restaurant, where the Israeli pop band played music from the mass, complete with irreverent lyrics; noticing my frozen face as I prepared to leave, the leader apologized and changed the repertoire. Both Mike and I know reacting to prejudice shouldn't be the cornerstone of a person's religious identity. Such definitions-by-default are little help concerning the perennial problem of the children.

Like me, Mike says he would like our kids to have a religious background. When our twins were born, I was amazed at how adamant he was that our son be circumcised. Yet, like so many neoagnostic couples, we have dealt with the religious hot potato of what to do about the kids by supplying them with a Disneyish sense of comparative religion that stresses holidays and food, God and goddesses, candles and gifts, and above all—thanks to Native Americans—nature.

Over soup in her kitchen one night, Rabbi Rachel Cowan describes a complicated path to a family's religious identity and her own conversion that began when a lapsed Christian woman married a secular Jewish man. Recalling her New England childhood in an intellectual home, she says that her socialist parents were "antireligious. For me to become religious involved this endless thing of proving to my father than I wasn't a fool—a weak person who needed a crutch." Nonetheless, Rachel had some experience of church, first with her Episcopalian grandmother, then in a Unitarian congregation that suited "Democrats in a Republican town," she says. "This church stood for something in the fifties, which was wonderful." Theologically as well as politically liberal, the church taught that Jesus was a great teacher and the Bible was written by human beings. "It all made sense and was radical and exciting," says Rachel, "but the idea of faith through Christ just never worked for me. I never got it."

When Rachel married Paul Cowan, like her a liberal political activist of the sixties, he was totally assimilated and completely untutored in Judaism. When their son Matt was small, recalls Rachel, they took him to a Purim party. Knowing nothing about the holiday, which marks the foiling of an ancient pagan plot to kill the Jews, Rachel was struck when Matt ran up to her saying "Mommy, they won't kill me, will they? I'm just half Jewish." For some reason, she says, "Paul and I decided to take that seriously, rather than just as a cute little comment. It led us in a whole direction of trying to explain why Jews live, not why they die, and what it means to be 'half Jewish.' That moment changed our lives, but it could easily not have. Often we just don't let ourselves listen to such things. Something happens, and we just kind of dismiss it."

If she hadn't married Paul, Rachel says, "I don't know if I'd be Jewish. We got into it together. He felt deracinated and wanted to figure out more about who he was and what it meant to be a Jew." Paul eventually wrote *An Orphan in History,* a book about his process of discovery. For Rachel, who has written a book about mixed marriages,[1] the first priority was "giving some texture to our family life that was deeper than being political liberals and community, peace, and civil rights activists, which we certainly were. I realized I would never be a Christian or a Unitarian, and Judaism just seemed really old and fascinating and full of people who were struggling to make it relevant to their lives." At first, she recalls, " 'adding Judaism' seemed like a sort of decoration. I loved the Jewish holidays and Shabbat and thought, This really makes our family life richer and more interesting, and we can do it at home with the kids. I didn't know anything, from Hebrew to recipes, but friends helped. At first, I didn't think of converting but just enjoyed being part of it."

As Rachel continues her story, I'm struck by how her religious evolution in some ways resembles mine since I began my reporting. "When I started to study," she says, "I loved what I studied, and the way you study. I realized I had actually come to believe in the reality of God. For me, Judaism was a path to that understanding. It wasn't about perfect faith or some epiphany. It was about coming into a vocabulary and rhythm of life and way to see the world through those eyes."

The way in which Rachel talks about God reflects her complex religious development. First, she says that Judaism's traditional attitude about theology reminds her of its approach to the afterlife: There's no point in being preoccupied with something that you can only guess about, particularly when there's so much else to be done in the here and now. Pressed for her own definition of God, like many modern, well-educated Americans, including clergy, Rachel searches for the right vocabulary—one that's neither too dry, abstract, and rationalistic nor too soupy and incompatible with her degree of sophistication.

"I think God has both a universal and particular aspect," Rachel says slowly. "There's a God who's very personal. I wouldn't say lover or friend . . . more a source of comfort and a partner in a dialogue when I feel great grief, loss, sadness, fear—or tremendous joy. There are times when I just totally experience God's presence. For me, a Quaker or Unitarian definition of God as something within us that aspires to perfection or is capable of love and beauty isn't enough. It doesn't explain the power of the feelings I have. Sometimes, as when I was hiking with my children recently, I can translate that into traditional blessings—thank you, God!" And, laughing, she adds, "I truly don't think that God intervenes in such things, but I always pray when the plane takes off, because it makes me feel better."

In addition to this more intimate sense of the divine, Rachel also thinks of God "as the very abstract and remote essence, or life energy, of the universe. So when I think of Paul [her husband, who died prematurely of cancer], I think of his spirit as being part of this very abstract universal aspect. Whether a personal God is the creation of our desire, in the sense of our needing that so badly, is really irrelevant to me, because it helps."

While I sit at Rachel's table, she takes a call from a beloved elderly rabbi and his wife, who have heard about some crank phone calls she has received: Someone rings up and asks for "the Christian" Rachel Cowan, to which Rachel replies that no such person is there. When I go to B'nai Jeshurun, I say, I'm struck by the tribal feeling: The congregation is united because they share not only a religion but also language, ethnicity, and culture. I sense how supportive and comforting that must be, but it also makes me feel like an outsider in a way that's impossible amidst the diversity of a *zendo* or the cathedral. I ask Rachel if, as a convert, she always feels like an insider. "I do," she says, "but I know my history is really different. It takes time."

Because we're sitting in a kitchen, we end up talking about keeping kosher, which Rachel does. "You can do it for a variety of reasons," she says. "Because your grandparents did. Because Jews throughout history did. It gives you a sense of who you are. That stuff is very attractive to me, having grown up Unitarian, which lacked that density and emotion from the interaction of religion and history that provides meaning in the present. On the other hand, I believe that Judaism is about more than that. Why would I convert just to be a cultural Jew? My conversion was really to be religious rather than Jewish. With a Jewish framework, I became a religious Jew."

When I tell Jonathan Omer-Man that I suspect my husband subliminally wishes I'd convert to Judaism and take him and the children with me, the rabbi remembers a congregation he once led in which almost everyone was in a mixed marriage. "In almost every case," he says, "it was the non-Jewish partner who drew the other back to Judaism." On the other hand, he says, "maybe your husband married an Irish wife because he doesn't want to be Jewish. That kind of marriage can be a way of blocking. . . . There's some pain and fear about coming home."

CHAPTER NINE

NO PLACE
LIKE HOME?

SINCE A CRISIS thrust me into a headfirst collision with Christianity, I've often thought how easy it would be if I could just go home again. In that dark hour of my son's illness, I learned that just as I speak English, I speak Christian—native languages acquired in the same way from my family in early life. In important respects, even the Catholic dialect still sounds sweet. Its experiential, personal spirituality was millennial long before the last millennium.

In honor of my parents' fiftieth wedding anniversary last year, I accompanied my eighty-two-year-old mother to her Catholic church one Sunday. Mom is a "greeter" at the crowded eleven o'clock mass. Too frail now for churchgoing, Dad receives the Eucharist at home. (Once a year, he and Mom also make their annual confession there, although, as she says rather wistfully, "We don't really have sins anymore.") Our Lady of the Angels, near the Victorian beach resort of Cape May, New Jersey, is a bright, open new church; on winter Sundays like this one, it is mostly filled with retirees and the pink- and blue-collar people who keep the community, from fishing fleet to medical center, operating year-round.

Lady of Angels is suffused with natural light, rather than the medieval gloom of my childhood's sanctuaries. The altar is a simple table facing the congregation, and the sometimes zany shrines that used to punctuate Catholic churches are conspicuously absent. A guitarist strummed folksy songs that might have been hymns. Girls served at the altar. In some respects, from its clouds of incense to its flying buttresses, the Protestant cathedral seems more "Catholic" than this. But certain things haven't changed. As in my youth, every pew was occupied, often by families including grandparents and wriggling babies. Unlike most mainline churches, Catholic ones often fill up several times each Sunday. The draw isn't the preaching, aesthetics, or social cachet that some other churches are renowned for, but the experience of the Eucharist, not as a symbol of God, but as God, period.

The Gospel story was a good one: Jesus' forty days of meditation in the desert and triple temptation by Satan. The sermon, which was given by an older, visiting priest who was there to lend the busy pastor a hand, concerned personal spirituality, discussed in utterly unembarrassed, everyday terms. Father began with some remarks about Admiral Richard E. Byrd, the famous polar explorer, who once spent three months alone in the antarctic wilderness. During this extended *sesshin,* which the priest described as a frigid version of Jesus' desert experience, the admiral "asked humanity's great questions. 'Who am I? Why am I here? Is there a God?' Because there was no one else there, he talked to God day and night. Later, this man who had done so many extraordinary things said that this period of solitude was the most important experience of his life."

Neatly, the priest segued to our own more pedestrian lives. Unlike Byrd and Jesus, he said, most of us don't have the luxury of long retreats. The best we can manage is an annual weekend, perhaps, or even a quiet day, or hour. "So what *can* we do?" he asked. "Make our own desert experiences. Turn off the TV, and think on your own. Spend ten to thirty minutes each day with Scripture or your rosary. Use a little mantra to remind yourself to practice self-denial—to get right out of bed in the morning and do what needs doing, to be nice to that person in your life who can be hard to take."

In short order and plain language, the nurses and contractors, teachers and housewives, kids and old folk, of this small Jersey community were neither lectured about public policy nor threatened with hellfire but reminded that like Jesus, no less, they were spiritual beings who needed spiritual refreshment. Busy as they were—nothing wrong with that—they nonetheless could and should, like the great explorer, make time to ask humanity's great questions. As the guitarist began the offertory hymn, the fine old priest turned to the altar and in the beautiful, ancient gesture of pleading for the people, lifted up his hands in prayer. At communion time, the guitarist sang "Panis Angelicus"—"Bread of Angels"—written by Thomas Aquinas. When Mom approached the altar, I surreptitiously wept into a wad of Kleenex that I had presciently thought to bring.

Considering my affinity for sacraments and grace, Latin and tradition, I decide that rather than just continuing to duck my religious childhood, I'll reexamine it as an adult. The easiest explanation for not returning home is disagreement with church doctrine. At St. Paul's Church in Cambridge one morning, I have a conversation with Father J. Bryan Hehir that helps clarify for me both what I admire about church teaching and why I can't just "accept" it.

Catholic-bashing is said to be the anti-Semitism of intellectuals, but few could support it after five minutes with Father Hehir. A brief summary of his endeavors inspires in me a new respect for celibacy and an interest in what vitamins he takes. A priest for thirty years, he's a professor at Harvard's divinity school and at its Kennedy School of Government who teaches ethics, international relations, military issues, human rights, and foreign policy, as well as issues of the church's role in American social policy. He is also counselor to the Catholic Relief Services, an agency sponsored by the American bishops. To the conservative jurist Robert Bork, the Catholic bishops "often look like the Democratic Party in robes."[1] Much of the progressive social policy he deplores is informed by Father Hehir's work, contributed during his twenty years on the staff of the National Catholic Bishops' Conference, those lonely supporters of health care reform and the welfare safety net who are, arguably, America's last liberals.

When I ask how people's spiritual needs differ today from those of pre-sixties America, Father Hehir says, "There aren't lots of places in our society where you can get a stable, structured moral vision, or even a proposal of that." As we face the millennium, he says, "the abiding moral issue is a coherent, consistently structured defense of human life in all the situations that threaten it and its dignity. There is no way to be Catholic, or Christian, and not be responsible for others."

Everyone knows that the Catholic Church is against abortion. Fewer are aware that the same "pro-life" rationale underlies its strenuous opposition to the death penalty and nuclear arms, and its support of social and racial justice. The pope's writings and travels demonstrate that the church puts as much thought and effort into its pro-life policy's social applications, such as human rights, as into the bioethical and sexual ones, such as genetics and contraception. (Remarking on John Paul II's trip to Cuba in 1998, a prominent rabbi told me admiringly, "The pope has balls!") Nonetheless, Father Hehir often gets phone calls from reporters who "literally ask the same questions they did in 1979 about birth control and so on. It doesn't enhance one's view of the depth of the media's analyses." With relish, he recalls that a Senate aide once said to him, " 'If the church would change its position on abortion, it would be the most liberal force in the country.' And I said, 'You're confused about what the liberal position on abortion *is*. We stand for inclusion in the circle of human community. *That's* the liberal position.' The standard secular liberals' position is great on welfare, but in most cases, they don't even seriously struggle with the abortion question. The Christian Coalition crowd are at the barracks on abortion, but what happens once the child is born?"

Despite its many controversial dimensions, the vast potential of the Catholic Church's moral vision is brought home to me when Father Hehir mentions the insistence of the pope, who is an academically trained philosopher, that there is such a thing as an objective moral order. When I say that surely all the great cultures agree about certain ethical basics, Father Hehir says, "No!" He reaches for his Thucydides, which illustrates the "realist position" regarding the behavior of victors to vanquished in wartime: A general says, "Come now, let us not talk about justice. Let us talk about how things are." By this standard, says Father Hehir, "the strong do what they will, and the weak what they must. From this perspective, we don't even all agree about 'Thou shalt not kill.' If you're strong enough to get your way by killing someone, you do it."

While the church supports the "hotly debated" notion of an objective moral order, he says, other thinkers maintain that agreement on such a code is beyond a pluralistic society. Still others insist that there are only ethical "hunches," he says, "so that each person has to think each issue through from scratch. Who can do that?"

Whether or not there's such a thing as a universal code of ethics isn't simply an abstract debate topic for Father Hehir. In addition to his regular courses, twice a year, he discusses the morality of war with an elite military gathering at Harvard's Kennedy School of Government. "In the spring, I face ninety colonels and in the summer, a hundred generals and admirals," he says. "There's no institution in society in which people struggle more with moral questions." In these closed sessions, he says, even the top brass can "really open up and talk to each other." One year, Father Hehir lectured on bombing policy in the Gulf War. "A guy raised his hand and said, 'I led the first raid over Baghdad,' " he recalls. "I take that kind of experience very seriously. What I don't want to say, however, is that the person who has it therefore has unique moral insight into war. Or that because generals have the most experience, their perspective has added ethical weight. The whole idea of a moral position is that it's a constraint on everybody's experience." For Father Hehir, war's fundamental moral issue isn't killing per se, "because I think there are certain times when the taking of human life is justified," he says, "as in the protection of certain values. But one should never legitimize in warfare the directly intended killing of civilians."

Moral clarity is very appealing. When the church fights to ensure that civilian areas cannot be targeted for bombing, that strikes me as magisterium at its best. Yet experience has taught me that clarity is only one of morality's criteria. Although I make a qualitative distinction between bombing civilians, say, and abortion, Father Hehir "sees the same moral principle at work in two distinct cases." When I question the church's efforts to impose its view of abortion on Americans who disagree, he brings up the bumper sticker that reads: "If you don't want an abortion, don't have one." To him, such statements "miss the point that civil law always influences society's moral tone. Imagine saying 'If you don't like segregation, don't be a racist.' Don't tell Martin Luther King that you're not going to change the laws. The church wants to press, force, push, and compel a debate about the nature of the moral order. We do want to legislate our position on some issues, but the only way to do that is to lay it out there, defend it, and convince people."

Switching from moral to doctrinal theology, I ask what Catholics today must believe. Part of "an intelligible structure of faith," says Father Hehir, "certainly means that one has to decide whether Jesus is the son of God or a really interesting historical figure, like Lincoln. The intellectual structure of Jesus' identity is really important." When I say that to me, it isn't an intellectual decision, he says, "You're right, it isn't ultimately. But it's not devoid of intellectual content. Take the Arian heresy."

Now we're heading for deep water. In the fourth century, the Council of Nicaea was convened largely because of a profound division among the faithful over a single question: Who was Jesus? One contingent was led by Arius, "a very well-intentioned priest," says Father Hehir, "who held that if Jesus was God in his humanity, God's holiness would be diminished. He wanted to protect that, yet still say Jesus was special. So his view was that Jesus was not God, but God's first creature." I say that I can't hate Arius for this idea, which seems perfectly reasonable. "No," says Father Hehir, "nobody wants to hate him. But you don't want to go down that road, because if Jesus isn't God, what's the difference between his offering of his life on the cross and the sacrifices of the Old Testament?"

As the water grows deeper still, I say that the whole divine death trip, known as the "atonement," really turns me off. As a mother, I'd never demand that a child suffer and die so that I would ease up on the rest of the family. Why would God behave worse than I would? Is God a dysfunctional parent? "Then why did Jesus come?" says Father Hehir. My guess, I say, is that somehow, through Jesus' experience of human life, of which death is a part, God showed a new solidarity with our ridiculous, sublime species, inaugurating a new kind of relationship. "This gets at the question of where we stand before God," he says. "Your position is a classical one in theology, but it used to come up in a different way. The argument was that if the human race was not in sin, would God have become man? Aquinas argued no, Jesus came because the human race was in absolute need of salvation." When I say that *of course* my little babies weren't born in sin, we both have to laugh. Between Arius, atonement, and original sin, we're now lost at sea. When I say that a multiple heretic like me really doesn't belong in the Catholic Church, Father Hehir kindly replies, "Now, don't draw that conclusion."

In many ways, I wish I didn't. On a recent spring vacation, I was reminded of the appeal—and utility—that black-or-white moral and theological certainty can have in an increasingly complicated world. On Palm Sunday, on the Caribbean island of St. Kitts, Mike, our twins, and I went to the Anglican church of St. George with St. Barnabas, in the town of Basseterre. Dating from the seventeenth century, the stone structure, built by slaves, had the Romanesque's solid simplicity. Clear windows slatted with tropical shutters illuminated a hand-carved wooden Madonna and saints. Tropics or not, no formal Anglican nicety of ritual went unobserved. After a stirring procession with homegrown palms, we followed the Mothers of the Church—twenty formidable black women in dazzling white dresses and hats—into the sanctuary for an eight o'clock service that, despite the heat, lasted well over two hours. Every pew was filled. All the congregants enthusiastically belted out easily twenty hymns, mostly stirring, straightforward greatest hits like "Rock of Ages" and "Amazing Grace." If Mike or I failed to join in, one or another kindly lady would meaningfully raise her hymnal and point out the right page. At one point, I closed my eyes for a bit of recollection, only to be tapped cordially and presented with a prayer book.

The rector's sermon made even more plain that this was not the time or place for dreamy self-indulgence. The Episcopal Church is sometimes fancifully pictured as a country-club religion that reserves hell for people who use the wrong fork. This notion would surprise the rector, a vigorous black man who seemed very little tortured by indecision. He spoke of us as Christian soldiers who, even in this holiest of weeks, must wage a constant struggle against the encroaching forces of darkness. We were exhorted to eschew sloth and drugs, promiscuity and thievery, and to do right: most particularly, to discharge our duty to the young, old, and poor. When the children whose birthdays fell that month came forward to receive a small gift, the benediction that came with it had the same martial tone: The Lord was exhorted to uphold them in this struggle we call life and to make them proof against its myriad temptations.

Notwithstanding the palm trees and Caribbean voices and complexions, St. George's seemed curiously familiar. Looking at the women in long sleeves, hats, and stockings and men in jackets and ties, I eventually realized why. I felt surrounded by my grandparents, whose churches, too, had helped them lift themselves up, fight the good fight, and prove that Irish Catholics were as good as anybody. By the time I was born, my parents and their siblings had moved to the suburbs and more austere, upscale churches. But I can just remember St. Carthage's, Nana's dark urban Gothic fortress, where shrines and votive candles offered solace in a hard world, particularly to women, and where sermons were concerned not with letting go or finding yourself but with self-control and doing right. The citizens of St. Kitts and bootstrapping American immigrants and strivers, now as then, look to their churches and temples not just for religion but for a sense of belonging and some additional steel in the spine that will help them catapult their children into a hard-won better future. From experience, I know that they toe the hard line not only because of law, but because of love.

Although it's the simplest excuse, ideology isn't all that keeps me from going home again. Dissent from church teaching isn't an obstacle for more than half of American Catholics, who also disagree with doctrines regarding abortion, birth control, extramarital sex, remarriage after divorce, married clergy, and the ordination of women.[2] They're able to concentrate on the good things they get from the church and remain. Indeed, many people of all faiths who aren't entirely happy with their religious birth tradition decide they're happy enough. An expert on pluralism and its challenges, Diana Eck is firmly convinced that, certainly in the three monotheistic faiths, some of the most difficult "dialogue" happens within each tradition. The deepest passions are aroused in those who are nourished by the same soil, she says, "because you have some basis for calling one another to account. The language of love and justice is so strong in the New Testament that when white supremacists wear crosses, I have to say, 'This isn't Christian.' But the Bible-pounding televangelists would say the same thing about me, because I've been in a relationship with a woman for twenty years. We're calling on the same God, but we argue over the story."

About the question of whether it's better to stay in your original tradition and fight what you don't think is right or switch to a more congenial community, Eck says, "That's a tough one, isn't it?" She feels she has no choice but to resist her Methodist coreligionists who have launched a "witch-hunt for women who use the feminine language of Sophia, the Divine Wisdom, when speaking of God, and have fanned the flames of homophobia. There's a lot I really can't stand about my church!" On the other hand, "at least it's better than when I was growing up, when churches didn't even talk about homosexuality," she says. "Now it's part of the intra-Christian argument. Why should I give my Methodist Church to the conservative voices who call themselves the Good News people, when what they're saying is not the Gospels' Good News?"

No human institution, religious or secular, is perfect. Like many Catholics, Eck concentrates on what's best about her church. In the end, she feels, the decision to stay or go depends on one's deepest commitments. If she were a Catholic woman really feeling called to the priesthood, she says, "I might just say, 'I can't exercise my vocation—the thing I want most to do—in this church.' But over most issues, I'd rather stay and fight." Before I leave, Eck says something that sticks in my mind: "We need to acknowledge our own responsibility for the image of God that we're content to believe in."

Part of the reason why an easygoing approach to my birth tradition doesn't work for me concerns what psychologists call a poor person-environment fit. Sometimes, an individual's early experience of religion becomes inextricably but unwittingly tied up with his or her relationship with parents. In my circle, for example, I've often observed a correlation between a harsh—or kindly—father and Father, who's accordingly resisted or enlisted. Then too, long before Harold Bloom observed that religion is a matter of temperament—personality's more inborn, heritable component—Hinduism had recognized four types of individuals and the religious style best suited to each. A streak of what psychologists call conscientiousness inclines me to think too much in terms of "ought" and "should." (As my best friend observes, this hand-wringing doesn't mean I behave any better than anyone else.) For me, the more rules and requirements, the more potential for angst. One morning, I'm plunged abruptly back into my childhood experience of the church, and get an adult's insight into the pain that can result from the ill-suited pairing of institution and individual.

The day before, I had phoned the last Catholic priest I had known reasonably well and liked a lot. He does interesting work, and I hoped to interview him. We had last met some years before, when my first marriage was heading toward divorce. When he returned my phone call, I said hello, and Father said, "Is this the bad penny turning up?" I felt as if I had been punched in the solar plexus. Numbly, I made an appointment to meet with him, then spent the rest of the day trembling. Later, a secretary called to cancel the appointment, promising the priest would reschedule shortly. He never did. For someone else, perhaps, this incident would just have been one of life's unpleasant moments: hasty, careless words, followed by discourtesy. For me, however, it was a metaphor of my relationship with the religion that, because it seems to require the impossible from me, makes me feel sad, mad, or bad.

There are a lot of us bad pennies jingling around. One third of Americans change from one denomination to another, many of them[3] "wounded Christians" like me. In every such person I meet, I recognize traces of the so-called approach-avoidance conflict that the Catholic Church elicits in me. One day at the cathedral, Jeff Golliher describes grappling with the confusing combination of positive and negative offered by the fundamentalist church of his youth in what he calls "the fire-and-brimstone mountains of the Bible Belt." (Instantly, I recall the East Coast suburban parish of my girlhood, presided over by the granitic Father Cassidy, a Ward Bond type who once thrilled a crowded church by bellowing from the confessional, then occupied by the dreamboat of the eighth grade, "Good God, boy! Do you want to go straight to hell?") Jeff remembers "sitting in the church and thinking that there was a lot of truth to spirituality, but this was not it. The fear and emotional blackmail were all wrong." By the time he was eight or nine, the church confronted Jeff with an either/or, good/evil choice: Join us, or you are a bad person who will burn in hell. By supporting his refusal, he says, "my parents saved my life at that point, because this was some very serious hellfire religion."

Like me, Jeff remains marked by his early religious upbringing. Although his childhood's church "doesn't have authority in my life anymore," he says, "I haven't been able to transcend it completely." Our ambivalence is rooted in the good associations that coexist with the painful. As a child, Jeff experienced "some very strange things that are described in non-Western cultures, which I saw through material about the Holy Spirit that I had gotten from the church. Those experiences took me out of my small world even though I still lived there." When he encountered the Episcopal Church at the age of twelve, Jeff immediately found it "appealing, especially the intellectual freedom to be who I was." On his path to the priesthood, shamans and yogis have been teachers as important to him as theologians.

Christianity doesn't have a monopoly on bad pennies. Telling of how she came to be a rabbi, Susan Schnur describes a childhood in which religion was inseparable from just plain life. "I just loved being Jewish," she says. "In the larger sense of God, it meant trust. I loved the security of going to synagogue with my parents and grandparents. But the focus was the home—kitchen, holidays, Shabbat, with its singing and the Hebrew. On Saturdays we walked to study with a teacher, which felt really special. It was all very integrated."

Susie's bad-penny experience began when she decided to become one of the first women rabbis. She was "Conserva-dox"—a blend of Orthodox and Conservative Judaism—and neither of these branches ordained women. She had to study at a less traditional reconstructionist seminary, "which didn't suit me temperamentally or ideologically," she says. "Religiously, I wanted the other environment, but that became complicated by rage around the women's issues. Wanting to stay Orthodox for all the beautiful things, but the anguish . . ." Partly because she has experienced "all the beautiful things," Susie is tolerant of those who choose a Judaism that's too restrictive for her. "Fundamentalism is what some people want, and it's redemptive for them," she says, with a smile and a sigh. "The part about being the rabbi that's anticlimactic is that the magic is in you, and you can't turn to someone else in the robes."

When Canon Susan Harriss talks about Sunday school in the Salvation Army of her youth, I can almost smell the crayons and construction paper with which my classmates and I excitedly made decorations for Christmas and Easter. Describing little booklets that had black, red, white, green, and gold pages that represented each child's heart, she says, "The Army didn't use 'soul,' it used 'heart.' First your heart was black, then it was washed with the Lord's blood, then it became pure, then it grew, then it was in heaven, where the streets were paved in gold." After four generations in the Army, her family was "very devout, passionately religious," she says. Their home in South Carolina was suffused by an evangelical piety that Susan both loves and rejects. "There was constant talk of 'the Lord this' and 'the Lord that' and 'what Jesus means to do.' My Grandpa Graham would come and do revivals for my parents and beat his tambourine on his knee and elbow and sing from the pulpit. I probably had as complete an immersion in religious life as any American child can have, and I really, really liked it. I don't think I ever got over it."

After leaving home, acquiring a secular college education, and living through the sixties, Susan no longer meshed with her childhood religion. Like Jeff, Susie, and me, she can't help loving pieces of an institution that, for whatever reasons, she either rejects or is rejected by. "I don't go back to the Salvation Army anymore," she says, "but I miss it terribly. There's this sadness about not being there, because even the soap in the bathroom smells right! And I do think the people are holy. Sometimes it's painful—unbelievably so." Once Susan entered the nondenominational Union Theological Seminary, it took her three years to make a commitment to a particular church. The day she was finally confirmed as an Episcopalian, she arranged to have Roberta Flack on the church's sound system singing "I Told Jesus It Would Be All Right If He Changed My Name"—an old spiritual about one's family turning away. When a seminary teacher said that the real sign of maturity was going back to embrace your root church, Susan says, she "wanted to throw up and say, 'No! I don't have to go back there. I have choices.' " These days, when someone asks her how she got from the Salvation Army to the Episcopal Church, she says, "Because God has a really good sense of humor!"

When people attempt to revisit their religious pasts, " 'bad penny' is often what they hear," says Susan, "and I think that's good. It just confirms that it's time to go somewhere else." To her, the true damage is done "when bugaboos from the past get religion attached to them, and inhibit *real* religion. Or when people take up the bad-penny voice and begin to repeat it to themselves. That's called 'siding with the accuser,' and there's a wonderful image of Satan playing that role." She smiles mischievously. "The devil's good! He knows! He's trying to distract people from moving ahead—absolutely." More seriously, she says, "That priest was wrong to call you that name, and some of us have to stop being so loyal to such clergy. God is big enough for us to move on, and we grow in the understanding that that's okay."

For most of my life, I finally realize, I've had an all-or-nothing approach to religion: It's perfect, or it's worthless. Like many people brought up in a particular faith, I also had a certain snobbery and chauvinism about "the real thing." It must be Rome or nothing! Now, as I take responsibility for what I'm content to believe in—after decades of believing in nothing much—I'm acquiring a different attitude. My choices no longer seem limited to being a neoagnostic, a bad penny, or "anything but Christian." A conversation with a remarkable former nun helps me recognize and honor my religious past and move on from there.

There are some women who, no matter what they're wearing, look like the nuns they are or have been. Recently I recognized two of these ladies on an airport shuttle bus. Dressed in colorful slacks and sweaters, they were heading home after a vacation down South. As to how I just "knew" they were nuns, it might have been their scrubbed, rosy faces, plain haircuts, and no-frills accessories, but mostly, I think, it was that some combination of openness and composure I notice in many Zen monks. It turned out that they were Sisters of Mercy, the order that taught me in grade school. Although they now worked as counselors—one with the elderly, the other with troubled youth—they had previously been teachers. They inquired closely about how I had gotten on in life—education, career, marriage, children, health of parents— and were visibly pleased that a Mercy girl, who would naturally be a strong grammarian and speller, had become a writer. They would pray that my work would "go easily." For the length of the ride, I was home again!

Despite her thirty years in the cloister, I would never have "spotted" Ruth Brennan, the handsome woman who waits in my San Francisco hotel lobby, as a former contemplative nun. She looks like the corporate personnel director she became after leaving the Passionist monastery where she had been abbess. As we talk over cappuccinos, it's clear that while she's certainly not unfriendly, Ruth is not the gal next door, either. She has a certain gravitas. Before speaking, which she does in a deliberate way, she thinks. During these pauses, I find that I lean forward in anticipation. In my everyday milieu of perpetual "communication," conversation with someone who savors silence and tries to be honest rather than clever is like diving into a cold, clear lake on a hot, humid day.

First, Ruth tells me a little of her history. In the 1940s, at the age of seventeen, she entered a cloister in rural Pennsylvania. She had no doubts that this was indeed "the excellent way to live," although fifty years ago, it meant strict enclosure in a walled, two-acre plot and only rare parental visits, conducted through an iron grating. In contrast to her restricted exterior life, however, her inner one was very rich. There was much prayer, of course, but also intellectual stimulation. She read a great deal, enjoyed the teaching of visiting priests, and became her community's artist. In these respects, she says, "I was very well fed."

For Ruth, becoming mother superior, which meant more dealings with a world—and church—on the brink of the sixties cultural revolution, was the beginning of the end of the nun's life. "I pushed the envelope," she says. "There were hundreds of cloisters, but we had never met. There were lots of questions we needed to discuss—from canon law to property management to the issue of how being cloistered supports being contemplative." Ruth convened the first meeting of the Association of Contemplative Sisters, to which she still belongs. The event was held in Woodstock in the summer of 1969, she says laughingly, "but it was Woodstock, Maryland." In "A Position on Contemplative Life," the 135 nuns present "affirmed that the traditional forms of enclosure are detrimental to the human and Christian development of our sisters and consequently to the full realization of our vocation [and urged] that contemplative religious creatively appraise the concept of withdrawal from the world and respond to the insights discovered with creative self-determination."

After being elected as the ACS's first president, Ruth was frequently absent from her convent. When her term was over, she had "already separated." First, she stayed with her parents while taking a typing course and looking for a job. "Survival was hard," she says, "but wholesome. Jammed into the subway, I'd think, This is a stream of life that you have to know and deal with, even if you sometimes have to turn it off." To Ruth, the cloistered life is "one-sided. You become 'spiritualized,' and subdue, or set aside, basic human realities. All your emotional, sexual, and psychological needs are subordinated to this great spiritual thing—this better thing. But even with the best intentions, being behind a wall . . . for the person doing that, life is very unreal." Ruth is very big on reality. "Some of the things you see on TV that glamorize the cloister just make me grind my teeth! Young women still join, but what they're looking for is unreal, romanticized." Although she thinks some form of contemplative community will always survive, Ruth firmly believes that the days of enclosure and isolation from the world are over: "The old cloistered lifestyle is finished!"

Although she left the convent, Ruth didn't leave religion, which for her is "Christ's message coming from the Gospels." At first, she says, "I just hung on to what I felt was important, and coasted." More recently, retirement has freed Ruth to resume a contemplative life of her own design. Describing it, she reminds me of Mrs. Moore, in *A Passage to India*. First, she mutters in Latin, then quickly translates for me: " 'I am before thee as a pilgrim and a wanderer.' I value all my phases. I carry all that stuff with me. The nun, the superior, the rebel, and now, at seventy-two, the person struggling to cope with the relative insignificance of my life." Spending much time in solitude, studying and reading, she has especially enjoyed a video course in quantum physics: "I'm fascinated by that meeting place between the micro- and macrocosm." I ask if she sees something there that resembles the Hindu concept of Brahman and atman. "Yes," she says. "Like that. I don't know how I got there."

Although she sometimes goes to church, Ruth hasn't sought another community. "It's too hard to share what I'm working on," she says. "I just feel like seeking the center of things. I don't feel connected other than at that center. The outside world doesn't matter that much right now. Someone said to me recently, 'You're back where you started,' but not really." Then, too, she says, laughing, "I can't belong to anything without ending up running it! It drives me crazy!" Nonetheless, she has become active again in the ACS. When I ask what these sisters are like at the millennium, she shoots back, "Women like you. It used to be just for nuns, but many of us left the convent. We stayed members, and we find our own kind." She pauses. "We're contemplative sisters, but not nuns. We're on a journey, walking this road together and sharing where we're at. Very profoundly. We don't get together just to socialize. We're searching for a deeper place."

Looking over some of the ASC's newsletters, which include many letters sent to the group by sisters, I particularly notice one definition of what it means to be contemplative: "accepting things as they are and not how I would have them be." A hospital chaplain writes that being "on call" is like being "bound and led by another," so that each person who seeks her becomes her teacher. From Lima, Peru, during the hostage crisis in the Japanese embassy there, a sister confides that despite the national turmoil, "I trust God that something good will come out of all this pain, confusion, anxiety. I just pray: 'In God all is well and all shall be well.' " My favorite items, listed under regional news, are updates on several hermits, who apparently can dwell in apartments these days. A seventy-five-year-old woman living on her Social Security in Washington State writes that despite adding considerable volunteer work to her life, "days are peaceful and somehow alone with God." These publications' overall tone is an impressive combination of quiet confidence and good cheer.

Toward the end of our talk, I ask Ruth what being a contemplative means at the millennium. "I don't like the word," she says. "It has connotations of people like Teresa of Avila.

It suggests that something from outside is being given, which can make you abdicate your own personal search. What we call 'contemplative' is the most central, profound human search anyone can know. There's something in our basic human being that is what contemplative is."

PART TWO

A VARIATION

CHAPTER TEN

ZEN: "AND THAT'S THE WAY IT IS"

A S I GLOOMILY ring the bell at Dai Bosatsu Zendo, where I've come for another Zen refresher, I'm facing three long days of lots of meditation, starting before dawn. I'd prefer to be starting a little vacation on the Gulf Coast, with brunch on the beach. Once again, the world is too much with me. A recent visit to my old people found them much frailer, and one of my young ones is floundering in school. Unbelievably, Thanksgiving is around the corner, and just behind it, far more labor-intensive holidays. I've fallen behind in my work. Unlacing my boots—they'll be left at the door—I try to remember why I'm reporting for this tune-up.

I've come to accept that I feel Christian, much in the same way and for the same reasons that I feel American, or like a Gallagher: For better or worse, there you have it. Nevertheless,

I'm not a creedal Christian, any more than I'm an unconflicted American or family member. Because I have a busy life and a busy mind, *zazen*'s demonstrable ability to create quiet calm and expand my definition of the sacred seems like a good foundation for any more elaborate religious structure. As the Psalmist says, "Be still and know that I am God."

In a moment, I'm greeted by Entsu, an American monk. His rangy young-guy energy reminds me of my oldest, and how hard it is to keep him in carbohydrates. In short order he hands me over to Yayoi, a Japanese-American monk, whose shaved head complements her piquant features. It turns out that we're around the same age and both have two kids in their twenties; we each exclaim that the other looks younger. Yayoi shows me around this posh Hilton of a *zendo*. My small private room is furnished with a futon and linens, low desk and cushion—even incense. Down the hall are men's and women's lavatories and a unisex shower room complete with Japanese bathtub. Yayoi leads on to the laundry, where I get to choose a robe to wear during my stay. As a New York woman, I wear enough black. I go for a handsome chino model. Then we head to the dining room to rehearse the formal eating style for breakfast and lunch, taken silently in community; dinner for non-monks is serve-yourself leftovers in the basement lounge. The drill is less exacting than *oryoki,* which I learned at the Sonoma Mountain *zendo*, but already exhibiting mindlessness, I have trouble remembering the details. Hopefully, I ask Yayoi about pace, but it's breakneck here, too. One can finish on time, she says, if one just chews steadily.

In the late afternoon, I walk by the monastery's private Beecher Lake. Craterlike, it's ringed by forested mountain ridges. This is the first day this year in which winter has chilled the air. The silence is profound. A good half hour from the nearest gas station and beyond the pale for cellular phones, Dai Bosatsu lies a mile from its own gatehouse, so there's not even the hum of the occasional car. The moon, nearly full, is already a huge pale disc hanging in the clear, still-blue sky. The bare brown trees enveloped in the quickly deepening shadows are silvery with frost. I spend some time taking in this landscape, so unusual in both color and composition. From the other side of the lake, a seated stone Buddha looks back.

At dusk, I microwave some leftovers in the dormlike lounge. The spicy vegetable stew and rice pudding are good. While eating, I chat with Dai En/George Burch, a husky, bearded middle-aged computer entrepreneur who's to be ordained at the next *sesshin*. He doesn't really want to talk, I suspect, but out of courtesy, will. He strikes me as belonging to a Zen type characterized by a droll, even rascally, mien. He jokes that maybe when he's officially a monk, more people will come to the *zendo* he maintains back home in Massachusetts: "But that's very American, to think religion is about large numbers and proselytizing."

Like most of the Zen folk I've met, Dai En's interest began with reading and turned into practice under the gun of a personal crisis. "Eighteen years ago, I came here and it just cleared up my problems," he says. Really? I ask. Just like that? "Yes," he says. Dai En returns at least once a year, often several times, and sits "pretty much daily." Since he began to practice, he says, Zen has become "much more accessible and amenable to Americans."

At first glance, gruff Dai En seems an unlikely evangelist, but his testimony is as clear and emphatic as a born-again Christian's. It's not the Zen way to beat around the bush. Then, too, he's a successful businessman who's accustomed to making a decision and executing it. "Buddha was correct about suffering," he says. "I have seen that. My practice is an act of gratitude for a path that alleviates suffering. I want that for everyone." As it's bad manners to tell a person in distress that "everything will be all right," much less that their pain is an illusion, what Dai En might offer instead, he says, is something like this: "There's a path that requires discipline. Not everyone can follow it in this life. But if you do, you can end suffering for yourself and all beings."

As I eat dinner in this fluorescent-lit basement while making the opposite of small talk with a perfect stranger, it's still late afternoon. At home, I'd be facing a few more hours of work, returning calls, a martini, dinner, and maybe a video. Here, I sip my mug of cold water and steel myself for two and a half hours of chanting and meditation, followed immediately by bed. At least, I think, I get to wear the cool robe.

In the *zendo,* I settle onto my assigned cushion between Yayoi and Dai En. At Sonoma Mountain, one faces the wall for *zazen,* but here we sit in two rows facing each other, which seems sybaritic. There's even a window almost in front of my gaze. After chanting in Japanese, which I read from a kind of phonetic hymnal, we sit for forty-five minutes. At the bell, to restore circulation, we rise and walk quickly in a kind of cloister track that borders the main space. When we return for the second sitting, the stillness is so deep you can hear people swallowing; my rumbling stomach makes an embarrassing racket. The squeaks and tings from the baseboard heating system remind me of the California *zendo* sighing in the wind. Rather than breath-counting, I try a two-word mantra: I inhale with "Kyrie"—God, the mystery, the ineffable, big mind, Brahman—and breathe out with "Christe"—Jesus, bodhisattvas, the prophets, the human ones, atman.

The second the ritual is over, everyone hustles off to bed. We must get up and rigorously do nothing all over again at five in the morning. Lights here are used on an as-needed basis, which means that darkness pretty much falls indoors as well as out. Incense hangs in the silent moonlit air.

I sleep badly. When the bell ringer traverses the monastery, town-crier style, I wake to a cold, black morning. The daily regimen begins with a near-gallop around the *zendo.* I'm a fast walker, but an unseemly gap soon widens between me and Dai En. "Catch up!" hisses Yayoi, and I break into a jog. Moving to the smaller shrine room, we do some Japanese chants. In the final one, each repetition is done slightly faster and louder, until we end with a great shout, as if we had all run off a cliff. The ringing hypersilence that follows is powerful. When it's time to get up, one leg is so deeply asleep that it slides out from under me as if it were on ice, and I fall on my butt. Officially no one notices, except for the oldest monk, who kindly whispers, "It's okay!"

Predictably after last night's mellow *zazen,* this morning's is fitful and unsatisfying. Even in a religion that has no beliefs, it's possible to have doubts. It seems stupid to sit here and just breathe—particularly when it's so hard. I want to go back to sleep, or at least drink some coffee and read the paper. Don't these people know there's a big world out there? Like going to the gym and loafing through a workout, however, sitting badly is the only thing worse than sitting. From the darkness, the window across the aisle emerges first as a misty gray rectangle, then as a frame for the surprise of fat snowflakes catching on bare branches. Even when a deer wanders past this porthole to the universe, I remain resolutely grouchy.

We file into the dining hall for a shocking breakfast of rice gruel with seaweed, pickles, scallions, and what seems like fish, washed down with orange juice. I put sliced fruit in one of my three bowls, but the guys put theirs on the table so they

can have two bowls of rice. We eat nonstop, wash our chopsticks and bowls with tea—Dai En economically licks his
clean—and bundle up the whole kit in a napkin.

At eight, we proceed to a sunlit parlor, sit on black cushions on a white wool carpet around a low timber table, and
chant a bit more. When we finish, Shokan/Marcel Urich, a
Swiss monk, reads a passage from a modern book about Zen.
He mispronounces "sagacity," putting the stress on the first
syllable. As soon as the rituals are over and what's called
Morning Meeting begins, there's much ribbing: "Saga City—
that's out West, isn't it?" Coffee and tea are handed around the
circle in big tin pots and, wonderfully, there's a huge tiered
strawberry shortcake to celebrate the birthday of a monk
who has just turned thirty-four. "I remember when you were
thirty," jokes another. "It seems like only four years ago."
Checking on the provisions purchased on the previous day's
shopping trip, Jiro/Andy Afable, the head monk who runs
DBZ when Eido-roshi is away, grins and asks, "Any smokes?"

As a visitor, I'm the next item on the agenda. I'm officially
greeted by Jiro, handed the first piece of cake, and asked
about my project. Next comes a discussion of what sort of
trees to plant near the lake, where the beavers make particularly short work of certain species. Most of the neighbors
would simply shoot or trap the industrious mammals, but
these aren't Buddhist options. When the talk turns to plant-
ings for other locations, Entsu unaccountably declares that
apple trees are ugly. Another monk says, "Think what they
say about us!" When one person wonders aloud about what
is and isn't included in the Buddhist prayer for "all sentient
beings," someone says, "Ask your car."

When the day's business has been dispatched, I ask Dai En,
seated to my left, what the formidable-looking Eido-roshi
is like. "A Japanese Zen master," he says. But what is *he*

like? I persist. "They're all the same," he says. That's not possible, I say. What about individual temperament? "Get rid of it," he says. Whatever subject comes up during Morning Meeting is potentially hilarious.

Next, we head off for a few hours of "work practice." Correctly assessing my life experience, Jiro asks me to help prepare fourteen guest rooms for the coming weekend's Introduction to Zen retreat. This mostly involves vacuuming and making up the futons in a very particular way. Briskly showing me how to fold the two gray felt blankets and green duvet just so, Yayoi says that in Japan, monks do things even faster, which is hard to imagine. Zen was the religion of choice for the samurai class, and the order, speed, and formality of life at Dai Bosatsu have a distinctly martial cast. In most congregations, women outnumber men, but Zen groups seem predominantly male; only two women are living here. Then, too, the residents have a hard-driving New York energy quite different from those at Sonoma Mountain, where *kinhin* is creeping rather than speed walking. Here, there's more talk of suffering, too, but as a sinus victim, I know that could be the climate. Some differences are due to those between the Rinzai and Soto traditions. The former, followed here, puts more emphasis on intellect and the use of koans— riddles or paradoxical statements on which to meditate.

In a short essay called "What Is Zen?" Eido-roshi writes that while life and death, sickness and health, can't be ignored, they aren't our true nature, any more than self and Buddha nature are separate entities: "To be here, as an individual, and yet to be boundless—is this possible?" he asks. Those who think so aren't puzzled by a notion such as "your face before you were born and after you die." For the rest of us, struggling with such koans is a way to grapple with the "nonrelative reality" that Zen teaches is our true nature and which its practice can help us realize. In this Rinzai community, many beginners meditate on the one-word koan *Mu*—Japanese for a kind of "pregnant" emptiness—a nothingness that's not just nothing. When focusing on a koan, as when counting breaths, the practitioner is pushed to inquire where ideas come from, which eventually quiets down the brain's usual "monkey thoughts" and helps expose the underlying basis of what is.

After my housekeeping chores, I have some free time to talk to some DBZ folk. First comes a psychospiritual discussion about Zen and behavioral science with Rinden/Roland Sujimoto. In his native Austria, he's a doctoral student in psychology. While taking a break from academe to immerse himself in Zen, he has researched an interesting question: Are there any measurable correlations between the maturity of one's Zen practice and certain personality characteristics, such as truthfulness and independence? When he analyzed data from forty Zen practitioners and a control group, Rinden found a strong association between the number of *sesshins* a person had attended—one gauge of rigorous practice—and his or her score in the trait of immediacy, or the tendency to act promptly. In other words, the more intense a person's Zen regimen, the greater the inclination to approach life with a just-do-it attitude.

Privately expecting an association with a more obviously "spiritual" trait, such as compassion or even concentration, Rinden was taken aback by his result—the more so because outside Zen culture, immediacy isn't necessarily thought socially desirable. (Indeed, practitioners can sometimes seem brusque.) He concludes that after cultivating *zazen*'s be-here-now state of mind, people are more inclined to live that way, too. As Rinden says, "Experience actually supports the Zen theory of one-pointedness."

Although Rinden links a get-on-with-it attitude to the

practice of Zen, another explanation can't be ruled out. It may be that a highly engaged personality type is disproportionally attracted to Zen. Only a study involving identical twins separated at birth and reared apart can definitively show whether a trait has been largely acquired through experience or inherited through genes. Zen regards such individual differences as deriving from karma, which results from actions in our past lives. As Eido-roshi writes in his essay, "We know that there is something ghostlike about our life; it is temporary and fleeting. If we don't realize this, we complain about our parents, our social conditions, our historical context, and so on. . . . From the Zen perspective, however, the particular circumstance of each individual is inevitable, and somehow appropriate. With this acceptance, we can begin our practice."

Even as a small child, Rinden was interested in existential issues: Who am I? Where did I come from? Where am I going? In his essay, Eido-roshi writes that these are humanity's most essential questions, which "pursue us, and more urgently, as we get older." Because he's so young, when I ask Rinden why he does Zen, I'm surprised by his somber reply. "So many people die in a sad condition," he says. "I'd like to clarify the important questions before I die. Many people ask them when they're children, then get distracted by 'real life' and forget about them or regard them as just kid stuff. That's the big illusion, because it's really the other way round, as we see again when death approaches. We act like we're going to live forever, but life shouldn't be wasted. The big questions have to be confronted. As we say in Zen, 'Die on your cushion.' "

Later in the morning, I talk with Jiro about *zazen's* particular experiential quality. He brings up some scientific research, begun in Japan in the 1950s, in which Dr. Tomeo Hirai studied how sitting affects the brain.[1] In one experiment, he used EEGs to establish differences between the brain waves of subjects in a control group who weren't meditating and those of monks who were. In another EEG study, Hirai asked control subjects to sit in a dim room and relax into what they considered a meditative condition. When he rang a bell at short intervals, they soon "habituated" to the stimulus; that is, their brain waves no longer "blipped" at each noise. When Hirai tested the meditating monks, however, their EEGs demonstrated the principle of being here now; their brain waves registered each ring as if they were hearing the bell for the first time. "If the phone rings when you're sitting," says pragmatic Jiro, "you *could* answer it."

It seems unjust, I say, that some people experience "something else" and others simply don't. "And you can't communicate with them," says Jiro. "Thomas Merton said that knowledge of God can't be passed down from father to son." He grins: "But neither can that of vanilla ice cream!" Considering the various levels of competence, talent, and character among practitioners of any activity, from meditation to playing the violin, he says, "in terms of quality, I bet the numbers—doctors, plumbers, Catholic priests, professors, Zen monks—all break down the same way!"

When I persist in complaining that it's "not fair" that some people are far more temperamentally suited to practice Zen or other religions than others, Jiro smiles. "The roshi recently said that after many years of thought and answering people's questions, he has come up with two points that are all anyone needs to know about practice. First, everyone is equally 'divine,' whether they call it that or Buddha nature, and whether they know it or not. Second, everyone has specific karma—personality traits that lead each of us in a certain direction. Two people will face the same kind of serious event—even the Holocaust—but one will cope better than the other. There are individuals who by every standard measure should, but just can't, be happy in the *dailiness* of life. They can't get to that place where things are . . . okay. We can't do much about it, and it's not exactly fair. That's just life!"

For several of the people I talk to at Dai Bosatsu, Zen practice seems like second nature. After five years of eighty-hour work weeks as the manager of a large printing company, Shoshanna/Suzanne Triner decided it was time to relax. She took two months off and, hoping for a laid-back rural retreat, turned up here knowing nothing about Zen. The first few days were awful, she says, "but on the fourth, I had a breakthrough that embraced the whole world. I ended up staying for six weeks." Although she travels and offers seminars on personal development, she has mostly lived here for three years: "I love the community, the food, all the nature—the whole life."

Of the residents, Shoshanna seems closest to a New Age sensibility. As a small child, she had a religious sense of "the unity of all life. Even then, I saw these energy fields around all things, but people didn't know what to make of that. Here, it's taught as theory, as it is now in physics. We're each an expression of that one energy, which we should just bring out." Little Suzanne also had "these questions that no one would answer," she says. "I was brought up a Protestant, but I couldn't believe in Noah's ark, or 'this is a sin, but that is not.' I couldn't just *believe* things, without understanding or feeling."

Although the *zazen* condition "can't really be described," says Shoshanna, "it's more than just an empty mind. There are states that last only two or three seconds but nurture you for days—months. And the cushion isn't the only place to have these experiences. They happen in nature, too." She practices because "doing Zen serves me and others. Merging into the one energy is so nurturing that I overflow and can really give." Over time, she has become "more grounded and stable. I'm supported in what I feel and experience, so I trust myself more."

As I rise to prepare for the noon sitting, Shoshanna quotes Rumi, the Sufi mystic who advised, "Get up, get up, get up! Even if you fall a thousand times, get up and try again." Any spiritual practice, she says, is "a matter of not giving up. The goal is only an arm's length away." That may be so in a monastery, I grouse, but not at my house. "And all that stuff goes to your neck," Shoshanna says sympathetically. Have I been holding my head funny, I wonder, or is it my aura? "Life is a dance that we should enjoy," she says. "We do too much judging—'this is bad,' 'this is better.' Maybe it's all a game." Maybe, I think, neck crimping.

Although I'm still glassy-eyed with fatigue and culture shock, the noon sitting surprisingly goes better. Across from me sits Ippo, who previously had spoken to me about moving from his Jewish upbringing to Buddhism. Sometimes, I notice, he wears a little smile during *zazen,* which strikes me as quite an accomplishment.

During a lunch of noodles, cabbage soup, and broccoli, I'm diverted by a fat, two-pronged buck who wanders around outside the dining hall's large windows. I fall behind in the bowl-emptying process, although several of the guys have taken heaping seconds, which they bolt quickly. As I drain off my tea, the deer is lying in what is now six inches of snow, just looking around. It's the first time I've seen one of these animals so familiar to me at rest—a furry demonstration of the sort of calm awareness I should try to cultivate.

This goal will always be far more elusive for me than it has been for Shokan. When I ask about his previous profession, the Swiss monk says, "street sweeper." With his clear blue eyes, white skin, and seraphic composure, Shokan could be a medieval Christian saint sent by Central Casting. Not surprisingly, he, too, was an ontologically minded child. Later, he read a book about Zen and archery "and knew that was it." What was so compelling about this combination, I ask. "They hit the target without aiming," says Shokan. "They shoot outside, but the target is inside. If you're right with yourself, you're right with the whole universe. You just let the 'something else' do it."

Although he continued to read about Zen, intense knee discomfort kept Shokan from all but the occasional sitting. Like most people at Dai Bosatsu—and, from what I can tell, everywhere—he found that his religious life deepened following one of life's jolts of pain. Only when pushed by a personal crisis was he able to do daily *zazen*. In time, he moved on to solo *sesshins*. After nine years of this solitary practice, he finally found a Soto group in Switzerland and was ordained in a year. Four years later, Shokan met Eido-roshi, who was traveling in Europe, and immediately recognized him as his teacher. After moving to DBZ three years ago, he was initiated into the Rinzai tradition and plans to remain here.

When I ask why a person should do Zen, Shokan says, "No one *should*. I can't help doing it. I have to. It's a need. I love it." As a little child, he had instinctively devised a similar meditation. Pantomiming his youthful posture, Shokan curls up. "I called it the worm thing," he says, "because I went inside myself like a worm." When I ask if he'd describe his state during *zazen* as pleasure, he says it's more "like taking a rest. Being a spectator. It's not that you deny or diminish your uniqueness, but you give up your egocentric likes and dislikes. Instead of being involved in your mind's actions, you step back and watch. Nothing is yourself, but it's an aware nothing—an Asian emptiness that's full."

While working on this book, I've been around hundreds of

religious people from many traditions. A few have had a special quality that I must simply describe as holiness. Speaking
of the great American ballerina Suzanne Farrell, the choreo-
grapher Maurice Béjart said, "She is like a violin. The music
comes out from her body." So it is, I think, with holiness.
Rabbi or roshi, monk or nun, minister or scholar, those who
have it share three attributes. The first is a peculiar characteristic aptly labeled by a cloistered nun when she described seeing Huston Smith on TV: "He's so transparent," she said. The
second is an extreme degree of for-realness; the holy are the
most down-to-earth, least pious people I've ever met. They
also have an extraordinary gift: In their presence, *you* feel holy,
too.

In the late afternoon, I take a walk. My sneakers make a
satisfying, corn-starch squeak in the clean, dry snow. After a
long, mild fall that ended just yesterday, it's shockingly cold.
Against the whiteness, Beecher Lake looks like ink. As it has
throughout this volatile, changeable day, the sky clears, then
clouds over again. Through the intermittent snow squalls, I
glimpse Buddha on the distant shore. He's still sitting.

At the cosmopolitan hour of 4:50 P.M., I have another
early-bird special in the lounge. As I finish my microwaved
rice and vegetables, Dai En rings the big gong outside at five,
then comes in to polish off two thick slices of homemade
bread and jam. In this topsy-turvy world, it seems perfectly
reasonable to ask this near-stranger if, after nearly two decades
of practice, he has come to any conclusion about why we're
here. "We aren't," he says. After a good laugh, he continues,
"We're just here because of the coming and going of certain
relationships and sperm. We're not inherently different from
life's other forms." Responding to my look, he says, "It's hard
to reconcile the self and reincarnation. There's an ocean, and
the waves look individual, but they're not."

Turning to more practical matters, Dai En says he's concerned about how America's increasingly middle-aged and elderly population will cope with *zazen*'s physical stresses. Many people, particularly men, find the seated posture uncomfortable, even painful. My problem, I say, isn't joints, but thoughts. "Your thoughts are just karma interfering with mind," says Dai En. "When you stop them, you can experience mind. Everything is coming and going, but you try to experience big mind independently of that transitory stuff." When Dai En says, "Big mind is infinite memory," I think of Charles Hartshorne's similar definition of God. "Because mind was never born and will never die, but just changes in form," he says, "you should be able to remember being a speck of dust aeons ago."

This recollection must elude me, I say, if it depends on maintaining an empty mind for more than a few breaths. Dai En says that I shouldn't assume that *zazen* must be so hard: "When you listen to music, your mind isn't all over the place, is it? It just follows." People make too much of sitting's difficulty, he goes on, when in fact, it's no more so than many of the other things we do without undue moaning and groaning: "If there were something you could do to avoid all suffering for all time, wouldn't that be worth some effort?" When I ask if he really believes that's possible, he fairly snorts, "I *know* it." I allow that I enjoyed a long run of good spirits after *sesshin*. As Rinden's experiment suggests, Zen practitioners don't spend much time worrying and brooding, says Dai En. If there's something to be done about a situation, they do it; if nothing can be done, they move on to the next order of business. "That can sometimes be a problem itself," he says, laughing. "But we don't have a lot of ups and downs. I'm a happy camper."

The evening sittings seem long and difficult. Returning to my experience of working out, I remind myself a circuit-training regimen seems endless too, but if you keep turning up, you get results. Minutes after the final gong, I fall onto my futon and don't stir until the five A.M. bell.

During the dawn sitting, the window slowly emerges from blackness to grayness to brilliant blue, sparkling with crystalline gusts of fresh snow. Observing this is cheating, I suppose, but then again, maybe watching nature naturing, as the deer did yesterday, is as good as counting breaths. I take heart from Dai En's comparison of *zazen* and music. Perhaps sitting—religion—is just listening to reality. My leg goes to sleep again, but when the bell rings between sittings, I abandon decorum and give it a good rub before trying to stand.

Once again, Morning Meeting is a merry cosmic kaffeeklatsch, this time embellished with chunks of homemade chocolate sent by a grateful retreatant. Like schoolkids, two monks get the giggles as Shokan does the daily inspirational reading and simply can't stop until Jiro speaks sharply. The steaming pots go round, followed by a book I wrote called *The Power of Place,* which concerns how our surroundings affect behavior. The first chapter examines the effects of light, the lack of which becomes a problem for many people at this very time of year. There are lots of jokes about monastic mood swings and the seasonal vicissitudes of life here in New York's dark, damp, cold rain belt.

For the book's epigraph, I chose a passage from *Glory,* a novel by Vladimir Nabokov, which one monk reads aloud:

". . . he saw the flaming, restless nest of fire a short distance away, and the silhouettes of people around it, and someone's hand adding a branch. The crickets leapt crepitating; from time to time there came a sweet whiff of burning juniper; and above the black alpestrine steppe, above the silken sea, the enormous, all-engulfing sky, dove grey with stars, made one's head spin, and suddenly, Martin again experienced a feeling he had known on more than one occasion as a child: an unbearable intensification of all his senses, a magical and demanding impulse, the presence of something for which it was alone worth living."

Although I didn't know the term at the time, I say, I now wonder if what Martin experiences is *kensho.* Around the circle, heads shake no, and faces take on a Clint Eastwood expression. Bragging about one's experiences, spiritual or otherwise, is bad form, but this degree of circumspection strikes me as machismo. Finally, one monk says kindly, "Well, the unbearable intensification of senses . . ." "No, no," says another. "It's missing the oneness of all life."

The next order of business is a long, funny conversation about a year-end gift for Eido-roshi. Apparently, he'd like a cell phone for his travels. New York being New York, there's a *zendo* member who's a dealer, and he has a special price. There's much discussion about whether the phone should ring or vibrate. For sartorial reasons—Zen masters wear robes with no pockets—the ringer is deemed best. Outside, a stiff breeze blows diamond sprays of snow from high tree branches.

After the meeting, a monk privately volunteers his experience of *kensho.* During a period of great stress, he decided to attend a *sesshin,* not for the sake of Zen practice but to try to "approach my life like a koan," he says. "The question I assigned myself was What am I going to do? When I wake up tomorrow? The next day? There were very practical things I had to solve." By the third day, he had made little progress: "I was sitting in the *zendo* thinking Oh shit, I don't want any of this stuff. This is not what I'm here for—to have *experiences.*"

Suddenly, the monk recalls, a hazy light that had been filtering down from a ceiling fixture entered his body, lodged in his diaphragm, and "just exploded. I could see every molecule of my body . . . just gone. All that was left was this consciousness that was aware. I ran to *dokusan* and got halfway through the story when Roshi said, 'No,' and rang his bell—the signal to leave. I understood what he meant: Fine, it happened, don't put too much value on it, just move on."

A well-educated, pragmatic man, the monk knows that a psychologist would probably explain his *kensho* as a release of great tension during a traumatic time. But, he says, "I'll never forget it. I understood something from it that has to do with the loss of self." Although far more dramatic, the experience also resonated with his frequent dreams of disintegration and merging. "They're powerful," he says. "It's always about losing myself. As a Buddhist, I can't recant my own experience and feelings, but I stress that *kensho* isn't of particular interest to the Roshi, or to me. It's nothing to envy, nor should someone who hasn't had one feel somehow deficient. People make much more of it here than in Japan. Americans have that hard style of 'going for it.' When someone has one, I just say . . . 'Fine!' "

A little later, Entsu hands me a photocopy of a letter, addressed to Eido-roshi, that describes the writer's *kensho.* One morning toward the end of a *sesshin,* the writer despaired of his practice and wished to "turn back to the 'normal' world." For some reason, he recalled the roshi saying "Keep your eyes open or you will miss it!" Suddenly, he wrote, "the teacup in front of me seemed to 'fly apart' and all the constituent matter in the cup, and in my body, and in the universe, were the same from all past to all future for endless time. I saw that what seems to be me or a cup is only due to where my self was sitting. This experience totally freed my self from the coming and going and caused the greatest gratitude to well up in my heart. . . . I am now like a kite. When strong winds blow I rise up, in light winds I drift. Without thinking a thought I do the right thing, just like a kite. . . . Now I need no practice. But I am not arrogant."

Before my final *zazen* at noon, I ask Jiro about the role of religious experience in practice, and in life generally. He's not crazy about the question. "I don't pursue special states of mind," he says. "There's no difference between a state of mind outside or inside the *zendo* that's important. Otherwise, we have a bunch of people who are special when they're in there and ordinary when they come out." To him, a major difference between East and West is that in the former, "the absence of goals is accepted. You continue practice, but you have no goal. We attach a lot of importance to the things we do, but in the large view, they actually don't count for very much. But we might as well keep doing them! Whether it's music or carpentry or whatever, people who pursue something and find meaning in it are happier than those who don't. I'm in bed for seven hours, and the rest of the day is family and *zendo* time. If you don't have any activities, what are you going to do? It's a very practical question."

Over the past several years, Jiro has followed the debate about whether *kensho* is just one of the "peak experiences" of the sort studied by Mihaly Csikszentmihalyi, the respected University of Chicago psychologist who wrote the bestselling *Flow*. These episodes of intense fusion with the business at hand are reported by fly fishermen and runners, surgeons and basketball players, musicians and lovers. As Reinhold Messner, the Himalayan mountaineer, said, "The longer I climb, the less important the goal seems to me, the more indifferent to myself I become." Throughout Zen's history, its masters developed a series of queries to determine whether a special experience was *kensho*, says Jiro. "They tried to establish that the experience had an authority that hadn't diminished in five years. That's my answer to people who want to consider all peak experiences as *kensho*."

From a psychoanalytic view, the images of union with the

divine or the cosmic that are characteristic of vivid spiritual experiences from different religions are re-creations of the baby's blissful contentment at the mother's breast. Jiro recalls that one day soon after he had started to sit, "an image came to me of a photograph of me as a baby with my mother during the war. She was holding me. For no reason, I started crying. I called my sister and told her I felt this great surge of joy and gratitude. She said, 'You better talk to somebody.' I said, 'I don't think so. What's happening to me is really good and healthy.' "

Like other thoughtful people dedicated to one form of religion, Jiro wonders whether the modes of spiritual experience and awareness of the numinous are socially determined. If so, Christians, say, and Buddhists would experience the same phenomena in different clothes, as it were. Christianity's imagery is peculiarly tied to the life of Jesus, but Zen's is so universal—rocks, trees, streams—that Jiro feels it can transcend its Japanese cultural roots.

No matter what the specific content, as far as Jiro is concerned, religious experience has a very practical application. "Every religion is the same in the sense that each provides some release from suffering," he says. "Each person can say, 'If I didn't practice my religion, my life would be different, because I would suffer more.' *Kensho* provides that succor in times of pain, stress, and death. Its validity is determined by whether it holds for all time and gives you that resource."

During my stay, I've decided that I want to make a real commitment to *zazen,* rather than just doing it when I feel like it. As Jesus so neatly put it, "The spirit is willing, but the flesh is weak." Patchy as it has been, my practice has given me a lot, and I want to deepen it. It helps me to function better, and brings me into the shadow of the mountain. Some people here have urged me to return for a *sesshin,* but I doubt that I have what it takes for a week in which the evening sittings alone last from five to ten o'clock. "The best thing, really, is to sit at home," says Jiro. "It's like practicing the piano. Twenty minutes at the same time each day is the key. It will take on an energy of its own, and you just go with it. You can throw the clock away and just have a sense of when to get up."

Giving me some final tips on technique, Jiro says, "When you breathe, tag it at the end of the exhalation. Not one, two, three, but one, one, one. It takes some people six months to get a taste for breathing, and others two minutes. But if you can just get it down, it becomes very sweet. Your whole body reaches an equilibrium. If you lose focus, just go back to the breath. It's not so special per se, but just the simplest thing to be aware of. You're not really thinking, but you're aware. When you get better at it, you can be aware of birdsong or rain."

Would a koan help? I wonder. "It's a mystery to me why koans started," says Jiro. "Supposedly students started asking questions, and teachers gave illogical answers because logic was inadequate. In time, they discovered that this method of talking paradoxically was actually effective. It's a time-tested technique. I've seen it work." Observing that traditional Zen masters "always give you a hard line," he says that D. T. Suzuki's teacher offered him no instruction in sitting or theory, but simply told him to "do *Mu*," which he worked on in a library by himself. "Some people find that kind of thing attractive," says Jiro, "and some don't. The point of a koan is that you can't clarify the mysterious. You have to just get into it!" After spending a lot of time studying a particular collection of koans, Jiro realized that "all this guy is asking me to do is to try. That really is the message. Keep going. Keep trying. The practice gets viewed as a difficult and demanding discipline because you have to set aside time for it. But it doesn't have to be such a heavy thing!"

When Robert Frost was asked why he didn't write in free

verse, he said, "I don't like playing tennis with the net down." This is how Jiro regards practice: The net is one's resistance to *zazen,* and without it, nothing happens. After the astronauts started spending time in space, he says, scientists found out that weightlessness, which eliminates resistance to movement, causes the bones to break down. "We need gravity. That's just the way it works. When we climb a mountain, gravity pulls us down, and it's the same with practice. You have to work, and your muscles will hurt, but that's what makes something else possible. The resistance you've expressed—about it being hard to sit or taking too much time or having other things to do—is a necessary condition for the practice. The dream of transcendence—to be aloft, above it all—is such a delusion. I love to put it down!"

Reminiscing about his own beginner's practice, Jiro says that some people get awfully precious where conditions are concerned, complaining, for instance, about the sound of the wind in the *zendo,* but he has never needed total silence. When he began to sit, he and his wife lived in a small apartment. He did *zazen* in the living room for a half hour while she watched the evening news in the bedroom. After a while, he says, "the semantic content of the news just dropped away. Then, after thirty minutes, Walter Cronkite would say, 'And that's the way it is.' That's one of Eido-roshi's favorite sayings."

My last sitting feels good and goes quickly, no doubt for the unspiritual reason that it's the last. After lunch, I wash my bowls and store them in the kitchen, strip my bed and take the linens to the laundry, and stop by the shop to buy sitting cushions and incense, called "Clouds over Pine." To jump-start daily practice, I've decided to set up, within sight of my computer, a permanent niche for *zazen.* Like working, cooking, or going to the gym, it will become part of my routine.

As I put my things in the car, I realize that despite the generally poor quality of my sittings over the past three days, the heaviness and obsessions that I lugged here have been replaced by a calm exhilaration. Nothing has changed, but everything feels different. When I settle into my seat and slam the door, I set off a small snowstorm that feels like a baptism of sorts. The kind oldest monk pokes out from the furnace room to wave: "Come back soon!"

Before I come back here again, however, I must make a trip back home.

CHAPTER ELEVEN

JUDAISM: TURNING THE TORAH

The essence of Jewish religious thinking does not
lie in entertaining a concept of God but in the
ability to articulate a memory of moments of
illumination by his presence.

—ABRAHAM JOSHUA HESCHEL,
Between God and Man

ONE SATURDAY MORNING, as the last section of the Book of Genesis is read out in synagogues around the world, I hear the Hebrew text in perfect company: Rabbi Burton Visotzky, the scholarly author of *The Genesis of Ethics* and the edgy star of Bill Moyers's television series *Genesis.*[1] We are neighbors, and he has kindly invited me to a Shabbat service at Ansche Chesed, where I've attended a healing service. This Conservative synagogue, like other vibrant millennial institutions, is really a constellation of several *havarot,* or small communities of people who pray with and care for one another. While Rabbi Michael Strassfeld presides over the main service in the big sanctuary downstairs, the Learners' Minyan, a group geared to raw beginners, meets upstairs. Mike, my husband, has begun to attend from time to time, and is reading *The Five Books of Moses,* spectacularly translated by Everett Fox.[2] In another classroom, we join the scholarly Minyan M'at, or "group of the small sanctuary," to which Burt belongs.

Although they overlap, there are three basic styles of being Jewish. One emphasizes observance of religious law, or halakah, as the Orthodox do. The second path accents spirituality, or relationship to God, as Hasidim and, recently, many millennial congregations do. The third mode stresses the intellectual: the study of Judaism's sacred texts. Casting about for a new way in which to reapproach the God of Jews and Christians, I've decided to begin at the beginning, with the Torah.

The more Orthodox the synagogue, the less it seems like a church and the more it feels like a kind of library. In this respect, Burt's minyan resembles a traditional shul. There's nothing ethereal about this hot, crowded room or our metal folding chairs—or even about the portable ark and plywood table covered with a velvet cloth. The atmosphere is respectful, but not especially subdued. The two-hour service, conducted in Hebrew, began at ten in the morning. I was surprised when Burt said we should arrive at ten-thirty, but people trickle in well after that until all seats are taken.

Nodding and greeting, Burt, who is a professor at the nearby Jewish Theological Seminary, points out numerous distinguished academics and rabbis, including the woman presiding over the service. Although Ansche Chesed is in many ways very traditional, it differs sharply from Orthodox Judaism regarding women's equality. When the big Torah scroll is unfurled, several pairs of learned eyes search vainly for the correct place to begin the day's reading. Finally, yet another rabbi emerges from the congregation and, to much acclaim, instantly sets his finger on the right spot. The man's father was a cantor, says Burt, who immersed his son in the Hebrew text when he was practically in the cradle. At Minyan M'at, *this* is status.

Glorying in his element, Burt says, "You won't find a congregation with such knowledge of Judaism anywhere west of Jerusalem!" Community is clearly important, too. The middle-aged old-timers have buried one another's parents and attended all their children's bar and bat mitzvahs. But, says Burt, "different congregations have different needs. At a service at BJ, they give the edge to prayer. Here, we give it to study. At least half of these people hear the Torah reading as if it were in English. That and the comment"—the Jewish equivalent of a sermon—"are the high points."

After the Romans destroyed the Second Temple in 70 C.E., Judaism changed from a religion in which priests offered blood sacrifices to one in which teachers direct study. Because culture changes over time, and even the Torah is the product of a certain civilization, scholars must uncover the meanings in the text and make them clear and relevant to each generation of readers. Their commentaries, called midrash, are so integral to the Bible that they're considered part of Torah; neither is complete or makes sense without the other. In Genesis, for example, there are two versions of the creation story; assuming there's a reason, "the rabbis"—an august body of scholars whose midrash has been written down and collected since the mid second century C.E.—have come up with explanations of why the story is first one way, then another. Comparing midrash to snapshots, Burt says, "the more you have, the better your overall picture of the Torah." Not surprisingly, scholars struggle to add to this vast composition, or "get on the page," by having their midrash published and read by a wide community. Just as American midrashists had to fight for their European predecessors' acceptance, now women are vying for recognition in this hitherto male world.

By using the midrash process, all readers, not just experts like Burt, can grapple with the text given by God and find new meaning for themselves. Great respect is given to legendary rabbis such as Rashi, who, in eleventh-century France, interpreted every line in the Torah and Talmud. Judaism's way of wrestling with revelation, however, rules out a single, sanctioned interpretation of a text, much less the equivalent of a catechism or creed (although acceptance of the unity of God, the unique situation of the Jewish people in history, and observance of halakah figure in most definitions of Judaism). Regarding belief, says Burt, "Jews really are different. Belief is nice, but for us, how you behave—your mitzvoth, or good deeds—is far more important." One of the best deeds is to pore over Torah. "That's what Jews do," he says. "We study."

A muscular worshiper, Burt recites and sings Hebrew in a strong voice from memory, acknowledges friends, monitors my prayer book, checks on his family, supplies arcana. After reading along in the Torah for a while, I ask him whether we're studying or praying. According to the rabbis, says Burt, prayer happens in the morning. Later in the day, the same activity becomes study. On record as describing Genesis as "an ugly little soap opera about a dysfunctional family," he sighs over today's passage, in which Jacob inexplicably gives the firstborn's blessing not to Manasseh, his oldest adopted son, but to Ephraim: "Some things never change!" He shakes his head, too, over the quality of the midrash that accompany the readings: "The text is the text, but this commentary!"

When it's time for today's spoken comment on the Torah portion, which happily for me is delivered in English, a woman congregant comes forward. Ansche Chesed's do-it-yourself Judaism doesn't rely on rabbis. Her focus is the gloomy scene in which the dying Jacob "blesses" his sons, who are the leaders of Israel's twelve tribes. My reaction to the reading is, with blessings like these, who needs insults? To his father, Benjamin is a "ravening wolf," Dan a "viper on the path," Reuben "uncontrolled as a flood," Simeon and Levi "accursed" for their ruthless rage. The speaker, however, sees a light at the end of this tunnel of a text. A parent's honest assessment of a child can indeed be a gift if given and received in the right spirit and at the right time, she says. Unlike Jacob, however, we shouldn't wait for a deathbed to speak or hear such blessings. This insight gets Burt's nod of approval. In the old days, he whispers, "before we all had kids," Minyan M'at's members, afire with youthful zeal, sometimes exchanged comments on the Torah portion for an hour.

In keeping with the elegiac tone of today's readings, the service finishes with the story of the death of King David, including his beautiful blessing to Solomon, his son and successor: "I am going the way of all the earth. Be strong and show yourself a man." At the cathedral, after the Sunday liturgy, we have coffee and cookies. At Minyan M'at, there's a small feast, including wine and even a frosty bottle of vodka. Whether studying or partying, says Burt, "we don't fool around."

Contenting myself with a piece of rugalach, I ask Burt what he thinks is the best way for a neoagnostic to approach religion. He points out that although Tertullian said, "I believe because it's absurd," that doesn't work for many people today. "Temporarily suspending the intellect means leaving something very important at the door," he says. "The other approach is to brace yourself for a battle. Going to the synagogue or the church may not be the warm, cuddly, comfort food you thought it would be. It may be the battle of your life, but emotionally and intellectually, it could also be the most exhilarating one you've ever engaged in. Whether you experience God's reality or are just intellectually intrigued by the idea, God can be a very powerful force in people's lives—

spiritual, emotional, supportive—that almost no other system can offer. But you must gird yourself for a fight and know that you're going to have to try to reconcile very difficult things. Or at least hold them in suspension and bounce them back and forth and get tired. There's no quick fix, but we have the benefit of drawing on thousands of years of religious thinking. You can't learn it over a weekend. It's an engagement for the rest of your life."

One morning, Burt generously offers to be my *hevruta* for an hour. Opening my King James Bible to Exodus 3: 1–6, which tells the story of Moses and the burning bush, I read the first sentence aloud: "Now Moses kept the flock of Jethro, his father-in-law, the priest of Midian." When Burt asks if I detect any funny business so far, I have to admit that I don't. But as I know, he says, pointing to Exodus 2:18, Moses' father-in-law is called Reuel, not Jethro. So which is it? The rabbis' answer: There are "ten names" for Jethro, all of which are wordplays on his biblical function, which boils down to "acceptance." After one line, I see that Torah study isn't just atomistic—breaking down every word and phrase—but also holistic. "Harmonizing the problems is part of the process," says Burt. "It's all about reinforcing Torah."

When Burt asks if anything *else* about the line bothers me, I look hard at the remaining three words, but sadly remain untroubled. "Priest of Midian" seems pretty straightforward to me, but not to my *hevruta*. I had assumed Midian was a place, and Jethro the local Jewish clergyman. At that point in history, however, the lines between the Jews and other peoples of the region were still very fuzzy. Midian might even have had its own local god, says Burt, so that Jethro might have been a pagan priest. Moving on to the next sentence, I read: "He led his flock to the backside of the desert and came to the mountain of God, even to Horeb." When I smile at "backside," Burt says the English term is a very good approximation of the earthy Hebrew. "And what else?" he asks. With a little prompting, I recollect that "the mountain of God" is later called Sinai. Thus unbeknownst to him, Moses is about to meet God in the same place where he'll eventually receive the Ten Commandments.

Getting to the text's juicy part, I read, "And the angel of the Lord appeared unto him in a flame of fire out of the midst of a bush: and he looked, and, behold, the bush burned with fire, and the bush was not consumed." Afraid, Moses turns away from this weird sight. Then, "God called unto him out of the midst of the bush." What's fishy here, I say, is that first it's an angel in the bush, then it's God. What's going on? To the rabbis, says Burt, an angel, which means "messenger," is not another order of being, but a manifestation of God. The angel who wrestles with Jacob looks like a man, but usually they appear as fire. "A miracle is not God," says Burt, "but that which calls your attention to God, as pyrotechnics do. You have to stop, look—pay attention—before you hear God's voice. Otherwise, you miss the miracle." I smile, remembering the Zen monk at Dai Bosatsu who, writing of *kensho,* recalled Eido-roshi's advice: "Keep your eyes open, or you will miss it!"

Whenever I pass the famed Jewish Theological Seminary, where Burt teaches, I read the phrase carved above its gates: "And the bush was not consumed." When I ask why these words were chosen, Burt says, "I can only see that with post-Holocaust eyes. After all those fires, we're still here."

Going back to our text, we read that next God gives Moses some good news—his people are headed for the land of milk and honey—and bad news—it's currently occupied by others. Then, in Exodus 14, the pair engages in an intriguing wrangle over the divine identity. To get to the heart of it, we shift from my Bible to three photocopied Torah pages, in Hebrew, that Burt has brought. In the upper right corner of the first are five words spoken by God, which are usually translated as "I am who I am." This biblical text is accompanied by three Targums, or translations of it: a formal Aramaic one from the second century C.E. and two more creative ones from the eighth or ninth century. The third element on this particular Torah page is midrash. These commentaries take up most of our three sheets; the eight Burt has marked come from Babylonia (now Iraq) and Palestine, Africa, and Europe, and from antiquity to the fifteenth century. I don't read Hebrew, but even the look of the page bespeaks the history behind it, while it also, as Burt says, "blurs time."

For me, "I am who I am" evokes Shakespeare: "What's in a name?" asks Juliet, in *Romeo and Juliet*. "That which we call a rose / By any other name would smell as sweet." For Moses, things are not so simple. In his day, and within Judaism still, says Burt, "to name something is to acquire power." By this reasoning, the true name of God—by definition, the most powerful thing—is simply too hot to handle. It can neither be written nor spoken, although it is sometimes alluded to by the letters YHWH. (In fact, says Burt, the translation of our text that reads "I am who I am" is a bit of wordplay on those four letters.) It's not surprising, then, that Moses is too scared to come right out and ask God, "Just who are you, anyway?" Instead, he beats around the bush, so to speak. It's not that *he's* curious, he tells God, but when he tries to explain his divinely ordained mission to the other Jews, *they'll* want to know exactly who sent him—by name. Hardly one to be upstaged, God responds in kind to Moses' "coyness," says Burt, telling him to say to the people, "I AM hath sent me unto you."

A prosaic modern reading of our text, says Burt, would be something along the lines of "I am who I am so shut up already! Mind your own business!" On a more poetic level, it speaks to Burt of "presence," so that it means "I am who I am right now and right here." A piece of midrash from a fifth-century Palestinian adds a Romantic note: "I will be with whom I choose to be with." Another from the same time and place suggests, "I will be with you in the future, even when you're enslaved." In the end, however, God remains mysterious. In different anthropomorphic passages of the Torah, God is described as having hands, fingers, nose, mouth, face, even a behind, as well as human feelings. Yet, asked Maimonides, what do these emotions or still less these body parts have to do with that which by definition is Wholly Other? The best plan, says Burt, is to "stand humbly before the unknowable God."

That said, it's not just informative and uplifting but also enormous fun to consider the different midrashists' reflections on the sacred personality. A Babylonian writer of the sixth century points out that God tells the cheeky Moses that Abraham, Isaac, and Jacob never asked for the holy name, but Moses makes like a detective at their first meeting—and before lifting a finger to fulfill the divine mandate! Doesn't he know that Judaism is more about getting the job done than about theology? Maybe because they're Western and among the "newest" of our midrashim, dating from twelfth-century Europe, "I was, am, and will be" and "I am described by my deeds" feel most familiar to me. The subtlest, prettiest interpretation, in my opinion, was written in North Africa in the tenth century: "My name is I am what I am. Just as you are with me, I will be with you." Does this mean, "I'll hang out with you, just as you do with me," I wonder aloud, or "I'll treat you as you treat me?" Burt smiles and says, "Ambiguity is the way that divinity identifies itself."

This is the kind of theology I like. In this golden age of English translations and newly accessible scholarship, says Burt, "even a modern doubter, a cynic, can still get a lot out of the Bible." Educated readers can employ academe's critical tools: historical and literary criticism, deconstruction and semiotics. Yet part of the pleasure of Jewish thought is that it's not only intellectually rigorous but *different*. As Burt says, "Talmudic thinking is Middle Eastern, not European." In classical Western reasoning, for example, one works from the general principle to the particular: All men are mortal; Socrates is a man; Socrates is mortal. Talmudic thinking, however, proceeds from the minor to the major: It's forbidden to write on Shabbat; how much *more* forbidden is it to write on Yom Kippur, a far holier day? In this tradition, it's also permissible to "argue from silence," or from what the text *doesn't* say. "Suppose I go to a wedding, and later tell you the groom was happy and the bride beautiful," says Burt. "You would conclude that it was a happy occasion. But in Talmudic thinking, that same description could mean that the groom looked like a gorilla and the bride was crying her eyes out."

When I ask Burt if his scholarship ever gets in the way of his belief as a Jew, he smiles. "If a page says, 'Rabbi X said that . . .' my first thought is Did he *really* say that? How do we know? What was the background at the time when he lived?" However, after a ritual protest—"Would that I could achieve the innocence of a reader unschooled in these things!"—Burt allows that the modern critic's questions, too, can add a layer of spiritual nuance. When I assert that God has nothing to fear from the workings of my mind, he says, "I'm with you on that. I can read Torah as critically as I can, but it's not going to suffer for that. One of God's gifts to us is intellect, so it behooves us to bring all of our critical acumen to our reading of sacred texts."

No longer the exclusive province of synagogues and yeshivas, the midrashic attitude toward text and the custom of working with a *hevruta* have spread beyond universities to churches. Just about every small group I've attended, no matter what the denomination, has incorporated these techniques, which I find invaluable. As Burt says, reading and thinking on one's own promotes individualism and soul-searching, "but the rabbis thought it was important to study with a partner, not only because it keeps you honest, but because it builds community."

Like millennial Christians, Jews look for fresh things to add to, or reemphasize in, their ancient tradition. After lecturing at perhaps a hundred Conservative congregations, Burt says, "it hasn't escaped me that some Jews are awfully thirsty spiritually." In the old days, he says, meaning the fifties, involvement in a synagogue meant politics; now, it's about looking for meaning, learning Hebrew, and studying classical Jewish texts, almost all of which are available in English today. In his travels, Burt has noticed another significant change: "Jews are unbelievably hungry for talk about God."

Just as many Christians are becoming less interested in theology—at least the formal conceptual and systematic sorts they've been bogged down in since the Enlightenment— many Jews are becoming more so. Within Judaism the search for greater spirituality means more emphasis on personal relationship with God, which in turn encourages God talk in a religion whose language didn't have a word for "theology." If one does the mitzvoth and observes the law, said the rabbis, one will feel God's presence. There's no need to try to figure out who God is, which is impossible anyway. God is simply part of daily life. In the Middle Ages, the great Jewish philosopher Maimonides was almost excommunicated for probing the mystery of God, the nature of good and evil, and such recondite matters. The rabbis' position was that theology and philosophy were for those who didn't have Torah. In a religion that long regarded talking about God as nearly blasphemous, the new ways of doing so preserve a lot of mystery, and change according to person and circumstances. Yet extremely rationalistic interpretations that were popular not long ago, such as defining the divine as the community, certainly no longer prevail in millennial congregations such as B'nai Jeshurun and Ansche Chesed.

One Wednesday night I join some forty people in B'nai Jeshurun's basement meeting room for a class called Prayers and Prophets. Long-haired Roly Matalon, a Conservative rabbi à la J. Crew, adjusts his yarmulke and the zipper on his hip black cardigan, takes a seat in the horseshoe of chairs, and begins talking about God. Starting with the evening prayer, Roly points out the repetition of the word "love"—particularly the all-embracing divine sort. "The master of creation, time, the seasons—of all of that—is also the God of loving," he says. "The idea that in Judaism, God is concerned only with the law and not with love is anti-Semitic. God loves humanity, particularly his people Israel. When God chose Abraham, there were no laws. First came the falling in love, then the law, which is the substantiation of the covenant, which is based on love."

Developing the theme of God's love and mercy as inextricably bound up with divine law and justice, Roly says, "Here, right in this prayer, we read that first, God loves. But immediately, God also commands, requires. The Orthodox read the law and just do it. Here at BJ, we don't see God as commanding all the details—whether you can eat monkfish or not. But to be a Jewish community, we must share certain standards. What should we require to see ourselves in covenant with God? Prayer? Social service? Membership dues? In the Jewish view, you have to go that next step."

Considering the pat assumption, particularly among neo-agnostics, that "all religions are the same," talking about the divine, even within the so-called Judeo-Christian tradition, can be a tonic experience. During a question break, I get a sense of how Christian theology sounds to Jewish ears. Raising her hand, a woman asks, "Why don't we Jews talk much about 'God loves you,' like the Christians do?" Quoting St. John the Divine, another agrees, saying " 'God is Love'— that's what *they* say." In Judaism, says Roly, "too much of that talk is like Sweet'n Low. It's superficial and belies the responsibilities on both sides that go with the covenant."

Without patronizing, Roly slips in much information of the Judaism 101 sort for those present who didn't learn it with their mothers' lullabies: Judaism is about a relationship with God, not just about dietary details. For the more knowledgeable, he digresses from time to time, extemporizing on, say, the Jewish attitude toward time. For legal reasons, the precise scheduling of certain things, such as weddings and divorces, is important, he says. "But in Judaism, there's no eleven fifty-nine P.M., and then one minute later, it's the next day. No. Night and day are not so simple. The law tries to bring sharpness, justice, sternness, to it, but most of the time, life is not like that. Instead, it's filled with gray areas and transitions."

Moving from prayer to prophet, Roly sounds the theme so dear to millennial clergy's hearts: relationship. First, he reads a passage from Amos that says Israel is about to be destroyed forever, then follows with another in which Israel is rebuilt. The Bible in general, says Roly, and prophecy in particular are full of such apparent contradictions. Rather than regarding them as flaws, we should see them as the kind of alternating closeness and distance that characterize all real relationships, including God's with humanity. The role of the prophet, in fact, is to be an "official experiencer of the tension between God and the people," says Roly. "Thus, Moses pled for Israel before God, and for God before the people." Instantly, a woman says, "So how did he live to be a hundred and twenty?"

After the laughter dies down, Roly says, "People aren't logical all the time, and neither is prophecy. We sometimes act as if consistency were the highest value, but it's not. Hitler was consistent. Jonah wanted God to be consistent—a Nazi—and destroy the city he had threatened. What *is* consistent in prophecy is the God it's about. His law and love, justice and mercy—the world is regulated by these two forces in tension. On Yom Kippur, we're frightened because of God's justice, but by the end of the day, we say, 'Pity us and save us. We have nothing that balances our evil deeds. Just be merciful.' Our safety net is God's mercy."

Although I don't like the Enlightenment-driven, rationalist God-as-perfection-machine Christian model, I find the more idiosyncratic sacred personality that Roly alludes to somewhat alarming. Voicing the question hanging almost palpably in the air, Roly says, "Where was this safety net in the exile? The Holocaust? The rabbinic mind says that we can't blame God, but rather our sins. But in some midrash, there are hints of something else. Of 'We don't accept this, you're not nice, we don't understand.' God is not the distant unmoved mover, but intensely involved with us. What we do *matters* to him."

One day, I walk up Broadway to the fortresslike Jewish Theological Seminary to ask Burt Visotzky about God talk. In professorial plaid shirt and khakis, he meets me at the huge black iron gates and leads the way, through odd doors and serpentine hallways hung with old paintings of bearded rabbis, to a small, cozy office. This seminary was the home of the legendary Abraham Joshua Heschel, who changed American Judaism by reinfusing its intellectual content with the intense spirituality of the Hasidism into which he was born. No ivory tower ascetic, he insisted that religion belonged in the world. Heschel helped guide the Catholic Church toward its official reconciliation with Judaism, marched in Selma with Martin Luther King, and protested the Vietnam War.

The room we sit in is lined floor to ceiling with Hebrew, Aramaic, Greek, Syriac, Latin, French, German, Yiddish, and English texts. When I express wonder at such learning, Burt says it's nothing compared with that of some of his peers, and particularly his teachers of yore: rabbis who, in their eighties, studied from seven-thirty in the morning until ten at night and knew the whole Torah and Talmud by heart. As we talk about scholarship, Burt says proudly that in this regard, and others, America's Jewish community surpasses any Jewish group "since our heyday in Babylonia. What will we do with that? In the fifties, we defined ourselves between the poles of the Holocaust and Israel—victimization versus might. But neither of those involved U.S. soil, so they can't function as the be-all and end-all of our consciousness. In the nineties, we're groping toward a new definition of what it means to be a Jew in America." That definition seems to include increased spirituality.

Another missionary to neoagnostics, Burt helps the spiritually starved, Christians as well as Jews, to find what they're looking for by addicting perennial-grad-student wannabes like me to the pleasures of study, delighting their minds and then their hearts. "Most people don't get paid to think all day, as I'm privileged to do," he says. "They just eat up the opportunity to re-create that heady experience they had in college, when they could talk about ideas." Over years of doing this work ("a little bit study, a little bit group therapy, a little bit congregational"), Burt has learned that "if given a no-risk environment—the risk being that they'll make fools of themselves by admitting to peers that they're interested in God—people will take the jump. There's a lot more God talk in Jewish circles today than there was twenty, or even a hundred, years ago."

Burt's own millennial perspective shows when I ask him if strict observance alone—an intensely Jewish life-style, from modest dress to Shabbat rest to kosher kitchen—can bring one to know God. "Would that that were true!" he says. "In some circles, that's the sine qua non of Judaism. But I think one can be a very good Jew without being observant in the traditional sense, or be very observant and miss the whole point—know nothing about God, social justice, kindness. You can be observant, in other words, and not be a mensch. Observance is nice and puts you inside a group and identifies you with that, but by itself, it's insufficient. You can see all the details and miss the big picture."

In Burt's big picture of Judaism, religion is "a constant struggle to learn. The study of Torah is the one commandment that has no parameters. We're obligated to do it all the time, as long as we live. We read Torah each year. The words are the same, but we've changed, so the text has whole new layers of meaning. The rabbis say, 'Turn it and turn it, all things are in it.' I used to think they meant that if one looked at the jewel of Torah from enough angles, one would finally understand it. Now, I think they meant that if you just keep turning and turning, the text will always serve you."

In sharing his approach to his own religion. Burt has given me keys to several more bolts on the door to mine. In contrast to the neoagnostic's open-ended I-can-be-anything-I-wanna-be attitude, his embrace of Judaism as integral to his own identity is bracing. But accepting that the faith—or faithlessness—of one's fathers is part of who one is, and that one is destined to wrestle with it, is also scary.

A just-believe-it Christianity simply doesn't work for me. But perhaps, by adopting a midrashic attitude toward Scripture and the process-oriented *hevruta* method of finding meaning, I can find a new way of understanding the central figure of my own ancient tradition—and my life.

While hardly regarding the New Testament as a literal biography of Jesus that has been fact-checked by God himself, I haven't read it "Jewishly," as revelation that requires midrash. I know little about the context in which it was written, or for that matter, that of its main character. Much of its verily-I-say-unto-thee speech didn't speak to me. But perhaps, I think, if I turn it and turn it, I'll find something in it that I hadn't found before.

CHAPTER TWELVE

CHRISTIANITY: WHAT IF GOD WAS ONE OF US?

WHITE-WATER RAFTING doesn't sound like something one would do in the Holy Land, but I spent an adrenaline-soaked hour shooting down the roiling green-and-white headwaters of the Jordan. A grade-four wild river studded with boulders, stalked by tall herons, and nearly canopied in places by fragrant, whiplike willows, it resembled the roaring streams of the American West more than the desultory desert dribble I had anticipated. Just as one can't visit Yellowstone without imagining the Indians who once roamed it, one can't travel in the rugged rural Galilee without summoning up characters from the New Testament. Certainly rocketing over the Jordan's rapids with the handsome, tough young Israeli guides changed my idea of biblical farmers and fishermen. In the dense reeds of the riverbanks I could almost see John, who dressed in skins, lived on locusts and honey, and baptized people in these rushing waters.

One of them was his peculiar cousin Jesus, who emerged from the Jordan to spend forty days in the desert. Following this equivalent of a Native American vision quest, for a period lasting between nine months and three years, he walked about the Galilee. He talked with and taught people, becoming the first person to be recorded in Scripture as a "rabbi." He spent a lot of time eating and drinking with his friends, including rascals and loose women, and healing the sick. A Jew, he wasn't terribly interested in theology. He addressed the awesome God of Abraham and Moses as "Dad," and told people to relax, because "it is your Father's good pleasure to give you the kingdom." He questioned the political and religious status quo, particularly concerning who's "in" and who's "out." To paraphrase the bumper sticker, Jesus practiced random acts of kindness and advised others to do the same—not only for friends, but foes.

"Love your enemies, do good to those who hate you, bless those who curse you, pray for those who abuse you. If anyone strikes you on the cheek, offer the other also; and from anyone who takes away your coat do not withhold even your shirt. . . . If you love those who love you, what credit is that to you? . . . But love your enemies, do good, and lend expecting nothing in return. Your reward will be great, and you will be children of the Most High; for he is kind to the ungrateful and the wicked. Be merciful, just as your Father is merciful" (Luke 6:27–36).

A few days before in Jerusalem, I visited Jesus' so-called garden tomb just outside the Old City's walls. This pretty place is merely a proposed alternative to the site inside the walls, now paved over by a huge church, that has traditionally been honored as his burial place. Although no one really knows exactly where Jesus was crucified and temporarily laid to rest, the Gospels' simple Easter-morning picture is more easily imagined here than in the dark, teeming official shrine. Jesus was crucified at a spot called Golgotha, or the "place of the skulls," and part of the argument for the garden tombsite is a sinister-looking adjacent cliff. Under its skeletal rock sprawls an ugly parking lot and bus terminal—a blasted wasteland that testifies to what the Chinese call bad *feng shui*. Inside the garden is a small, seamless cave carved out of the rock, just as the Gospels describe. Entering the tomb alone on a quiet afternoon, I got the chills as I looked at the smooth ledge cut into one wall to cradle a dead body and wondered about that morning so long ago that changed the world.

After our long, unhappy history, I can hardly claim that Jesus is a stranger. I have become intrigued with that idea, however, as a result of one of postmodern America's most surprising cultural phenomena. Since 1980, university-trained biblical scholars have transformed the exegesis, or literary deconstruction, of the compact New Testament's twenty-seven short books into something approaching a craze. Some are members of the much-publicized Jesus Seminar, a group that tries to figure out what Jesus did and didn't say and do. Once guaranteed lives of near obscurity, several of these interpreters have even become impresarios. Hooked on the new scholarship's addictive combination of literature and history, detective work and religion, a huge readership clamors for the latest "historical Jesus."

Much of this popular enthusiasm for New Testament scholarship can be traced to the democratizing influence of computers and the Internet. Anyone with access to a PC can compare Greek and Aramaic terms, simultaneously view three or four different translations of a line from Mark or Luke, or exchange ideas with others on one of many religious-studies websites. Some people just want a better understanding of arguably history's most influential figure, who has long been obscured by religiosity. Even many of the devout, however, share the millennial insistence that faith jibe with reality, whether it comes from physics or papyrus fragments, and are stimulated by wrestling with a text's ambiguity and contradictions.

Although he was from a humble background, quite a bit is known about Jesus. Compared with the information about another legendary person from antiquity, Alexander the Great, the biographical resources on Jesus, particularly concerning what he thought, are better.[1] Most scholars agree that he was born in the Roman province of Palestine about 4 B.C.E. and spent most of his life in rural Galilee. His hometown, Nazareth, was only five miles from the Hellenized city of Sepphoris; there he must have seen something of the bright lights of Empire, although his worldview remained resolutely Hebraic. Like John, Jesus belonged to the long tradition of reforming Jewish prophets. Typically delivered in parables—stories—his teaching centered on a God of tender mercies and an enigmatic "kingdom," very different from his world or ours.

Around 30 C.E., after a short public ministry during a time of simmering political tension between the Jews and Rome, Jesus and his followers went to Jerusalem to celebrate Passover. After creating a public disturbance there, suggested by the Gospel story in which Jesus drove the money-changers from the Temple, he was arrested on the order of Caiaphas, the Jewish high priest, who was responsible to Rome for maintaining order among his people. Caiaphas sent Jesus to Pontius Pilate, the local Roman authority, who sentenced him to crucifixion. After his death, many claimed to have seen Jesus. His early followers, who were noted for their mutual solicitude and good cheer, rapidly spread throughout the Mediterranean world. Calling Jesus various enigmatic names, from Lord to Lamb of God, they considered him holy, but not necessarily divine. For some time they remained a movement within Judaism.

As I learn more about Jesus and the first-century Hebrew and Roman world, I begin to develop an admiration for him that doesn't require a lot of supernatural bells and whistles. Understanding the historical Jesus means understanding that he was, first of all, as the title of one notable biography puts it, "a marginal Jew."[2] When he told his listeners that his Father, who knew of every sparrow's fall, also numbered the hairs on their heads, he was paraphrasing the prophets. To devise Christianity's Great Commandment to love God and to love one's neighbor as one's self, he simply joined up pieces of Deuteronomy and Leviticus. Jesus didn't overturn, but rather extended, his people's tradition, which was unique in antiquity.

Their neighbors had many deities, but the Jews worshiped one. God was not only holy, but just and merciful, and expected them to be so, too. Because every event and life was part of the unfolding of God's grand design, for the Jews, time wasn't primarily cyclical, but historical. Eschewing an Asian philosophical resignation, they regarded life's good times as the result of their virtuous behavior and God's benevolence, and hard times as God's judgment or trial. Rather than questioning Judaism's core—its God, its sense of everyday sacredness, its historical nature, its passion for justice—somewhat like millennial Americans, Jesus seems to have regarded it as a toolbox, or resource. Concentrating on the spirit rather than the letter of Jewish law, Jesus stressed the elements, such as God's loving-kindness, and sensitivity to the poor and oppressed, that complemented his own temperament and philosophy. Writers know that the best way to present a subject is through a "profile" of a person who illuminates it. To me, profiles of Jesus explicate a Jewish theological and moral vision made so broad, welcoming, and accessible that any human being so inclined can engage with it.

Although no one, including Jesus, seems to have considered him divine during his life and for some time afterward, he was perceived as one of those people in all cultures, from Crazy Horse to the Lubavitcher Rebbe, who are close to the sacred. Some decades before Jesus, a Jew known as Honi the Circle Drawer was famed for the efficacy of his prayers for rain. Once, Honi stepped inside the circle he had drawn in the dust, and informed God, "I will not stir hence until you have pity on your children." When his demand brought a mere sprinkle, Honi complained: "Not for such rain have I prayed, but for rain of good will, blessing, and graciousness." It poured until the people had to seek higher ground. Jews don't speak casually or familiarly about God, and a religious official declared, "Were you not Honi I would have pronounced a ban against you! But what shall I do to you—you importune God and he performs your will, like a son who importunes his father and he performs his will." Like Honi, Jesus was close to God, popular with the folk, and vexing to the authorities.[3]

To his listeners, Jesus sounded more like a prophet than an ethicist. The figure I encountered in youth was first and foremost a moralist. However, scholars see little new in Jesus' teachings concerning personal do's and don'ts of the sort outlined in the Ten Commandments. To E. P. Sanders, a New Testament scholar and authority on Judaism in the first century C.E., "prophet" is the simplest way to define this person, who felt fated to prepare people for the coming of God's kingdom. What makes him unique among prophets is his air of authority: "Jesus didn't say, 'Study with me,'" says Sanders, "but 'Follow me.'" His stunning confidence that he spoke for his Father inclines Sanders to describe him as "God's viceroy—the king's representative. He was a person recognized to be very intimate with God."4

If Jesus sounded like a prophet, he was busy as a healer—particularly an exorcist. This sounds exotic to us, but healers were a dime a dozen in the ancient world, where mysterious cures weren't necessarily considered miracles, much less signs of divinity. Judging by his close followers' blasé reactions, Jesus' weren't seen as such. Some of his healings resonate with modern research that shows that most visits to the doctor are prompted by psychosomatic problems. After curing one woman, he told her, "Your faith has made you well."

Prophet and healer, Jesus was also a rabbi—Hebrew not for "priest," but for "master teacher." His first great lesson concerned a new interpretation of the divine personality. Instead of talking about the Creator who banished Adam and Eve from Paradise, he talked about the joyful father of the returning bad boy. Instead of evoking the awesome cloud over Sinai that disclosed the law, he spoke of a good shepherd who would search zealously for a lone lost sheep. Because they were in such good hands, he said, people should be compassionate and slow to judge, like God who "maketh his sun to rise on the evil and the good, and sendeth rain on the just and on the unjust." The Sermon on the Mount, with its odd assurance to the poor in spirit, mourners, and the persecuted that they are "blessed," even "happy," is classic Jesus: Address their pain, but make people think, too.

If such ideas sound strange today, so they did to many of Jesus' first listeners, who asked, "Is this not the carpenter's son?" Early on, his embarrassed family tried to restrain him, fearing that he was, as Scripture says, "beside himself," or even "out of his mind." In eulogizing Gentleman Jimmy Walker, one of New York City's most charismatic mayors, Toots Shor, the legendary restaurateur and man-about-town, said, "Jimmy, Jimmy! Wherever you walked in, you livened up the place." So it was with Jesus. One day, when he was teaching in a crowded building in Capernaum, two friends of a paralyzed man cut a hole in the roof and lowered down the cripple's stretcher in front of Jesus. Moved, he said to the man, "My son, your sins are forgiven." This zany response, as apparently irrelevant as it was blasphemous, understandably occasioned some grumbling. Jesus' answer: "Which is easier—to say to the paralytic, 'Your sins are forgiven,' or to say 'Get up, pick up your stretcher and walk?' " Only then did he so instruct the man, who rose and complied.

Christianity is Western, but Jesus and his Judaism were not. There's much in his teaching that resonates with that of Asian spiritual masters. Like Buddha, Jesus acknowledged that suffering was part of life, and that the way to avoid being crushed by it was to remember what's important and what's not. For Buddha, this meant relinquishing desire for and attachment to the ephemeral. For Jesus, it meant remembering that because a loving God is in charge of reality, somehow or other, everything will be all right. As he said to his friend Martha, the stressed-out homemaker: "You are worried and distracted by many things; there is need of only one thing." As if speaking for Buddha, Jesus said, "Do not worry about tomorrow. Tomorrow will take care of itself." Both Eastern masters taught that people who had attained the wisdom that relieved their own suffering should in gratitude ameliorate others'. "Be merciful," said Jesus, "even as your heavenly Father is merciful." If Jesus' first great teaching was his emphasis on the infinite loving-kindness and mercy of God, his second concerned an attitude of all-embracing inclusiveness and compassion toward others. To get people to think about this radical idea, he continually raised questions about the status quo: economic, social, political, religious.

One day I gather my courage and ask Rabbi Burton Visotzky how he sees Jesus. I may be flustered, but Burt, who often works with Christian biblical scholars and knows all the pertinent texts, is not. (It's an endearing feature of many religious people to want those of other faiths to be "orthodox," and several times, Burt nudges me away from the wilder shores of New Testament scholarship toward a "traditional, solid, Vatican II thinker.") "Jesus was a great rabbi of the first century," he says. Some of what he taught was pure Judaism; some was stricter, such as his prohibition of divorce; and some was more liberal. " 'Not that which goes into the mouth defiles a man, but that which comes out of the mouth' is a profound piece of Torah," says Burt. "In the Judaism of Jesus' era, however, such a statement would have been worrisome, as were his failures to observe Shabbat."

Some of the liveliest debates in New Testament scholarship concern the degree to which Jesus observed, bent, and broke the principles of Jewish religious law. In ordering the Jews to "be holy, as I am holy," and giving them halakah to spell out the particulars, God imbued every aspect of life with meaning and morality. They were to behave ethically, particularly regarding justice, to the point of according what we call human rights to paupers and even treating slaves decently— amazing ideas in the ancient world. They were not only to worship in certain prescribed ways and observe the Sabbath, but to observe a code of "purity" in matters of daily life, such as eating, washing, burying the dead, and physically relating to others.

Although the concept of purity has been common in other times and places—and is still symbolized by ceremonial use of water and incense—it is difficult for modern Westerners to comprehend. Being "unclean" meant something close to "untouchable," rather than "evil." Everyone was in this state from time to time—women after childbirth, men after intercourse, anyone who had touched a corpse—which required ritual purification. (When I was a child, Catholic women were "churched," or blessed by a priest, when they resumed attending services after a confinement.) Those who observed the laws of ritual purity, many of which concerned food, were "the righteous," and those who didn't were "sinners"—a group often mentioned in the Gospels. Like those born into India's lowest caste, however, some people were innately impure: not only Gentiles, but, say, lepers with sores. Because for various reasons it was harder for them to maintain ritual purity, some scholars argue, impurity was also associated with women and the poor, as well as with the chronically ill and maimed.[5] Politically, the purity system helped to maintain a society of many distinctions.

As a child, I secretly couldn't see why everyone made such a fuss over Jesus' behavior, which boiled down to egalitarianism and kindness. There were plenty of Americans who believed that all men were created equal and who were good to the poor and the sick. As I learned more about its historical context, however, I began to see why Jesus' radical inclusiveness, epitomized by his dining with impure "sinners," created a ruckus. Jesus sometimes observed the purity code by which his society was structured. But his willingness to break it and thus compromise his own religious status, often for others' sakes, must be regarded as either scandalous or revolutionary.

Perhaps because I'm a woman, my favorite Jesus-the-iconoclast story concerns a humble female complaint. In Mark's Gospel, after long, painful, useless medical treatments, a woman who had been bleeding for twelve years crept up behind Jesus and, reaching through the crowd, managed to touch his cloak. Immediately, she was healed. "Aware that power had gone out from him," Jesus turned around and asked who had brushed his clothing. The woman was frightened; as a bleeding female, she was ritually impure. For a Jewish man, her touch meant defilement, which could be cleansed only by ceremonial purification. For that matter, her gender alone ruled out contact with men outside her immediate family. However, when the woman came forward, instead of scolding her, Jesus addressed her as "daughter," saying "Go in peace and be free from your complaint." In another challenge to the status quo, Jesus came to the rescue of a woman who, as the law then allowed, was about to be stoned to death for adultery. To the irate men ready to kill her, he simply said, "He that is without sin among you, let him first cast a stone at her."

They may not be as cinematic as walking on water, but to me, such small incidents are Jesus' real miracles. He not only preached an all-embracing God, but embodied that quality. Because they, too, befriended and touched and dined with the "unclean" whom most of us avoid, in September 1997, the world mourned two women who died in the same week. Both Mother Teresa and Princess Diana could get on my nerves, but I fear that it's just such absurdly simple, annoying, even abrasive compassion as theirs, extended indiscriminately, that is Christianity's moral core. It's as magnificent and contagious as it is difficult and disturbing.

What Jesus said and did is one thing, and who he was is another. In New Testament scholarship, the most heated battles concern what happened right after his death. His ghastly execution was significant enough to be recorded by Flavius Josephus, a Jewish historian, and Tacitus, a Roman one. Probably because the male disciples had fled for their lives, the Gospels give a poor account of the events of Easter morning. Mark's stark rendition ends abruptly with three women disciples discovering the empty tomb: a spare scenario that works symbolically or literally.

The Gospels make plain that many people—perhaps

hundreds—reported seeing Jesus during the forty days following his death. Paul doesn't say that Jesus was "raised," but that he "appeared." Mark simply says that Jesus "showed himself." He was no ghost, people asserted; he ate and could be touched. Something that intrigues me is that after Easter, Jesus was clearly changed, so that even his inner circle didn't immediately recognize him; on Easter, his disciple Mary first mistook him for a gardener. This confusion is the kind of thing the evangelists might have fudged, but they preserved it. Paul says that after Easter, Jesus had a spiritual body, and that he was "the same," yet "totally different." That the disciples, frightened out of their wits after the crucifixion, soon rallied and devoted their lives to the Jesus movement, even to the point of martyrdom, leads Sanders to regard their resurrection experiences as "a fact. What the reality was that gave rise to the experiences I do not know."

As his three-hundred-year transition from an obscure executed rabbi to "the Lord" to the second person of a "Trinity" suggests, clarifying Jesus' nature was a gradual concern of the Christian movement. If he thought he was God, Jesus never directly said so, but spoke of himself as the "Son of Man"— a term whose meaning remains opaque. Outside monotheistic Judaism, many leaders of the ancient world, such as Alexander and Augustus, were deified. Allusions to Jesus as divine began about twenty years after his death, but only as spontaneous outpourings in hymns and prayers, not as formal theology. To the communities who first heard the Gospels and Epistles, Jesus was somewhere between being "very God," as he became in 325 at the Council of Nicaea, where the Nicene Creed was formulated, and being one of us.

As I learn to place the familiar Gospels in their unfamiliar cultural context, I begin to see the Jesus of my childhood in a very different light. At the cathedral one Sunday, Canon Susan Harriss reads a passage starring the Jesus I've always found least palatable. As in other stories in Matthew, this Jesus is very concerned with sorting the good from the bad: A fisherman nets a huge catch, but keeps only the best, throwing away the inferior specimens. In the typical sermon, God is the fisherman, and we are the fish.

Susan offers a different take. "What we hear is 'You're bad and stupid and awful, good-bye,' " she says. "But the story really isn't about condemnation at all." What the Gospels say, and how, often speaks to hot political issues at the time each was written, says Susan. Matthew's good fish–bad fish parable dates to a time when Jesus' early followers were deeply engaged in sorting out an "in-house Jewish conflict." Most were still Jews, but were they still within Judaism? Could Gentiles join the movement? Women? Slaves? Did the men have to be circumcized? Other stories reflect the same painful, troubling transition. In Matthew, "the Jews" demand Jesus' death, despite the better judgment of a tormented, soft-hearted Pilate (in fact, an unpopular brute). In Mark, the earliest Gospel (around 70 C.E., although some scholars date it earlier) and probably the basis for the later ones of Matthew and Luke, Pilate condemns Jesus; Mark lived during a time of great political unrest that culminated in his fellow Jews' war with Rome. Who wears the white and black hats depends on the particular Gospel's times and concerns.

Along with Matthew's historical context, says Susan, the personality of the apostle colors the Gospel that bears his name. Before joining Jesus, Matthew had been a tough, socially ostracized Jewish tax collector for the Romans: just the type to see the world in terms of sorting and measuring. Then, too, to be properly understood, each story must be read as part of a whole Gospel. Along with the good fish–bad fish parable,

Matthew also tells of a Jesus who says, "My yoke is easy, my burden is light" and "Judge not that ye be not judged." When she prepares a sermon, Susan considers all these matters, then asks herself, "What would God's intention be in telling us this *now*?" Today, her answer is, "We don't have to worry about sorting out who's good or bad, because that's God's job." This sounds much better to me than being a bad fish.

Jesus is, and always has been, in the eye of the beholder, both individual and institutional. For a Christian, he is both the historical person and what St. Paul described as the same Jesus, totally different, seen through the filters of the individual's own nature and nurture. This realization is both liberating and confusing. Reacting to both sensations, the church has understandably if not always agreeably tried to set Jesus in stone, whether of scriptural inerrancy or of creedal dogma. Responding with the secular version of this just-say-amen approach, the most hard-nosed of the historians have debunked Jesus nearly into oblivion. As I continue to read, my interest increasingly focuses on the question of why, whatever the truth of the matter, so many people have considered Jesus divine. Different scholarly portraits give different answers.

For three beautiful spring days at Auburn Seminary, I join a group of clergy and civilians to learn about John Dominic Crossan's picture. A former Catholic monk and codirector of the Jesus Seminar, he's a pioneer of the historical Jesus scholarship.[6] In the 1970s, as an expert on the Gospel of Mark, he decided to "clear the mind of holy stuff," he says in a fine Irish brogue, and examine Jesus as he would any other important figure. To him, the great advance of modern New Testament scholarship is its honest confrontation of the relationship between history and faith. "They are Christianity's longitude and latitude," says Crossan, "and you must know the difference between the two. In the hard dialectic between belief and objectivity, fundamentalists go one way and secularists the other. But to be human is to respect both reason and revelation. Faith is the meaning of history. It asks the question, 'Do you find God in this?' "

Informed by research on the Galilean Judaism and Mediterranean peasantry of the day, Crossan draws his Jesus from the Gospel of the roughshod Mark. To this plainspoken Jew, says Crossan, Jesus and his fate were inextricably bound up with an enigmatic "kingdom of God." Then as now in Israel, religion and politics were fused, so that Judaism was both a faith and a social identity. Then as now, Jews believed that there was God's kingdom and "the world"—in Jesus' day, the Roman one. Then as now, Jews believed that one day, God would also reign on Earth, redeeming Israel. Constantly evoking God's kingdom, Jesus talked about a mysterious realm so different from ours that there, the lowly, not the privileged, will be exalted. But he left much about this unworldly world unresolved, especially whether bringing it about is the business of the present or future, humanity or God, or some combination of these. Crossan's conclusion is that the "kingdom isn't just a community, but God's empire—political, social, and economic as well as theological—as opposed to Caesar's."

If pressed to sum up Jesus' kingdom, message, mission—even identity—in a single word, Crossan, like the so-called liberation theologians, would say "justice." In Judaism, he says, "justice is not just an idea that God had, or a law, but what God *is*. In the kingdom, justice is the way it is—like the principle of gravity." Thus Crossan's Jesus, who lived in non-violent resistance to systemic inequity, is the incarnation of God's and the kingdom's most essential quality.

To convey how radical Jesus, who fed and healed all comers for free, would have seemed in his day—and how troubling to political and religious institutions alike—Crossan brings up segregated America in the 1960s. "Jesus wasn't advocating just some nice, free-floating philosophy of 'love your neighbor,' he says. "Nobody gets killed for that, but for saying 'Let's sit together at the lunch counter and in the church pew.' " As with Martin Luther King, the proof of the political nature of Jesus' message was his violent death. Traditional Christians believe that he died to atone for humanity's sinfulness, but Crossan says, "Jesus was killed because he attacked the system, saying it wasn't God's."

Not surprisingly, then as now, most people, especially comfortable middle-class and rich ones, aren't eager to change the system. The far more popular brands of Christianity that are based on personal piety or religious experience would be "okay," Crossan says, "if 'spiritual experiences' didn't sometimes convince people to kill others, and if we weren't social beings organized by politics. That being the case, religion and politics have to talk."

As the people of the Earth increasingly divide into two megaclasses called rich and poor, says Crossan, "the first step toward the kingdom is deciding that God isn't on the side of X—racism, oppression, whatever. Then we must ask, How radical must we be?" A church that doesn't answer that question is "hypocrisy—a transcendental Prozac, a little vacation each Sunday. Rather than giving coins to beggars, we should change the church so that it makes the world a better place— that's what it's for. We want to talk about Jesus, but Jesus wants to talk about justice."

Not all scholars see Jesus in such a political light or regard "kingdom" as shorthand for social reform, if not revolution. Although Jesus talks constantly about it, says Sanders, he never clearly says he is, or even has brought, the kingdom, but rather that he prepares people for it; only God can bring about this mysterious realm that, like invisible leaven or a tiny mustard seed, quietly produces a transformation. Although they can't create the kingdom, says Sanders, people can nonetheless "enter" it by right living, loving God first and neighbor as self, and showing mercy. To Sanders, the notion of the kingdom as a just society created by men of good will began as camouflage for an embarrassing fact: God's reign on Earth simply failed to materialize as Jesus predicted, which required an explanation. Indeed, some scholars reason, because Jesus and his disciples expected the kingdom in the immediate future, it *couldn't* depend on revamping society. Although Jesus expected a lot from his inner circle, Sanders finds his basic teaching and requirements in the Lord's Prayer: not social upheaval, but reliance on God and forgiveness, even of enemies.

Describing the politicized, sociological view of Jesus as "a huge slippage," Huston Smith says he accepts Jesus "as God in human form, although he may not have thought of himself that way or known exactly who he was. Jesus was a Jew, so he appropriated with conviction the presiding view of a personal God who created and controls everything, so that we need not worry. Although he perceived God in very personal terms, he also regarded God as being the ultimate reality. Jesus is back, but is his view of the world, which has us in the loving hand of an omnipotent being? Do we have confidence in that today?"

Drawn from psychology as well as history and theology, Marcus Borg's intensely spiritual Jesus is the most millennial portrait.[7] He belongs to the tradition of the great Hebrew social prophets and raises radical questions about systemic secular domination. He is also, like the Asian sages, one who subverts conventional thinking. In what Borg calls his sketch, however, Jesus' identity as a "spirit person"—in some cultures a holy man or shaman, in his case, a Jewish mystic—is "foundational" to these other two dimensions. His spirituality, or "existential awareness of the Spirit," says Borg, was "the source of everything that he was." As a sage and "spirit person," he transcends the Judeo-Christian tradition. His experiential kingdom resembles a state of mind that Buddha called wisdom. Like Buddha's, this Jesus' mission was to lead people from a life of anxious distortion and grasping toward one based on true perception and giving.

The status quo Borg's Jesus challenges is the commonplace perception of reality. "Is not the life more than meat," he asked, "and the body more than raiment?" To provoke doubt about whether life was really about what the establishment—religious and secular—said it was about, he used koanlike aphorisms: "Where your treasure is, there will your heart be also." Mostly, he relied on homely parables: God is like a vineyard owner who pays each worker not according to his labor, but according to his needs. In the face of a providence more loving than fair, said Jesus, those who anxiously focus on worldly gain rather than on God's peace and neighborly compassion are like the blind led by the blind.

Far from being overly mystical or subjective, this millennial Christology presents stiff challenges, particularly for the church. Describing what makes neoagnostics out of so many potential Christians, Borg traces a chain reaction that begins when conventional wisdom turns the psyche into a storehouse for society's "oughts." Life becomes a matter of "How am I measuring up?" Even religion is reduced to a code of rules and regulations: the "good works" emphasized in Catholicism and the "right beliefs" of Protestantism. Grim, legalistic forms of Christianity may be accepted for a while, says Borg. But by adolescence, as happened with me, childhood's pious verities clash with the modern material worldview, and many find a Jesus who requires one to try to do the impossible or believe the unbelievable either unreal or harsh. When it strays from Jesus' mandate of compassion into legalism, Borg argues, the church can return to the mentality of a purity system, as when it condemns homosexuality by citing a ritual principle from Leviticus. Borg prefers to paraphrase Paul: "In Christ, there is neither straight nor gay." Similar insensitivity to marginalized "impure" groups becomes public policy when a rich, predominately Christian nation fails to provide health care to all.

If neoagnostics have one major problem with Jesus, it's his nature and his relation to God. Eschewing theological definitions, Borg feels it's enough to say that Jesus is so deeply related to God that it's "as if" he were God's son. By stressing the orthodoxy of beliefs symbolized by events in Jesus' last week over the bulk of his teaching, says Borg, the church can distort his life and Christianity itself into a "priestly saga of sin, guilt, sacrifice, and forgiveness." This focus on Jesus' death as atonement, particularly in a society keenly aware of abusive parents and dysfunctional families, "simply makes no sense," says Borg, "and I think we need to be straightforward about that. Modern people don't want to be forgiven, but freed and enlightened."

Portraits of Jesus, whether done by New Testament scholars, Christians, or other interested persons, are always more like paintings than photographs. Each image reflects the artist as well as the subject. Those I like best leave a lot of room for mystery. A gifted novelist as well as an amateur biblical scholar, Reynolds Price presents a Jesus whose message is "Trust me" and "Love one another."[8] Light years away from creedalism, this theology is roomy, mysterious, helpful, pithy, and optimistic without going overboard. Price's remarks about Jesus in an interview sent me into highly unusual orgies of agreement. This is my kind of evangelist! "Under threat of torture," said Price, "I would describe myself as a renegade Christian." Although not a member of any particular church, he "wouldn't at all be comfortable being a Unitarian and saying that Jesus was a lovely sort of guy who presented a high moral standard for us all to follow." To Price, Jesus seems "to have stood in demonstrably but inexplicably intimate relation to the creator of our world." Although he doesn't have a bumper sticker that says "Honk if you love Jesus," Price said, he "absolutely" believes that Jesus is alive today, and prays to him.[9]

Curious about the way in which a theologian who's also a scientist addresses such matters, I asked Robert John Russell, of Berkeley's Graduate Theological Union, how he thinks about Easter. "If you suppose linear time and reductionistic materialism," he said, "the Resurrection is really hard to accept." But suppose, he continued, there were another "time line"? One that starts with an eternal future that God is preparing for the whole cosmos and reaches back into human history to the life of Christ? In that case, he said, "the Resurrection marks the beginning of the transformation of the whole universe into what Christians call 'the new creation.' It signals the *eschaton* [last element] that inaugurates the transformation of the cosmos into a 'new heaven and a new Earth.' " This kind of talk forces words to the edge of their meaning, he said, "but that's inevitable when we try to think carefully in light of science about what is, in the end, the central mystery to which Christianity points."

In the Hungarian café one morning, I ask Jeff Golliher about his Jesus. "The Jesus I know is something else," he says. "Someone who has access, in the most compassionate way, to what our hearts and whole being are really like? This person is the same as God, because only God can do that?" In the church's more hands-on functions, such as sacraments and healing, Jeff finds "an understanding that there's a descending force—like light, or cool rain on a hot day—that's thought of as Christ's spirit." Through his experiences in his earthier ministries of healing and ecology, he has come to believe that the resurrection somehow involved "Jesus doing something pragmatic with the way the universe works. My intuition, too, is that with people, Jesus did things directly on the soul level that we don't know about, or only a little bit." Jeff smiles and shrugs. "There's a certain level of truth that I'll never have access to—Jesus as son of God, his special relationship to the ultimate mystery. It's not what we think."

Later, I ask Dean Harry Pritchett about his Jesus. "He never says anything that denies or opposes generosity, graciousness, openhandedness, risking it all, giving it away," says Harry. "Jesus never says, 'Play it close to the chest' or 'Take as much as you can get.' His stance is always open, vulnerable, naked—'Here I am. I'm yours.' "

Doggedly, I ask Harry what Jesus thought people are supposed to do. Change the world? Pray? To assert either one of Christianity's classic polarities strikes Harry as "trying to define that which is not quite clear. In my theology, if you establish two truths, they need to talk to each other. It's more comfortable to perch on one pole, but we live on a tightrope stretched between those two, which bounces us around some." Personally, Harry favors "activist mystics and mystical activists."

Relentless, I ask just who Jesus was. Harry says that every time he celebrates the Eucharist, like all priests, he says, "Christ has died. Christ has risen. Christ will come again." At least for himself, and the people I'm writing for, he says, "I can't say exactly what that means . . ." After a little silence, I say, "But I'm for it." Harry is tickled. "Yes!" he says. "Yes! I'm for it! On the simplest level, resurrection is about believing that no matter what we do, from that *mess,* God can make something new and beautiful. That life doesn't end in a dung-hill or on a cross, not because of anything that we do, but just the goodness and lovingness of the heart of the universe it-self. It would be ridiculously inappropriate to say to someone in terrible grief or distress that 'it will be all right' "—he snorts at the very idea—"but there's a sense in which I'm for it." We smile, hearts peculiarly warmed.

One hot morning in Jerusalem, I made the circuit of the leg-endary Christian sites. Still jet-lagged, I trudged unmoved through the hulking shrines that long ago paved over the ground on which the main events of Jesus' last days allegedly transpired. Finally, just outside the Old City's walls, I stopped to rest outside the Garden of Gethsemane. In this olive grove, Jesus spent the night before his death racked by a massive pre-monitory panic attack, from which he emerged still trusting in God. The site's official attraction is an awful "modernistic" chapel reminiscent of late 1950s tail-fin automotive design; I preferred to stay outside. As I stared dully through the tour-bus fumes and iron fence at the garden's ancient trees, the hair on my arms suddenly stood up. From nowhere, tears boiled down my cheeks. Embarrassed, I slunk into the hideous but dark church. For a few more minutes in a back pew, I was overcome with a kind of tidal wave of compassion: an in-tense, highly unusual awareness not only of the suffering of that great soul so long ago, but of all creatures. I felt what Jeff calls "more than empathy," what Cardinal Newman called "heart speaking to heart." Different traditions use different terms, but because of its strong outward focus, I know this was a religious experience. Because it had to do with Jesus, I call it a Christian one.

I had once hoped that I could reason my way either into or

out of Christianity, but I suspect that in the end it's a matter of being, in one way or another, like St. Paul, "struck from your horse." I admire Thomas Jefferson and Leonardo da Vinci, Martin Luther King and Mahatma Gandhi, but I don't experience them. I don't mean that Jesus appears or talks to me. When I listen to people describe Jesus as a kind of best buddy squared, their experience sounds so different from mine that I sometimes wonder if mine is even "religious." It not only lacks much creedal content but seems oddly, for lack of a better word, impersonal. In John, Jesus says, "I live in you and you live in me." To me, a Christian is someone who "gets" that. Many people who are just as good or holy or wise, or more so, simply don't.

Compared with the fairly rational way in which many Jews, say, or Buddhists, can discuss their religion, Christians sound a little crazy talking about theirs. Even St. Paul referred to the "folly" (which Crossan translates as "moronicity") of the cross. Acknowledging the "intractable *strangeness* of the ground of belief" in Christianity, the Oxford theologian Rowan Williams says, "The problem was, is, and always will be the Christian attitude to the historical order, the human past. By affirming that all 'meaning,' every assertion about the significance of life and reality, must be judged by a reference to a brief succession of contingent events in Palestine, Christianity—almost without realizing it—closed off the path to 'timeless truth.' " Even the greatest Christian saints are, says Williams, "left speechless by that which lies at the centre of their faith."[10]

I'm with them there. Last year, thinking of Christianity's folly, I would once again have failed to "get to the bottom of it" and dismissed it as superstition. This year, I'm less inclined to think that a thing must be logical in order to be true, or that being faithful is the same as believing. My portrait of

Jesus isn't theological enough to be traditional, but it's not sociological enough to be modern. Regarding his raison d'être, I imagine that it had little if anything to do with atonement and much to do with a divine-human learning experience. God, I think, is also working on us. As to Jesus' nature, I really don't know. God's viceroy and the idea of the bodhisattva seem right in their seemly reticence. Much like his very first admirers, whose enigmatic names for him have come down through a hundred generations—Lamb of God, Son of Man, Lord—Jesus is special, but I'm not sure just *how* special. In short, I've discovered that I'm an Early Christian.

One evening in Israel, at Kibbutz Ginosaur near Capernaum, I sat on a pier jutting far out into the Sea of Galilee, watching the sunset. As the glorious violet and orange faded into a night sky, I breathed in the damp, marshy air, listened to the waterfowl, and enjoyed that peace that passes all understanding that must have kept Jesus' followers in his fateful orbit. Writing to the Philippians, who like him and me never saw the historical Jesus, Paul said, "Beloved, I do not consider that I have made it my own, but this one thing I do: forgetting what lies behind and straining forward to what lies ahead, I press on toward the goal for the prize of the heavenly call of God . . ."

CHAPTER THIRTEEN

GOING HOMELIKE

The Lord Yahweh speaks.
Who can refuse to prophesy?

—AMOS

ONE SUNDAY AFTERNOON, with the mixed feelings that often attend a visit back home, I arrive at the Mother of Perpetual Help Monastery. The cloistered Redemptoristine nuns, whose new convent my friend Steve is designing, have invited me for an overnight visit, during which I'll join them for meals, recreation, and prayer. As I ring the bell, I know these two days won't be easy. In the nuns' contemplative approach to religion I hope I'll find some insight into how to reconcile my own Christianity and Zen. Yet through the cloister's stout door, I feel the emotional equivalent of gravitational pull.

I'm quickly greeted by smiling, white-haired Sister Mary Regina. She shakes my hand, shows me into a sitting room off the foyer, and disappears behind a door. I'm sitting in the cloister's "public" part, which is closed off from the nuns' private areas not by the iron bars of old but by a network of halls and doors. In a few moments, Sister Paula enters. The prioress, too, smiles and greets me as a very welcome guest.

Understanding that I'm curious about the cloister, Paula explains that some of its customs are rooted more in secular history than in religion. When women's religious communities began, "the Vandals were running through Europe and families sometimes tried to snatch their daughters back." Somehow, she says, the walls first built in self-defense gave rise to "the idea that these women lived their lives in there for other people but had no contact with them, because their recollection and prayer would be disturbed. There are still such communities, but generally, that's changing very much."

The Redemptoristines' way of life would astonish their predecessors. During the monastic renewal begun by the Second Vatican Council, the contemplative life was rid of many of its time-honored hardships, such as strenuous fasting, sleep deprivation, and other potentially damaging "penitential" practices. Paula is proud that the Redemptoristines "never had as much of that as some traditions. Our order has aimed to make the contemplative life accessible to people of ordinary good health. We never broke our sleep. Once a week we had the discipline"—a self-inflicted flagellation meant to "subdue the flesh"—"but early in renewal, psychology told us that wasn't healthy. And it could stimulate feelings you didn't want. Most contemplatives today wouldn't support that kind of thing. There's a comfortable way to live our life that has time for prayer, privacy, and community. Its values must be human ones that supply the things people need."

Despite reform, some sexist anachronisms remain. Paula hopes that church law will change so that each women's monastic community can govern itself, as men's do, instead of being ruled, at least officially, by the local bishop. Over the years, however, Paula says, "the essentials of contemplative life have stood out stronger, and the inessentials—things that prevented people who met us from seeing that you don't have to live behind bars or wear a habit to be contemplative—have fallen away."

Soon, Regina returns to lead me through a maze of halls and rooms in the cloister's "semiprivate" section and up a flight of stairs to the spacious guest bedroom and bath. Furnished in motel style, it's cheerful and comfortable, but plain, in keeping with the monastic attitude about "stuff." Everything is very, very clean. Like Proust's madeleine, the monastery's particular fragrance brings back the convents of my old teachers. (Later, when I mention this elusive scent, which seems to include beeswax and soap, fresh air and lavender, to my friend Steve, the nuns' architect, he immediately says that he, too, has remarked it.)

After a walk outdoors, I try to find the nuns' semiprivate living room, where they gather daily for recreation. Sister Paula has asked me to meet with the whole community there at three-thirty. One quiet yet enormous difference between monastic life and regular life is that the former runs by the clock. One doesn't do something if and when one feels like it, but because it's time. If our private lives operated more on this principle, I suspect Prozac sales would decline. After a few wrong turns, I reach my destination.

The large, pale-green parlor, with its linoleum and overhead fluorescents, could be a lounge in a school or community center. It, too, is furnished in the endearing spiritual-eclectic style—a mix of inspirational artwork, antiques, and seventies "modernistic" furniture—that prevails in so many religious facilities. The Redemptoristines help support themselves by sewing fine liturgical vestments, and their decor also features lots of needlework. There are several tables for cards and board games, and, in one corner, a handsome, greatly indulged cockatiel in a capacious cage. He's a special favorite of eighty-five-year-old Sister Mary Catherine, who is wheelchair-bound. When her back is to him, she checks the bird from time to time with a small mirror of the sort once used for powdering noses.

In a carpeted area ringed with chairs and sofas, the sisters, all of whom, including Mary Catherine, have a direct gaze and a firm handshake, introduce themselves and take their seats. They wear simple, pretty costumes in a burgundy color, which symbolizes God's love, but there's no habit per se. Each nun chooses her own style of dress, jumper, or skirt, which are all sewn here. Most wear short black veils, but some are bareheaded. Footwear is of the sensible Rockport/ Birkenstock sort, comfortable indoors and out. One of the covert thrills of Catholic schoolchildren in my youth was getting a glimpse of what lay beneath the nuns' old-fashioned habits. Were their heads really shaved? What *did* they do with their bosoms? I can't help noting that the Redemptoristines' stockings are the knee-high kind. Of the thirteen sisters, several look either "young" or "old," and most somewhere in hearty later middle age.

After some general chatting, Sister Paula asks me to talk a bit about what I've learned about millennial religion. If my remarks strike these women, most of whom have spent decades in intense spiritual life, as the random musings they seem to me, the cordial sisters don't let on. Not in the least pious or solemn, their expressions are receptive, as if waiting to be pleased. Like Zen monks, they smile and laugh a lot. Occasionally, they chime in with suggestions of books or scholars they've found informative. They especially seem to like Sister Elizabeth Johnson, a theologian at Fordham and author of *She Who Is;* Basil Pennington, a contemplative

priest and writer who's a popular teacher of spirituality; and
Thomas Merton, my own favorite monk. When I lament that
he'll probably never be canonized, everyone agrees. However,
when I assume that the obstacle is his pluralistic sensibility,
particularly regarding Asian religion, the nuns shake their
heads. "His drinking," says one. "And he . . . fell in love," says
another.

Like other millennial Americans, the nuns speak of spiritual life as a search. When I ask what "cloister" means in the
postmodern era, Sister Mary Jane says, "We're still figuring
that out." In discussing their way of life, the sisters often refer
to the Venerable Maria Celeste Crostarosa, their foundress.
Charmingly, they call her simply "the Venerable": an hon-
orific given to a person in the first phase of the three-step
canonization process. An upper-class mystic and mother superior along the lines of Teresa of Avila, she was an eighteenth-
century Neapolitan born with what she described as a "very
precocious and ardent nature." Her sixteen literary works,
written in an obscure Italian dialect and only partially translated and edited, include poems and an autobiography called
Jesus Christ Is My Life.[1]

At a time when Jansenism cast its puritanical pall over Europe, Maria Celeste described God in Tantric language. She
writes that after God ordered, "Love me alone. . . . I am jealous of your heart for I have chosen you for Myself alone," she
entered a Carmelite cloister. "I remained in my cell as much
as I could," she writes, "enjoying the Presence of my Beloved." When not rapt in religious ecstasy, the formidable
Maria Celeste struggled against a disapproving male hierarchy
to establish her own religious order. Her determination was
rooted in her God-given mandate to establish a community
that would be "a living memory of Jesus Christ." This principle of "viva memoria" continues to guide the Redemptoristines today. It doesn't simply mean following Jesus'

example, as all Christians are enjoined to do, they explain. Rather, they must be "living images" of him, thereby amplifying the divine presence in the world.

The Redemptoristines are well aware of America's increasing interest in religious experience. Research over the past twenty years shows that a consistent third of Americans have had a "particularly powerful religious insight or awakening." Like Maria Celeste, almost a half—particularly women, persons over thirty, the college-educated, and the religiously inclined—say they have "been aware of, or influenced by, a presence or a power—whether you call it God or not—which is different from your everyday self."[2] Where mysticism is concerned, however, the nuns have that feet-on-the-ground attitude that I've come to expect from those who don't just talk the talk but walk the walk. Amused, one sister says, "Let's put it this way. We don't wake up in the morning and rush to choir to see if he's still there. He is." In my world, expressing oneself is nearly a religion. Here, where another prevails, the sisters automatically take turns speaking. Seconding her sister, a nun says, "This life is sheer faith most of the time. Very sheer."

Traditionally, contemplative monasteries have been portrayed as the spiritual equivalents of power plants: Their prayers fueled "the world." Paula compares this notion to "the Zen idea of an energy that circulates in the world that comes from contemplative people." Regarding the future of this way of life, she sees a growth edge outside traditional communities like hers. Among what the nuns quaintly call "the public," she says, "there's a lot more interest in the things that we do, such as taking time for reflection and finding ways of stepping back. Thomas Merton once said that we contemplatives 'hold a treasure that our busy modern world needs.' "

In their quiet way, the Redemptoristines symbolize traditional religion's predicament on the cusp of the second millennium: They must preserve what's most important and must also change. When I bring up Buddhism's spiritual technology, Paula brings up "centering prayer." In this increasingly popular Christian practice, which has much in common with *zazen,* one silently meditates on a word or simple phrase that expresses openness to God.[3] Before benefiting from such a practice, she says, "a lot of people have to learn receptivity. They don't have to create God's presence. It's there." Although the sisters try to "live it full-time," says Paula, "to be human, everyone needs centering time."

Responding to popular interest in spirituality and their own need to "stay in business" and attract new recruits, many monasteries of different faiths have opened retreat centers and otherwise become more involved with laypeople and their needs. The Redemptoristines' new constitution urges each convent to be a "center of prayer" for the local church. Regarding the matter of "what can people join us in," says Paula, "we haven't worked that out." Part of the challenge is that many American Christians, who have traditionally focused on the so-called social Gospel, don't even know their faith has a contemplative tradition. When the sisters recently invited local Catholics to vespers, those who came liked it, says Paula gently, "but it was something a little different. If we had had a mass, more would have come."

In their most successful outreach effort, each month, the sisters host a group of "lay associates," who spend an afternoon at the monastery studying spiritual life, and then attend vespers; those who come from a distance sleep over. Last year, twelve associates made a commitment to recite daily some of the Divine Office—set prayers, including psalms, that are chanted at certain hours—and spend at least fifteen minutes in private prayer. Recently, one associate said that "just being with the Lord for ten or fifteen minutes each morning is wonderful," says Paula. "She had no clue that you could just relax with God, and that's prayer."

Because I like the sisters and want them to prosper, I can't help but think of PR schemes. When I ask Paula how anyone outside the immediate environs could know that the Redemptoristines exist, she lists a directory of Catholic religious orders, word of mouth, and the Redemptorist priests. Advertising and corporate growth are thought of differently here. Then too, the nuns are still grappling with the right modern ratio of public and private, says Paula. "Stephen [Katz, the architect] is always challenging us about the issue of privacy. It bothers him that, for example, we'd like two dining rooms, so that everyone—our families on visits or people on private retreats—doesn't come into ours. By vocation we're on the fringe of the busyness, but by prayer, we're right at the heart of the world."

At five-thirty, it's time for vespers. Just down the hall is the chapel, a simple space with a tablelike altar backed by some modern stained-glass windows. The sisters take their assigned seats in the modern version of choir stalls, which flank the altar in diagonal rows, like pews. As in other Christian communities around the world, the nuns gather throughout each day for the office of the hours. If there's one crucial element to spiritual growth, I've learned, it's some daily ritual. Like nothing else, it shows that while everything changes, something else stays the same.

Responsively, in pure, clear voices, the sisters sing the Magnificat—Mary's gorgeous outpouring, humble and proud, upon the angel Gabriel's "annunciation" regarding her future: "My soul magnifies the Lord, and my spirit rejoices in God, my savior. . . . For he that is mighty has done great things with me, and holy is his name." Just as there's no place for egotism and melodrama in monastic life, there are no solos or flourishes in the beautiful plainsong. I know the words and music by heart, but keep silent, afraid my stinging eyes will overflow.

After vespers, the Redemptoristines lead me to the refectory for a buffet of leftovers; the nuns take their main meal at noon. As I help myself to some good homemade soup and a bagel, I notice a tray of the various vitamins and other dietary supplements that are so much a part of millennial America. Because it's Sunday, we chat at table, but on other nights the sisters listen to spiritual reading or an audiotape while eating. As at Zen monasteries, dining and other daily routines are handled differently here.

During the recreation hour, I sit next to Mary Jane, a pretty woman with salt-and-pepper hair who "entered" twenty years ago at the age of thirty-three. These days, a girl's decision to join a convent right after high school, which was once the norm, would be looked at askance. Sister Mary Ann, who joins us, says that most novices are in their thirties, and near forty is best, "after the 'window-shopping' is over." Before entering, says Mary Jane, she had had her own apartment and "possessions." Then, she lived in a house with five other women also interested in the spiritual life, gradually realizing that, as she says, "I wanted more." In a process resembling looking at colleges, Mary Jane first visited the Poor Clares, a contemplative order founded by St. Clare, the "spiritual sister" of Francis of Assisi; then she found the Redemptoristines. "I really liked the spirit here," she says. "These women are my family. In some ways, we're even closer." Perhaps because she's near my age, I'm startled when Mary Ann says matter-of-factly, "I know I'll die here."

Soon we're joined by Sister Moira, one of the community's "babies." A hairdresser before she entered, also at thirty-three,

Moira styles the nuns' attractive, individual coiffures. She has just given a perm to Mary Ann, who shrugs in women's timeless gesture of "I can't do anything with my hair." With the candor that obtains here, she says, "I asked Moira if yours was dyed, and she said yes." I laugh, and Moira adds, "But *that* job would be beyond me." I make a mental note to pass on this rather ambiguous remark to my tattooed, punky colorist.

When talk turns to the decline in vocations within the Catholic Church, which requires celibacy for priests and nuns and refuses to ordain women, I repeat the observation of a priest I know: Judging from his parishioners, the costs and benefits of religious and married life, though different, are probably equal. The nuns nod, and mention a sister who left their community and now returns for periodic retreats—with her husband. With the ecclesiastical and cultural changes of the sixties, which nearly emptied many convents and seminaries, "contemplatives began to move about in the world," says Mary Ann. With no bitterness, she adds, "Some of those who joined young in the old days discovered they had other vocations."

I suspect that back in the prefeminist—and precontraceptive—era, many Catholic girls, particularly from working-class families, were attracted to the convent as much by the promise of a "ladylike" professional world run by women as by the prospect of a spiritual life. Back then, when most careers were off-limits to women and mothers were nearly forced to stay home, nuns enjoyed a status and serenity denied to many of their secular sisters. Reflecting on the lot of married women before the era of the planned parenthood that the church still forbids, Jane Austen, a spinster who lived in her father's vicarage, wrote: "Anna has not a chance of escape; her husband called here the other day, & said she was pretty well but not equal to so long a walk. . . . Poor Animal, she will be worn out before she is thirty.—I am very sorry for her.—Mrs. Clement, too, is in that way again. I am quite tired of so many children." Perhaps the number of Catholic women unwilling to become "poor animals" before the cultural changes of the 1960s gave the church a false sense of security about the number of vocations. As Buddha knew, the contemplative's path is narrow and not for everyone.

At eight-fifteen, we return to the chapel for compline. In a sweet translation of Psalm 91, my favorite, the nuns chant, "God will cover you like a nesting bird, and under his wings you will find refuge. . . ." Sitting in the chapel, I try not to look at the stained-glass windows and their pious scenes. Going to church is often an immersion in the most popular and familiar form of Christian spirituality, known as the kataphatic tradition. This so-called *via positiva* employs material things—music and pictures, Scripture and sculpture, bread and wine—to illumine the elements of faith and inspire devotion. To draw even illiterate people into a relationship with Jesus, who was a real, flesh-and-blood person in history, Francis of Assisi created two kataphatic masterpieces: the Stations of the Cross and the crèche. The tradition's more meditative dimension was profoundly shaped by Ignatius of Loyola, the founder of the Jesuits, whose famous *Spiritual Exercises* gives readers a sense of participating in biblical events.

For me, the exoteric, you-are-there kataphatic approach doesn't work. Like the stained-glass windows, its words and images often seem just too much. As with exercise, I'm now addicted to daily Zen practice and its interior and exterior silence. Last December, I stumbled upon a bridge between this part of my life and Christianity in another, more ancient and esoteric prayer tradition known as apophatic spirituality, or the *via negativa*.

As the little girl in the joke prays, "Forgive us our Christmases and those who Christmas against us." By Thanksgiving, the holiday's demands were already threatening my small store of equanimity. Its kataphatic symbols, from Nativity scenes to St. Nicholas, only added to the static in my head. In the effort to mine something of value from the seasonal pit, I picked up a copy of a diary kept by Basil Pennington, a Cistercian monk whose work is highly thought of by the Redemptoristines. Pennington wrote the journal during a silent retreat at Thomas Merton's former hermitage.[4] It covers December 1 through 8, so I resolved to begin each of those days by reading the corresponding entry before getting out of bed.

In places, the book rang with a devoutness and certitude that I'm allergic to, but Pennington's approach to the technology of prayer stuck with me. When trying to pray, he writes, "we have a job letting go of things—especially our own creations: our thoughts and images. We try to get God to fit within them." Like the rabbis, he concludes, "But any 'god' who will fit into our thoughts and images will never satisfy our hearts. He is a false god, an idol that we have created." Like the roshis, he says, "We have to have the courage to go beyond our thoughts and images where, at first, it is very dark."

I followed this *via negativa* back through the centuries, to the writings of some of Christianity's earliest spiritual masters.[5] To these church fathers, knowledge of God comes not through *scientia*—cogitation—but *sapientia*—contemplation. Like millennial Americans, they were more interested in experiencing the divine than in making up doctrines about it. Informed by Asian and Hebrew ideas as well as Greek philosophy's search for the simple, beautiful, and true, their writings have a simple grandeur often missing from later religious works. Not infrequently, great scientists insist that the more they've learned, the less they understand. There's something similarly modern, even soothing, about the patristic acceptance of what Gregory of Nyssa called "unknowing." As if anticipating millennial skepticism about theological dogma, the fourth-century rhetorician-saint advanced the apophatic hypothesis: Unable to escape our human perceptions and imagery, we can only "not see" God. We can only know what God *isn't,* and long for the mystery that eludes us. In an age of information overload, this reverse theology is appealing, particularly to those strained by sometimes corny kataphatic language and tchotchkes. As Augustine put it, "Before experiencing God, you thought you could talk about Him; when you begin to experience Him you realize that what you are experiencing you cannot put into words."

Gregory's most poetic, evocative anti-images of the divine have a languorous, nearly melancholic cast: God is "a luminous darkness," "an unsatiated desire." Like a lover separated from the beloved or a lost child from a parent, we long most for what is hidden from us. In his *Life of Moses,* he describes how God first appears to the people of Israel as light, then as a cloud of darkness over Mount Sinai; the closer God is, the darker it gets. As happens in other relationships, too, says Gregory, the human-divine one brings not only joy and comfort but confusion and distress. Our only recourse, he decides, is *epektasis,* or "straining forward" beyond the self toward God's otherness. "To follow God wherever he might lead," says Gregory, "is to behold God."

Inverting our customary way of looking at things, this theology *noir* postulates that God is most present when seemingly absent. This apophatic assertion particularly suits the age of Buchenwald and Hiroshima, of AIDS and childhood cancer. When words fail, the *via negativa* winds silently through hell, social and personal. In what might be an apophatic hymn, Willie Nelson sings, "I been too sick to pray, Lord / That's why we ain't talked in a while / It's been some of those days, Lord / I thought I was on my last mile / . . . Never needed you more / Would have called you before / But I been too sick to pray." The most powerful—and shortest— sermon I ever heard was given by a priest who was too sick to pray. After reading the Gospel lesson at a weekday mass, he looked at the small congregation and said, "I feel absolutely desolate. Something terrible has happened in my life, and every friend and loved one has let me down. I feel utterly abandoned and alone. I wish I had something more to say to you—something hopeful—but I don't." Then, this apophatic witness walked back up the altar steps and finished the mass.

Like Zen, apophatic spirituality has a nonsectarian dimen- sion. Some of its insights, such as that only a mind emptied of thoughts can experience true reality, are as well suited to a Buddhist monastery as to a Christian one. St. John of the Cross, the sixteenth-century Spanish mystic, succinctly de- scribed the apophatic perception: *"Nada, nada."* To illustrate the universality of this mystical sensibility, Huston Smith jux- taposes two little poems. In the first, Angelus Silesius, a Christian contemplative, says, "God, whose boundless love and joy / Are present everywhere; / He cannot come and visit you / Unless you are not there." In the second, a Sufi mystic named al-Halraj writes, "I saw my Lord with the eye of the Heart. I said: 'Who are you?' He answered: 'You.' "

If the Redemptoristines' stained glass isn't to my taste, their simple responsive chanting is. Finally, Sister Paula circles the chapel with a small silver bucket, blessing us with holy water. As the Great Silence, which extends from nine in the evening to morning office at seven, draws in, I have a sense of being gathered up and protected—tucked in on a cosmic level— that I remember from bedtime prayers.

During the Great Silence, the nuns conduct much of their private spiritual lives, meditating and praying in their rooms. Whether to set the mood, economize, or both, when we emerge from the evening ritual, the lights are already out, as at Dai Bosatsu. Through the maze of hallways illuminated only by twinkling votive candles, the nuns move as if in broad daylight, but I get lost. Turning a corner, I come suddenly upon Sister Maria Paz, a petite Filipina who has just moments ago returned from a retreat at a Washington convent. Bumping into a tall stranger in pants has necessarily startled her, but without missing more than half a beat, she grins hugely, hugs me, and says, "Welcome! You're a sister here." I realize how wrong was my initial impression that life here is surprisingly "normal."

At seven in the morning, I join the nuns in the chapel. They kindly add my work to their prayer list, which makes me weepy again. A research psychologist who's an expert on touch once told me that a mother brushing the hair back from her child's forehead is the most comforting gesture in the world. For me, being prayed for or blessed—by anyone of any tradition—is the psychic equivalent. Perhaps because it's in God's first language, I especially like a Hebrew blessing. Sitting in the nuns' chapel, I realize that this moment is a kind of freeze-frame of my religious life: thinking of a Jewish benediction and missing my silent *Mu,* I'm nonetheless uplifted by the familiar words of the church's morning office.

After breakfast, I spend a little time with Sister Paula. Looking back on her own spiritual voyage, she's struck by how rigid her expectations of self and others were when she entered, and how poorly she was prepared for her new life. When she was growing up, she says, "I loved to look at prayer books, but they didn't answer, and nobody spoke about another way of praying. I listened to people who were full of devotion and 'Jesus is wonderful' and 'Isn't this beautiful?' but

I didn't know how to pray." Her first year or so in the monastery was "a journey of faith in a totally different world. I just knew this life was right for me, but I had to learn everything." She was baffled when the sisters would read a text, then turn the lights out to meditate on it: "I didn't know how to do that." Finally, just before her "clothing"—a ritual leading up to a nun's final vows—Paula confided in a superior, who gave her "a very simple little thing to do," she says. "I was just to think about some article of faith, turning it over and looking at it from all sides, like it was a jewel." I think of Burt Visotzky comparing the Torah to a jewel, and the rabbis' admonition to "turn it and turn it." Sitting out in the woods, says Paula, "I'd just be with the Lord and somehow or other, I learned to pray. But not like in any book."

Toward the end of our conversation, she says, "Yesterday you asked us, 'Why are you here? What sense does it make?' My reaction was 'I'd never be here, except that the Lord sort of . . .' " She pauses for a moment to think before continuing. "I like the image of Habakkuk, the Jewish prophet who was picked up by the hair and set down to do something for the people of God. I would never have had the sense to choose this. Somehow or other, it was the Lord."

For many reasons, I say, this kind of conviction is hard for me to imagine. "That's the struggle of the growth of prayer life," says Paula. "To become more and more attuned within God, who's within you. It's an immersion thing. Our foundress, the Venerable, has some interesting things to say about that. In one of her dialogues with God, he tells her, 'Live like a child in my womb.' "

At lunch, I chat with white-veiled Sister Marapa, the true baby of the house. A dark-haired, plump Basque novice from one of the order's Spanish convents, she has been in America only five months. Her quiet brimming joy is enormously appealing. As if she were a glowing fireplace, I'm drawn to her warmth and light. The biggest difference between her convent in Spain and this one, she says, is the individuality here, where the nuns are free to determine much of their own spiritual regimens. At home, more of the day is still structured by superiors. As if speaking of a mutual good friend, she smiles and says, "But God is the least authoritarian thing we can imagine!" Later, as if making normal conversation, she says that life here is "about preparing to receive. If you empty yourself out, God will fill you up. Like a cup. That's how he glorified Jesus."

Later, as I walk in the monastery's beautiful grounds, trying to glimpse the great river beyond the woods, I think of Ruth Brennan, who spent much of her life as a cloistered nun in rural surroundings. Our last conversation was full of references to nature and to apophatic spirituality. When I asked her again what being a contemplative means at the millennium, she thought for a minute. "Being conscious of a certain pulsing readiness," she said. "A disposition that makes one totally awake and alive to the moment. Why worry about tomorrow? There is no tomorrow. It doesn't exist. Yesterday is gone. I don't have anything in this world except my presence to you right here. You don't either! That's true. That's the realest thing."

When I asked Ruth how to cultivate this contemplative awareness, she paraphrased Rilke. While we should be patient, she said, "we shouldn't make the Lord's coming more difficult for him than the Earth makes it for the spring when it wants to come. After it has assimilated the cold and dying of winter, there's an energy of readiness in the Earth." As to what this state of readiness has to do with God, Ruth said, "I don't know. But I think that's where he touches us. If I have any connection to him, it's got to be there—that meeting place between the micro- and the macrocosm."

Unlike a nun or monk, I said, I'm up to my elbows in "the

world," where maintaining readiness isn't easy. Ruth got exasperated. "That's what I hate about the notion of cloister—that you can only achieve awareness by cutting that other stuff off! You can't. At this moment, all of that is right inside your presence to yourself. As T. S. Eliot said, in the end we come back to our beginning and know it for the first time."

Asking questions is my trade, so instead of letting that bit of poetry sink in, I kept trying to wheedle some advice about developing a contemplative stance. Finally, Ruth allowed that right awareness involves a process of "quieting down. But you can't do that by just sitting down. Space, time, and our five senses—that's our frame of reference. So any human ways of quieting down, from listening to music to watching the ocean—my fixation—are conducive. You have to honor your own total person in this moment, then make a place, or center, of readiness that's fully alert, with eyes in all directions." As to more specific techniques, she said, "That's very foreign to me—steps and everything. You need to get away from methods. There is no method. A lot of things go on in our heads on different levels, but there's a center."

No more interested in theological definitions than a medieval rabbi or a Zen monk, Ruth said that she thinks that God "is an energy in my life—an inherent sense of the good, of value. But God is beyond our mind's power to conceive of. 'Neither has eye seen nor ear heard . . .' Cosmologists say the same thing about the vastness of space." Her comments on Jesus were spartan. "I'm concerned not about the end of the road, but about the journey, and the person of Jesus shares the road. It isn't as though I feel his presence. I don't, and I don't have to, either. What we have to assimilate is Jesus' message, which is very clear and simple. It concerns a sense of what really matters and of okayness with what is."

When I asked Ruth to elaborate on what seems to me an

impossible dream, she said it's a matter of being "grateful for everything just the way it is. The things I can change and the things I can't—all fine. Where things look bad and out of order, the chaos all comes back to a rhythm." Of death, she said, "We don't know what will happen, and it's okay not to know. You get to a turn, and some people go this way and you go that way. The day you step over that threshold, then that's where you belong. But you'll recognize it if you've been there all along the road. Your life is relatively insignificant, and that's got to be all right with you. You can't hang on to anything."

If she absolutely had to describe God, Ruth said, " 'presence' says a lot."

Before heading back to "the world," I take leave of Sister Paula in the nuns' parlor. Whenever I've been in this room, my eyes have gone repeatedly to an old-fashioned framed photograph of an arresting woman with a mature, mobile, intelligent face, draped in the old-fashioned wimple and veil. It's a formal portrait, yet the nun looks as if she has just run in from outside. Caught on the fly, she is radiant. When I inquire, Paula identifies her as an English Redemptoristine, who came to North America, established the order's first Canadian house in 1947, and died at the age of forty-nine. She was teased for having trouble pinning her own veil. I return again and again to the nun's photograph, which is oddly familiar. Finally, I recognize the joyous, alert expression. It's Suzuki-roshi's.

Zooming down the thruway in my car, I remember that when I began my reporting I thought I was trying to resolve a conflict between religion and reason, feeling and thought. I've learned that the religious sensibility draws on the intellectual and emotional—even the physical. The best term I can think of for this faculty is "wholeheartedness." That's what you see when Jews sing the Sh'ma Israel, Buddhists bow, and the sisters chant the Magnificat.

Centuries ago, St. Anselm said that he didn't seek to understand so that he could believe, but to believe so that he could understand. I've come to agree with the medieval philosopher, although I'd substitute "trust" for "believe." For neoagnostics at least, the days of belief in the unbelievable are long gone. But the days of belief in the unlimited powers of intelligence and education are numbered, too. With these tools, we can build things that are smart and new, but not Jerusalem—not home. That requires a depth of wisdom and a sense of history that religion can supply, and that something else that all religion is about.

I began this book with a set of questions. Three years later, I have some answers. *What is real?* For me, what is real is right now, in the presence of the sacred. *How do I feel?* Ready— when I remember what is real. *What are my choices?* This one is more complicated. In principle, religious development is best fostered by immersion in one of the great faiths—in part because that means struggling with the inevitable thorns on the rose. Presumably, this kind of commitment works for many of the 40 percent of Americans who attend weekly services. For many of the remaining majority, however, particularly neoagnostics, this purist attitude is a roadblock on the spiritual path. At the millennium, rapid cultural change can, within a single generation, render nearly unintelligible religious knowledge that was once absorbed, almost like English, in the seamless context of family and community. Outside answer-oriented fundamentalism, among most Americans, the lines between believers, who often express doubts, and doubters, who often express spiritual concerns, are increasingly blurred. In this postmodern milieu, the expectation of orthodoxy must be questioned by anyone belonging to or interested in the unconverted—the majority. Something is not only better than nothing, I believe, but can be the first step toward a deeper truth.

After a long, bumpy trip, I've found my place in the inquirers' pew in a different church within the same great religion I was born into. I couldn't be an Early Christian without the gifts of a Jewish approach to the Bible to satisfy my intellect, *zazen* to organize my perceptions and emotions, and both traditions to challenge and expand my sense of the sacred. My hope is that the effort of holding steadfastly to different truths will ultimately be beneficial. Some will see my customized sanctuary as a folly. To me, it feels both familiar and new, complex and just right—homelike.

As I inch across the George Washington Bridge toward my secular city, I consider the most important question I hoped to answer. I believe religion is right. Even if it's not, it hasn't deprived me of any good thing and has given me many. In the age of anxiety, religion replaces narcissism and fear with compassion and *epektasis*—straining toward the mystery. It says you should do the best you can right now—pay attention to what's most true and be kind—and trust, like the great souls of blessed memory, that somehow, everything will be all right. If there's a better way to live, I don't know of it. I intend to keep working on God.

NOTES

INTRODUCTION

1. George H. Gallup, Jr., *Religion in America* (Princeton, N.J.: Princeton Religion Research Center, 1996).

2. Ibid.

3. George Steiner, "Books of Knowledge," a review of the *Routledge Encyclopedia of Philosophy, The New York Times Book Review,* July 5, 1998.

4. George H. Gallup, Jr., *Emerging Trends* (Princeton, N.J.: Princeton Religion Research Center, June 1997).

5. Robert Wuthnow, *Sharing the Journey: Support Groups and America's New Quest for Community* (New York: The Free Press, 1994).

6. Harvey Cox, *Fire from Heaven: Pentecostalism, Spirituality and the Reshaping of Religion in the Twenty-first Century* (New York: Addison-Wesley, 1995).

7. Gallup, *Religion in America.*

8. Ibid.

9. Wade Clark Roof, *A Generation of Seekers: The Spiritual Journeys of the Baby Boom Generation* (San Francisco: Harper-Collins, 1993).

CHAPTER ONE: SPIRITUALITY: JUST DO IT

1. Wade Clark Roof, *A Generation of Seekers: The Spiritual Journeys of the Baby Boom Generation* (San Francisco: Harper-Collins, 1993).

2. George H. Gallup, Jr., *Religion in America* (Princeton, N.J.: Princeton Religion Research Center, 1996).

3. Ibid.

4. Shunryu Suzuki, *Zen Mind, Beginner's Mind* (New York: Weatherhill, 1970).

5. Gallup, *Religion in America.*

CHAPTER TWO: RELIGION GETS REAL

1. Huston Smith, *The World's Religions* (San Francisco: HarperCollins, 1991).

2. Isaiah Berlin, *The Sense of Reality: Studies in Ideas and Their History,* ed. Henry Hardy (New York: Farrar, Straus and Giroux, 1997).

3. Freeman Dyson, "Is God in the Lab?" *The New York Review of Books,* May 28, 1998.

4. Walter Isaacson, "The Private World of Bill Gates," *Time* magazine, January 13, 1997.

5. Susan Harriss, *Jamie's Way: Stories for Worship and Family Devotion* (Cambridge, Mass.: Cowley, 1991).

6. John F. Burns, "Cyclone Rips India," *The New York Times,* November 12, 1996.

CHAPTER THREE: THINKING FOR OURSELVES

1. Robert Wuthnow, *Sharing the Journey: Support Groups and America's New Quest for Community* (New York: The Free Press, 1994).

2. Rebecca Johnson, "The Just-Do-It Shrink," *The New York Times Magazine*, November 17, 1996.

3. Harry Pritchett, *Morning Run: Sabbatical Reflections on the Church and Society* (Atlanta, Ga.: Cherokee, 1989).

CHAPTER FOUR: GOOD AND EVIL

1. "Halloween in Hell," *The New York Times,* October 27, 1996.

2. Urie Bronfenbrenner et al., *The State of Americans* (New York: The Free Press, 1996).

3. George H. Gallup, Jr., *Religion in America* (Princeton, N.J.: Princeton Religion Research Center, 1996).

4. George H. Gallup, Jr., and Sarah Jones, *100 Questions and Answers: Religion in America* (Princeton, N.J.: Princeton Religion Research Center, 1989).

5. Burton Visotzky, *The Genesis of Ethics* (New York: Crown, 1996).

6. Gallup, *Religion in America*.

7. Wade Clark Roof, *A Generation of Seekers: The Spiritual Journeys of the Baby Boom Generation* (San Francisco: Harper-Collins, 1993).

8. Nilton Bonder, *The Kabbalah of Envy* (Boston: Shambhala, 1997).

CHAPTER FIVE: BODY AND SOUL

1. George H. Gallup, Jr., *Emerging Trends* (Princeton, N.J.: Princeton Religion Research Center, June 1997).

2. Daniel Goleman and Joel Gurin, *Mind/Body Medicine* (Yonkers, N.Y.: Consumer Reports Books, 1993).

3. Charles Marwick, "Should Physicians Prescribe Prayer for Health?" *Journal of the American Medical Association,* May 24, 1995.

4. Harold Koenig and Harvey Cohen, "Religious Participation and Health," *International Journal of Psychiatry in Medicine,* October 1997.

5. Herbert Benson, *Timeless Healing* (New York: Scribner, 1996).

6. Abraham Joshua Heschel, *Moral Grandeur and Spiritual Audacity,* ed. Susannah Heschel (New York: Farrar, Straus and Giroux, 1997).

7. Charles Hartshorne, *Omnipotence and Other Theological Mistakes* (Albany: State University of New York Press, 1984).

8. Elie Wiesel, "A Prayer for the Days of Awe," *The New York Times,* October 2, 1997.

CHAPTER SIX: PLURALISM: SOMETHING FOR EVERYONE

1. Steven Holmes, "Census Sees a Profound Ethnic Shift," *The New York Times,* March 14, 1996.

2. George H. Gallup, Jr., *Religion in America* (Princeton, N.J.: Princeton Religion Research Center, 1996).

3. Diana Eck, *Encountering God: A Spiritual Journey from Bozeman to Banaras* (New York: Beacon Press, 1994).

4. Alan Wolfe, *One Nation, After All* (New York: Viking, 1998).

5. Wade Clark Roof, *A Generation of Seekers: The Spiritual Journeys of the Baby Boom Generation* (San Francisco: HarperCollins, 1993).

6. Gallup, *Religion in America.*

7. Ibid.

CHAPTER SEVEN: A NEW AGE

1. George H. Gallup, Jr., *Religion in America* (Princeton, N.J.: Princeton Religion Research Center, 1996).

2. Wade Clark Roof, *A Generation of Seekers: The Spiritual Journeys of the Baby Boom Generation* (San Francisco: HarperCollins, 1993).

3. Ted Peters, *The Cosmic Self* (San Francisco: HarperCollins, 1991).

4. J. C. Smuts, *Holism and Evolution* (New York: Macmillan, 1926).

5. Michael Murphy, *Golf in the Kingdom* (New York: Penguin, 1997).

6. Michael Murphy, *The Future of the Body* (Los Angeles: Tarcher/Putnam, 1992).

7. Don Hanlon Johnson, *The Body in Psychotherapy: Inquiries in Somatic Psychology* (Berkeley: North Atlantic Books/California Institute of Integral Studies, 1998).

CHAPTER EIGHT: BEYOND TOLERANCE

1. Rachel Cowan and Paul Cowan, *Mixed Blessings: Overcoming the Stumbling Blocks in an Interfaith Marriage* (New York: Viking Penguin, 1988).

CHAPTER NINE: NO PLACE LIKE HOME?

1. Robert Bork, *Slouching Towards Gomorrah* (New York: ReganBooks, 1996).

2. George H. Gallup, Jr., *Religion in America* (Princeton, N.J.: Princeton Religion Research Center, 1996).

3. Wade Clark Roof, *A Generation of Seekers: The Spiritual Journeys of the Baby Boom Generation* (San Francisco: HarperCollins, 1993).

CHAPTER TEN: ZEN: "AND THAT'S THE WAY IT IS"

1. Tomeo Hirai, *Zen Meditation and Psychotherapy* (New York: Japan Publications USA, 1986).

CHAPTER ELEVEN: JUDAISM: TURNING THE TORAH

1. Burton Visotzky, *The Road to Redemption* (New York: Crown, 1998).

2. Everett Fox, *The Five Books of Moses* (New York: Schocken, 1997).

CHAPTER TWELVE: CHRISTIANITY: WHAT IF GOD WAS ONE OF US?

1. E. P. Sanders, *The Historical Figure of Jesus* (London: Allen Lane/Penguin Press, 1993).

2. John P. Meier, *A Marginal Jew* (New York: Anchor/Doubleday, 1991).

3. Sanders, *The Historical Figure of Jesus.*

4. Ibid.

5. Marcus Borg, *Meeting Jesus Again for the First Time* (San Francisco: HarperCollins, 1994).

6. John Dominic Crossan, *The Historical Jesus: The Life of a Mediterranean Jewish Peasant; The Birth of Christianity* (San Francisco: HarperCollins, 1991; 1998).

7. Borg, *Meeting Jesus Again.*

8. Reynolds Price, *Three Gospels* (New York, Scribner, 1996).

9. Peter Steinfels, "Beliefs," *The New York Times,* 5/18/96.

10. Rowan Williams, *Resurrection* (Harrisburg, Pa.: Morehouse, 1982).

CHAPTER THIRTEEN: GOING HOMELIKE

1. Maria Celeste Crostarosa, *Jesus Christ Is My Life* (Esopus, N.Y.: Redemptorist Nuns of Esopus, N.Y., 1996).

2. George H. Gallup, Jr., and Sarah Jones, *100 Questions and Answers* (Princeton, N.J.: Princeton Religion Research Center, 1989).

3. Thomas Keating, *Open Mind, Open Heart* (New York: Continuum, 1996).

4. Basil Pennington, *On Retreat with Thomas Merton* (New York: Continuum, 1995).

5. Roberta C. Bondi, *To Love as God Loves: Conversations with the Early Church* (Philadelphia: Fortress, 1987).

ACKNOWLEDGMENTS

I am particularly grateful to five communities and the wonderful people who help guide them: the Cathedral of St. John the Divine and the Very Reverend Harry Pritchett, its dean, and the Reverend Canons Susan Harriss and Jeffrey Golliher; the Congregation B'nai Jeshurun and Rabbis Marcelo Bronstein and Rolando Matalon; the Sonoma Mountain Zen Center and Jakusho Kwong-roshi; the Redemptoristine Sisters of Our Mother of Perpetual Help Monastery and Sister Paula Schmidt; and the Dai Bosatsu International Zendo and Jiro/Andy Afable, head monk.

For their kindness in reading the entire manuscript, I particularly thank Jeff Golliher and Harry Pritchett. For generously offering many suggestions for its improvement, I'm deeply indebted to Rabbi Burton Visotzky.

For their invaluable insights and their patience in helping me make proper use of them, I also wish to thank Imam Talib 'Abdur-Rashid, Rabbi Nilton Bonder, Marcus Borg, Ruth Brennan, Susan Cannon, Rabbi Rachel Cowan, Harvey Cox, John Dominic Crossan, Diana Eck, George Gallup, the Reverend J. Bryan Hehir, Katherine Henderson, Don Hanlon Johnson, the Reverend James Karpen, Stephen Katz, Elisabeth Koening, Shinko Kwong, Michael Murphy, Rabbi Jonathan Omer-Man, Ted Peters, Wade Clark Roof, Robert John Russell, E. P. Sanders, Rabbi Susan Schnur, Huston Smith, the Reverend Minka Sprague, Rabbi Michael Strassfeld, Jeff Weber, Robert Wuthnow, and the many others whose ideas enliven these pages.

Finally, I thank Ann Godoff, my editor. This book is a kind of conversation with her.

INDEX

ABOUT THE AUTHOR

WINIFRED GALLAGHER is the author of *Just the Way You Are: How Heredity and Experience Create the Individual,* which was a *New York Times* Notable Book of 1995, and *The Power of Place: How Our Surroundings Shape Our Thoughts, Emotions, and Actions.* She has written for many magazines, from *The Atlantic Monthly* to *Rolling Stone.* She lives in Manhattan and Long Eddy, New York.

ABOUT THE TYPE

This book was set in Bembo, a typeface based on an old-style Roman face that was used for Cardinal Bembo's tract *De Aetna* in 1495. Bembo was cut by Francisco Griffo in the early sixteenth century. The Lanston Monotype Company of Philadelphia brought the well-proportioned letterforms of Bembo to the United States in the 1930s.